Lecture Notes of the Institute for Computer Sciences, Social Informatics and Telecommunications Engineering 317

More information about this series at http://www.springer.com/series/8197

Der-Jiunn Deng · Ai-Chun Pang ·
Chun-Cheng Lin (Eds.)

Wireless Internet

12th EAI International Conference, WiCON 2019
TaiChung, Taiwan, November 26–27, 2019
Proceedings

 Springer

Editors
Der-Jiunn Deng
National Changhua
University of Education
Changhua City, Taiwan

Ai-Chun Pang
National Taiwan Normal University
Taipei, Taiwan

Chun-Cheng Lin
Department of Industrial Engineering
and Management
National Chiao Tung University
Hsinchu, Taiwan

ISSN 1867-8211   ISSN 1867-822X   (electronic)
Lecture Notes of the Institute for Computer Sciences, Social Informatics
and Telecommunications Engineering
ISBN 978-3-030-52987-1   ISBN 978-3-030-52988-8   (eBook)
https://doi.org/10.1007/978-3-030-52988-8

This Springer imprint is published by the registered company Springer Nature Switzerland AG
The registered company address is: Gewerbestrasse 11, 6330 Cham, Switzerland

Der-Jiunn Deng · Ai-Chun Pang ·
Chun-Cheng Lin (Eds.)

Wireless Internet

12th EAI International Conference, WiCON 2019
TaiChung, Taiwan, November 26–27, 2019
Proceedings

 Springer

Editors
Der-Jiunn Deng
National Changhua
University of Education
Changhua City, Taiwan

Ai-Chun Pang
National Taiwan Normal University
Taipei, Taiwan

Chun-Cheng Lin
Department of Industrial Engineering
and Management
National Chiao Tung University
Hsinchu, Taiwan

ISSN 1867-8211 ISSN 1867-822X (electronic)
Lecture Notes of the Institute for Computer Sciences, Social Informatics
and Telecommunications Engineering
ISBN 978-3-030-52987-1 ISBN 978-3-030-52988-8 (eBook)
https://doi.org/10.1007/978-3-030-52988-8

This Springer imprint is published by the registered company Springer Nature Switzerland AG
The registered company address is: Gewerbestrasse 11, 6330 Cham, Switzerland

Preface

We are delighted to introduce the proceedings of the 12th edition of the 2019 European Alliance for Innovation (EAI) International Conference on Wireless Internets (WiCON). This year, it took place at Windsor Hotel, TaiChung, during November 26–27, 2019. This conference provides an opportunity to connect with researchers, developers, and practitioners from around the world so as to discuss recent findings in the area of the emerging wireless Internet and networks.

The technical program of WiCON 2019 consisted of 39 full papers in oral presentation sessions at the main conference tracks. These technical papers cover a broad range of topics in wireless sensor, vehicular ad hoc networks, security, blockchain, and deep learning. Aside from the high-quality technical paper presentations, the technical program also featured four keynote speeches. The first keynote speech was entitled "6G: Next Frontier in Wireless Communication Research," by Prof. I.F. Akyildiz from Georgia Institute of Technology, USA. The second keynote speech was entitled "Let IoT Talks: Examples on Smart Campus," by Chair Professor Yi-Bing Lin from National Chiao Tung University, Taiwan. The third keynote speech was entitled "Connected Autonomous Vehicles" by Prof. Mohammed Atiquzzaman from University of Oklahoma, USA. The last keynote speech was entitled "Smart Cities: Best Practices and Trends of Development" by Prof. Dagmar Caganova from Slovak University of Technology, Slovakia.

Coordination with the steering chairs, Imrich Chlamtac, Xudong Wang, and Der-Jiunn Deng was essential for the success of the conference. We sincerely appreciate their constant support and guidance. It was also a great pleasure to work with such an excellent Organizing Committee, and we thank them for their hard work in organizing and supporting the conference. In particular, the Technical Program Committee (TCP), led by our TPC co-chair, Rung-Shiang Cheng, who completed the peer-review process of technical papers and made a high-quality technical program. We are also grateful to conference managers, Lukas Skolek, for his support, and all the authors who submitted their papers to the WiCON 2019 conference and workshops.

We strongly believe that the WiCON conference provides a good forum for all researcher, developers, and practitioners to discuss all science and technology aspects that are relevant to wireless networks. We also expect that future WiCON conferences will be as successful and stimulating, as indicated by the contributions presented in this volume.

June 2020

Der-Jiunn Deng
Ai-Chun Pang
Chun-Cheng Lin

Organization

Steering Committee

Xudong Wang   Shanghai Jiao Tong University, China
Der-Jiunn Deng   National Changhua University of Education, Taiwan

Organizing Committee

General Chair

Der-Jiunn Deng   National Changhua University of Education, Taiwan

General Co-chair

Ai-Chun Pang   National Taiwan University, Taiwan

TPC Chair and Co-chair

Chun-Cheng Lin   National Chiao Tung University, Taiwan
Rung-Shiang Cheng   Overseas Chinese University, Taiwan

Sponsorship and Exhibit Chair

Viviane Su   Institute for Information Industry, Taiwan

Local Chairs

Shin-Ming Cheng   National Taiwan University of Science
                                   and Technology, Taiwan
Hui Hsin Chin   Overseas Chinese University, Taiwan

Workshops Chair

Bo Li   Northwestern Polytechnical University, China

Publicity and Social Media Chairs

Anthony Y. Chang   Overseas Chinese University, Taiwan
Chi-Han Chen   Overseas Chinese University, Taiwan

Publications Chair

Yu-Liang Liu   Overseas Chinese University, Taiwan

Web Chair

Chien-Liang Chen   Overseas Chinese University, Taiwan

Technical Program Committee

Rung-Shiang Cheng	Overseas Chinese University, Taiwan
Chien-Liang Chen	Overseas Chinese University, Taiwan
Yu-Liang Liu	Overseas Chinese University, Taiwan
Chun-Hsien Sung	Overseas Chinese University, Taiwan
Jen-En Huang	Overseas Chinese University, Taiwan
Lung-Ping Hung	National Taipei University of Nursing and Health Sciences, Taiwan
Ding-Jung Chiang	Taipei Chengshih University of Science and Technology, Taiwan

Contents

Security and BlockChain

Internet of Things

Wireless Internet

Services and Applications

Ad Hoc and Sensor Network

Design and Implementation of Automatic Following Technology for Mobile Devices

Ming-Fong Tsai[1]([✉]), Chi-Feng Chen[2], Chow-Yen-Desmond Sim[3], Chih-Sheng Li[4], and Lien-Wu Chen[5]

[1] Department of Electronic Engineering, National United University, Miaoli, Taiwan
mingfongtsai@gmail.com
[2] Industrial Ph.D. Program of Internet of Things, Feng Chia University, Taichung, Taiwan
dg2000@gmail.com
[3] Department of Electrical Engineering, Feng Chia University, Taichung, Taiwan
cysim@fcu.edu.tw
[4] Professional Master's Program of Information and Electrical Engineering, Feng Chia University, Taichung, Taiwan
hero.hero.g@hotmail.com
[5] Department of Information Engineering and Computer Science, Feng Chia University, Taichung, Taiwan
lwuchen@fcu.edu.tw

Abstract. Along with the flourishing development of Internet of Things, vehicles which assist move goods are developed as well, for example, automatic guided vehicle applied in manufacturing plants. Vehicles vary with pattern of goods to be moved. If it moves along magnetic tapes, it would lose its flexibility in moving directions. To make vehicles more dynamic and convenient, this study designs and implements automatic following technology of vehicles. Through relative position between vehicles and objects to be followed positioned by satellite and laser radar installed on vehicles which can detect relative distance, vehicles are able to automatically follow objects to be followed.

Keywords: Automatic following technology · Mobile devices · Position information

1 Introduction

To reduce manpower demand of factory, the application of robot arm and automatic guided vehicle (AGV) have become crucial. Along with the development of telecommunication technology and smart products, the development of auto follow technology of mobile vehicles has become an important field for research [1–10]. However, existing research technology are implemented via image recognition and laser radar which can easily affected by light in environment and cause misjudgments [11–20]. This study develops auto follow technology of mobile vehicles based on laser radar sensing modules combining with GPS or indoor positioning information to confirm relative position

© ICST Institute for Computer Sciences, Social Informatics and Telecommunications Engineering 2020
Published by Springer Nature Switzerland AG 2020. All Rights Reserved
D.-J. Deng et al. (Eds.): WiCON 2019, LNICST 317, pp. 3–9, 2020.
https://doi.org/10.1007/978-3-030-52988-8_1

between target to be followed and mobile vehicle. In this way, we can check whether distance and direction detected by laser radar module are correct and launch mobile vehicles to automatically follow targets to be followed.

2   Design of Automatic Following Technology for Mobile Devices

System framework proposed in this study is shown in Fig. 1. It includes mobile vehicle and smartphones. Mobile vehicles are combined with laser radar sensing modules and GPS modules. Laser radar module can be used to detect relative direction and distance of target to be followed, while GPS module is used to obtain positioning information of mobile vehicles. Smartphones can access to positioning information of target to be followed via GPS modules and transmit this information to mobile vehicle in real time through wireless communication module, providing mobile vehicles with relative position between target to be followed and mobile vehicles and check whether distance and direction detected by laser radar module are correct and launch mobile vehicles to automatically follow targets to be followed.

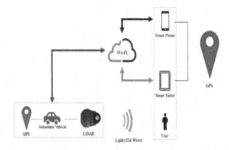

Fig. 1. System architecture

As shown in Fig. 2, the system flowchart of mobile vehicles shows it continuously monitors connection requests through wireless communication modules when it stands by. When the mobile vehicle receives connection requests from auto follow and complete connection, the mobile vehicle obtain relative position via comparing its GPS with constantly received GPS of target to be followed, it detects relative position and distance of target to be followed and automatically follow target to be followed and correct the following path in real time. Figure 3 shows how targets to be followed send auto follow connection request to mobile vehicles through wireless communication module and after the connection is completed, how it transmits its GPS positioning information to mobile vehicles.

This study proposed a laser radar sensing module based on mobile vehicles combing with GPS to determine relative position between target to be followed and mobile vehicles. Figure 4 shows the real-time distance with surrounding objects including targets to be followed, other users, obstacles and so on measured by laser radar sensing modules. It then determines relative distance of targets to be followed and mobile vehicles through their GPS. It then filters and obtain correct relative distance and position via

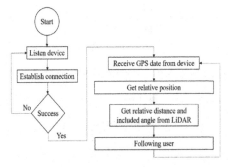

Fig. 2. System flowchart in mobile devices

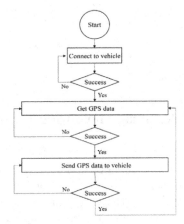

Fig. 3. system architecture in user

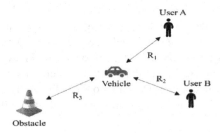

Fig. 4. Real-time distance with surrounding objects

results sensed by laser radar in Fig. 5. Figure 6 shows filtered GPS relative position. After it figures out the correct targets to be followed, and the laser radar sensing module obtains correct direction and distance, mobile vehicles can correct the following path in real time.

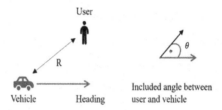

Fig. 5. Relative distance and position

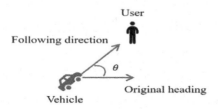

Fig. 6. Filtered GPS relative position

3 Implementation of Automatic Following Technology for Mobile Devices

This experiment adopted devices including TurtleBot3 Burger, Hitachi LDS-01 and HTC M8x. In this experiment, we included four moving approaches including go straight, go backward, turn left and turn right. The highest moving speed of mobile vehicles is 20 cm/s. We set targets to be followed move faster, equaling to and slower to this speed at 30, 20 and 10 cm/s. In this experiment, after mobile vehicles obtain relative position with targets to be followed via their GPS, laser radar would filter correct relative direction and distance of targets to be followed through information obtained from GPS and start to follow targets to be followed in various moving approaches. Finally, we record the final error distance between the two. Figures 7 and 8 demonstrate experimental results of auto follow in various moving approaches. From these results we know when speed of targets to be followed is equaling to or slower than mobile vehicles, its final error distance will be both lower than that when it is faster than mobile vehicles. Thus, it is recommended when developing auto follow technology, moving speed of mobile vehicles should be taken into consideration.

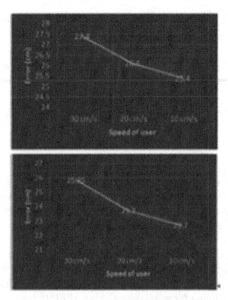

Fig. 7. Experimental results (forward and backward)

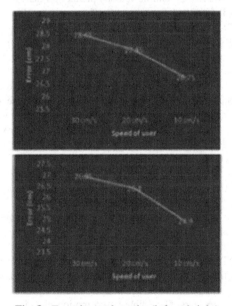

Fig. 8. Experimental results (left and right)

4 Conclusions

This study designs and implements automatic following technology of vehicles. Through relative position between vehicles and objects to be followed positioned by satellite and laser radar installed on vehicles which can detect relative distance, vehicles are able to automatically follow objects to be followed.

Acknowledgments. We thank the Ministry of Science and Technology of Taiwan for supports of this project under grant number MOST 108-2622-E-239-004-CC3 and MOST 107-2218-E-167-004. We thank co-authors and reviewers for their valuable opinions.

References

1. Lu, F., et al.: A low-voltage and high-current inductive power transfer system with low harmonics for automatic guided vehicles. IEEE Trans. Veh. Technol. **68**(4), 3351–3360 (2019)
2. Kamoshida, R., Kazama, Y.: Acquisition of automated guided vehicle route planning policy using deep reinforcement learning. In: IEEE International Conference on Advanced Logistics and Transport, pp. 1–6 (2017)
3. Han, Y., Cheng, Y., Xu, G.: Trajectory tracking control of AGV based on sliding mode control with the improved reaching law. IEEE Access **7**, 20748–20755 (2019)
4. Yoshitake, H., Kamoshida, R., Nagashima, Y.: New automated guided vehicle system using real-time holonic scheduling for warehouse picking. IEEE Robot. Autom. Lett. **4**(2), 1045–1052 (2019)
5. Raineri, M., Perri, S., Bianco, C.: Online velocity planner for laser guided vehicles subject to safety constraints. In: IEEE/RSJ International Conference on Intelligent Robots and Systems, pp. 6178–6184 (2017)
6. Lu, F., et al.: A tightly coupled inductive power transfer system for low-voltage and high-current charging of automatic guided vehicles. IEEE Trans. Industr. Electron. **66**(9), 6867–6875 (2019)
7. Xu, J., Liu, J., Sheng, J., Liu, J.: Arc path tracking algorithm of dual differential driving automated guided vehicle. In: IEEE International Congress on Image and Signal Processing, BioMedical Engineering and Informatics, pp. 1–7 (2018)
8. Webber, J., Suga, N., Mehbodni, A., Yano, K., Kumagai, T.: Study on fading prediction for automated guided vehicle using probabilistic neural network. In: IEEE Asia-Pacific Microwave Conference, pp. 887–889 (2018)
9. Aguilar-Gonzalez, A., Lozoya, C., Orona, L., Romo, S., Roman-Flores, A.: Campus kart: an automated guided vehicle to teach using a multidisciplinary approach. IEEE Revista Iberoamericana de Tecnologias del Aprendizaje, 199–207 (2017)
10. Yao, F., Keller, A., Ahmad, M., Ahmad, B., Harrison, R., Colombo, A.: Optimizing the scheduling of autonomous guided vehicle in a manufacturing process. In: IEEE International Conference on Industrial Informatics, pp. 264–269 (2018)
11. Rozsa, Z., Sziranyi, T.: Obstacle prediction for automated guided vehicles based on point clouds measured by a tilted LIDAR sensor. IEEE Trans. Intell. Transp. Syst. **19**(8), 2708–2720 (2018)
12. Mercy, T., Parys, R., Pipeleers, G.: Spline-based motion planning for autonomous guided vehicles in a dynamic environment. IEEE Trans. Control Syst. Technol. **26**(6), 2182–2189 (2018)
13. Herrero-Perez, D., Martínez-Barbera, H.: Modeling distributed transportation systems composed of flexible automated guided vehicles in flexible manufacturing systems. IEEE Trans. Industr. Inf. **6**(2), 166–180 (2010)
14. Xidias, E., Azariadis, P.: Mission Design for a Group of Autonomous Guided Vehicles. Robot. Auton. Syst. **59**(1), 34–43 (2011)

15. Tsai, M., Pham, T., Hu, B., Hsu, F.: Improvement in UWB indoor positioning by using multiple tags to filter positioning errors. J. Internet Technol. **20**(3), 677–688 (2019)

16. Tsai, M.-F., Pham, T.-N., Hsiang, C.-F., Chen, L.-H.: Evaluation of the effect of variations in vehicle velocity and channel bandwidth on an image-streaming system in vehicular networks. Mob. Netw. Appl. **24**(3), 810–828 (2018). https://doi.org/10.1007/s11036-018-1082-3

17. Lu, S., Xu, C., Zhong, R.: An active RFID tag-enabled locating approach with multipath effect elimination in AGV. IEEE Trans. Autom. Sci. Eng. **13**(3), 1333–1342 (2016)

18. Ching, F., Chen, P., Zheng, A., Tsai, M., Chen, L.: A prototyping for bluetooth connection of cleaning robot, national conference on web intelligence and applications, pp. 1–4 (2015)

19. Draganjac, I., Miklic, D., Kovacic, Z., Vasiljevic, G., Bogdan, S.: Decentralized control of multi-AGV systems in autonomous warehousing applications. IEEE Trans. Autom. Sci. Eng. **13**(4), 1433–1447 (2016)

20. Bacik, J., Durovsky, F., Biros, M., Kyslan, K., Perdukova, D., Padmanaban, S.: Pathfinder-development of automated guided vehicle for hospital logistics. IEEE Access **5**, 26892–26900 (2017)

Efficient Deployment Based on Congestion Control Delivery in Multi-hop Wireless Sensor Network

Chien-Liang Chen[1(✉)] and Ding-Jung Chiang[2]

[1] Department of Innovative Living Design, Overseas Chinese University,
TaiChung, Taiwan, R.O.C.
clchen@ocu.edu.tw
[2] Department of Digital Multimedia Design, Taipei City University of Science
and Technology, Taipei, Taiwan, R.O.C.
djchiang@tpcu.edu.tw

Abstract. Multi-hop Wireless Sensor networks are designed for various real-time applications, and it should be appropriately designed to avoid delivery congestion between linked nodes. For efficient transmission with minimum energy, our proposed work introduces a novel optimized method based on the congestion management algorithm. In our approach based congestion control algorithm was based on the cluster-based routing, since the energy consumption was effectively reduced throughout the network. Since it has to improve network lifetime for a plentiful simulation period, the delivery control process also reduces the access delay. Initially, cluster the nodes with the k means algorithm. After that focusing on the delivery control using Kalman Filter strategy, and this is suitable for minimum access-delay prediction. Finally, the delivery with high efficiency using optimized routing. The experimental results are implemented on the Windows platform, and the performances outperform average throughput, average packet loss, packet delivery ratio, energy-consuming, and system reliability.

Keywords: Multi-hop wireless sensor network · Kalman filter · Real-time delivery

1 Introduction

There are three key points, such as sensing, power-consuming, and communication in the wireless sensor network. Wireless sensor network allows various monitoring and sensing facilities in regions of energetic significance such as safety, security in the healthcare, efficient industrial production, traffic management, and monitoring. In order to attain valid and significant data, the sensor node collects information from its neighbor nodes and transmits data to an integrated location. The sensor node could function on a tiny battery for some existences

© ICST Institute for Computer Sciences, Social Informatics and Telecommunications Engineering 2020
Published by Springer Nature Switzerland AG 2020. All Rights Reserved
D.-J. Deng et al. (Eds.): WiCON 2019, LNICST 317, pp. 10–19, 2020.
https://doi.org/10.1007/978-3-030-52988-8_2

based on the applications. Even though wireless sensor network provides unlimited advantages, it is reserved through limit resources such as wireless bandwidth, available energy, a few memory, and delivery rate.

In the application of the Internet of Things, the wireless sensor network is identified as an essential component. It is challenging to consider an end-to-end congestion control method in a wireless environment. The deployment methods are removed from the initial development stage of the wireless sensor network. The congestion arrangements of wireless sensor network could be developed based on the sensible procedures that they function. Our approach focuses on the important issue of distributed sensor cluster selection for sensed linking in wireless environments. A subset of sensor nodes can only be used for sensing at each time slot. For each sensor node, it can transmit its message to its neighbors, and each sensor node makes its estimate in its group. Our goal is to minimize the congestion rate considering bandwidth utility and resource competition. For transmission efficiency, we provide a novel approach based on low complexity Kalman filter [6] to track sensor nodes. Each sensor node can make its own activity decision to construct an efficient path in the communication constraint.

The structure of our paper is as follows. The introduction describes our motivation and research issue. Paper survey describes the paper works about this research area in Sect. 2. We address the research issue and provide our approach in Sect. 3. The implementation and performance discussion are implemented in Sect. 4. Finally, Sect. 5 concludes our contribution and future work in our study.

2   Deployment Strategy of Wireless Sensors

Many researchers provide several deployment policies for wireless sensor nodes in wireless environments described in [1]. In view of network performance, we represent the greedy and dynamic programming algorithm, which is applied with efficient deployment over congestion management delivery in a wireless environment. But the performance is not excellent. Deployment management for wireless sensor nodes in a wireless environment is briefly described in [2].

The system model has studied in which the cluster head assigns network characteristics using deployment strategies. Our approach explains the traditional algorithms with a time constraint for network features like the followings:

- Earliest Deadline First (EDF) Algorithm: EDF is the optimum algorithm to process real-time scheduling. The highest priority assigns the data with time constraint which is the earliest.
- Requests Times Wait (RxW) Algorithm: RxW defines scheduling decisions for data items using the current state which appends a queue.
- Longest Waiting First (LWF) Algorithm: The data item with the longest waiting time of all pending requests have been requested and then it owns the highest priority. The data item will been scheduled next.

– Least Slack (LS) first Algorithm: The least slack time defines as $d - (t + E - P)$. d defines as the deadline, t expresses the current time, E defines as the execution time and the processor time consumed that defines as P. For data item without interrupting, if the time constraint is ≥ 0, the data item with slack time meets its deadline. The slack time expresses the access delayed time of a transaction and still meet its deadline.

For multi-path transmission with time constraint, the implementations represent that the EDF strategy is the best methods over the non-wireless environment. The RxW strategy measures a calculation using the LWF method to multiply the multi-path. For the sake of efficiency, the performance of the approximate algorithms has proven nearly LWF. In view of minimizing wait time, the LWF strategy has been proven to outperform all other policies. However, the LWF has been shown as expensive to implement described in [5]. In LS strategy, the data item with the priority based on the processing time it receives. The disadvantage of LS is that the transaction restarts, and its priority changes. When the system is under heavy load, LS strategy and EDF strategy decrease their edge, and even with the strategy of first coming and first serving, most data items face deadlines.

Some research work has been studied multi-path for wireless sensor distribution described in the following. In [16], a routing protocol used to organize the deployment of wireless sensor nodes, called adaptive information dispersion algorithms (AIDAs), which consider fault tolerance and assign nodes to schedules to reduce the overload of intermittent failures to utilize redundancy where sensor nodes must be routed periodically to meet timing constraints. AIDA strategy certifies the lower bound for the probability of meeting timing constraints. Similar paper works dealing with routing appears described in [8]. In [9], it points that designing strategies for routing based on pinwheel scheduling. This study obtained a pinwheel strategy, which uses mechanism to construct fault-tolerant routing. [9] differs from our work because, in our approach, we deploy all sensor nodes with time constraints using fitting methods over multi-path to minimize the congestion status.

In a multi-hop system, the cluster head periodically deals with a routing program with node access patterns. The routing cycle defines as the periodic routing program for one transmission. The deadlines have been integrated into the routing mechanism described in [10]. To reduce the congestion rate by using most effectively possible paths, the deployment strategy has to deal with key factors such as access frequency, time constraints, and path requirements. In [11], the deployment mechanism for sensor nodes is to minimize the delay caused by inefficient paths, but it is applicable for all nodes to optimize the average access time with the expected time.

3   The Proposed Method

Multiple hopping is a problem to be the real-time, dynamic deployment of sensor nodes. A cluster head is a cluster mainly constructed to process multi-path on sensor nodes. There are some features for traditional management systems that are different from dynamic systems. The data which the queries required to be dynamic and continuous in the service centers which expect dynamic data and continuous queries. In view of a large amount of required data, This assumption does not allow pending programs to be stored in their storage, nor can they query all program history. In general, the transactions executed over a set of data. A set of data is aggregated into the broadcast program, which is assigned to the current query. There are emerging applications, such as sensor networks, traffic control networks, and the healthcare system that brought important issues related to valid data.

We now represent a structure to support the deployment of the sensor node with congestion control. In this section, the deployment problem, cluster architecture, and solving mechanism are introduced. The prediction mechanism, problem formation, and cluster architecture are shown as Fig. 1 and solving mechanism is introduced. The versatility of wireless networks combined with the increase of ultra-light devices enables data processing applications and their design and use to be as deeply transformed as they are used. The hardware and software infrastructure is or is about to become available. First, the wireless network access is now operational, by the wireless local area network (WLAN) or by the ZigBee network. Also, the number of small-size nodes increases and connects to the network. All offer sensing capacities and communication in constant progress according to much research. Therefore, our purpose is to add the evolution in the field of processing technology based on proposing technologies to optimize information acquisition.

The Kalman filter focuses on the prediction problems which try to estimate the states of multiple asynchronous processes that are controlled using the linear stochastic difference equations. The definitions of the kernel define the important equations and the predict-update mechanism as followings:

Theorem 1. *Kernel Mechanism of Kalman Filter*
   Predict States:

$$ES_t = ST_t ES_{t-1} + CM_t CV_t \tag{1}$$
$$SV_t = ST_t SV_{t-1} ST_t^T + PV_t \tag{2}$$

   Update States:

$$ES_t = ES_{t-1} + KG_t \left(MV_t - MM_t ES_{t-1} \right) \tag{3}$$
$$KG_t = SV_{t-1} MM_t^T \left(MM_t SV_{t-1} MM_t^T + MVM_t \right)^{-1} \tag{4}$$
$$SV_t = SV_{t-1} MM_t^T \left(I - KG_t MM_t \right) SV_{t-1} \tag{5}$$

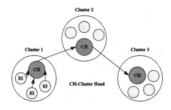

Fig. 1. Deployment of sensor nodes in wireless sensor network

where

- *ES: Estimated state.*
- *ST: State transition matrix.*
- *CV: Control variables.*
- *CM: Control matrix.*
- *SV: State variance matrix.*
- *PV: Process variance matrix.*
- *MV: Measurement variables.*
- *MM: Measurement matrix.*
- *KG: Kalman gain.*
- *MVM: Measurement variance matrix.*

Subscripts are as followings: t defines as current time period, and $t-1$ defines as previous time period. Random variable matrix PV represents the process and MVM represents the measurement noise. The matrices are independent, white, and with normal probability distributions. In practice, the process noise covariance PV matrix and measurement noise covariance MVM matrix change with each time step or measurement. We assume that the matrices are constant. The matrix ST in the difference Eqs. (1) and (2) is related to the state at the previous time step $t-1$ to the state at the current step t, there is absence for a driving function or process noise. The matrix A changes with each time step, but we assume that the matrix is constant. The matrix CM is related to the optional control input CV to the state ES. The matrix MM in the update Eqs. (3), (4) and (5) is related to the state to the update ES_t. The matrix MM changes with each time step or measurement, but we assume the matrix is constant.

We provide a simple sample demonstrating a way to measure the number denoted as N of sensor nodes in a wireless sensor network. This is shown in the Fig. 1. We are trying to estimate the number of sensor node in the cluster and the number of sensor node is unknown. We obtained the measurements which are from the known number. The definition is an assumed number or initial number. This number could be:

- Emptying, maximizing or static number.
- The relative measuring number to the average number of sensor node is static or is changing over time.

We assume that the model is the most basic model and the number is static (i.e., the number is constant $N = c$). Using the equations based on kernel definition, the state variables can be simplified to a scalars (i.e., $ES_t = ES$ where ES is the estimate of N). We assume a constant model which defines state $ES_{t+1} = ES_t$, so $ST_t = 1$, for any $t \geq 0$. The control variables CM and CV are not used (i.e. $both = 0$). In our model, we get the known number. The value is represented by $MV = MV$. We measure the value which could be a scaled measurement. In general, we assume that the measurement is the exact same scale as our state estimate (i.e. $MM = 1$). In this model, we assume that there is noise from the measurement (i.e. $MVM = mvm$). The process is a scalar and the value is $SV = sv$. The process is not well defined and we adjust the noise which define the value $PV = pv$. We show the effects which change these noise parameters. The filter can be described as followings:

Theorem 2. *Our Approach Model*
  Predict Equations:

$$ES_t = ES_{t-1} \tag{6}$$
$$SV_t = SV_{t-1} + PV_t \tag{7}$$

Update Equations:

$$ES_t = ES_{t-1} + KG_t \left(MV_t - ES_{t-1}\right) \tag{8}$$
$$KG_t = SV_{t-1}(SV_{t-1} + MVM)^{-1} \tag{9}$$
$$SV_t = (1 - KG_t) \, SV_{t-1} \tag{10}$$

We resolve our problem to make it a resolvable problem as following. Given a number of sensor node N to be deployed in multiple cluster K. Each sensor node is associated with an access probability. Every access of a node is only one delivery. Expected delay, w_i, is the expected number of ticks a node must wait for the delivery of sensor node d_i. Average expected delay is the number of ticks a node must wait for an average delivery and is computed as the sum of all expected delays, multiplied by their access probabilities, where w_i is expected delay and p_i is access probability for sensor node d_i respectively. With congestion rate of sensor nodes, a delivery for sensor node d_i has exceeded its maximum delay when deadline (expected delay time for sensor node d_i exceeds its total waiting time $t_i < W$) occurred at its time slot. The congestion rate for all sensor nodes is defined as following:

$$CongestionRate = \sum_{j=1}^{K} \sum p_i \tag{11}$$

Our approach predicts the number of sensor nodes in the cluster that minimizes the system overload. We define an policy referred as mechanism prediction of system overload described in [3] to enhance the system efficiency on a wireless environment. If the node number is minimized, system efficiency can be optimized.

Algorithm 1. Predict-Update

{The PU process estimates all states of system}
Input: The number of sensor nodes in the previous time step;
Output: The number of sensor nodes in the current time step;
    Use the previous state to predict the current state;
    To adjust state variance matrix based on process variance matrix;
    To update the current state by Kalman gain and measurement variables;
    To adjust Kalman gain using measurement variance at the current time step;
    To adjust state variance matrix using Kalman gain at the current time step;

---

4   Performance Results and Discussion

We randomly selected a scalar constant as the first step and then ran 100 different tests with an error value generally distributed around 0 and a standard deviation of 0.001. We can generate individual measurements in the filter loop. However, the pre-generated 100 measurements allow us to run several simulations with the same measurements (i.e., the same measurement noise) so that comparisons between simulations of different parameters are more meaningful. During the simulation process, we fixed the measurement variance at R. Since this is an actual measurement error variance, we expect optimal performance in balancing responsiveness and estimating variance. This will be more obvious in the following simulations. Figure 2 depicts the result distribution which represents the relationship of prediction and measurement. In Fig. 3, both prediction and measurement are close in some estimated values in term of accurate prediction from our model. In except of the initial state which is extreme assumption, the experimental result shows the better performance and verifies the fact that our approach model is an efficient prediction mechanism.

In our mobile simulation model, bandwidth is not explicitly modeled. On the contrary, it is similar to previous work described in [4], we use broadcast ticks as a measure of time. The greatest advantage of this approach is that the results are not limited to any particular path number. The measurement devotes to get the important features in the system described in [12]. The system implements multi-hop networking shown as [13]. The sensor nodes are allocated on fixed location in a cluster. Sensor nodes need to communicate to the cluster head via a link can be transmitted in [14]. The arrival rate of requests generated by sensor node follows a *Poisson* process and the inter-arrival time is exponential distribution with mean λ. Each node has a transmission *id* and arrival time.

We assume transmission generated by sensor nodes are random and no update transmission which is allowed. Our approach does not consider the concurrency control issues. At each tick of the time slot, a implemented transmission generator produces transmission with exponential distribution. The information of each transmission *id* and arrival time is stored. The transmission is then inserted to the appending queue. A node can require multi-path. We assume that transmission probabilities p_i follow the *transmission* distribution described in [15], where p_i represents the $i'th$ most popular path. The *transmission* distribution allows the path requested to be skewed.

$$p_i = \frac{\left(\frac{1}{i}\right)^{\theta}}{\sum_{i=1}^{M} \left(\frac{1}{i}\right)^{\theta}}, 1 \le i \le M \tag{12}$$

We only chose online heuristic algorithms to simulate the environment because we believe that these online heuristics are better suited to the dynamic changes in the intensity and distribution of system workloads. The off-line algorithms are not considered due to the fact that they are mainly for fairly stable systems. We implement the simulation model described in the previous section using visual studio. In each experiment, we run the simulation for 1000 time units, and we use an average of 100 runs of each simulation as the final result. The default total number of sensor nodes in the cluster called the number of nodes is 100 unit sensor nodes that reach another node exponentially, with an average arrival time of *lambda*, and the value of λ is varied from 1 to 100 in our simulation. The model is used to implement the system with rising, greatly dynamic populations. Congestion shows a skewed *transmission* distribution with parameter θ to control the skewness.

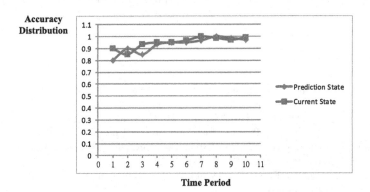

Fig. 2. Accuracy deployment between prediction and measurement states in WSN

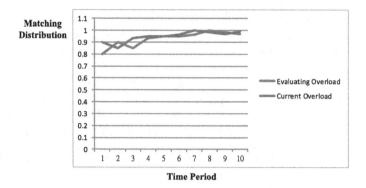

Fig. 3. Matching deployment between prediction and measurement states in WSN

5   Conclusion

In this paper, we present a prediction model based on the Kalman filter for deploying the sensor node to balance system overload over wireless sensor environments. In our demonstration, the traditional strategies that have proven to work cannot effectively balance system overload in wireless environments. We propose an efficient prediction mechanism based on an online heuristic algorithm, which is designed for timely balancing sensor nodes in wireless environments to minimize the congestion rate and reduce system overload. We simulate our model over wireless multi-hop environments based on heuristic deployment. The experiment results show that the proposed method is superior to the existing method in different accuracy distribution. In times to come, we intend to adjust our system parameters to decrease its time complexity. Other concentrations include estimated state of variance variables and matrices that can handle measurement errors, update processes, control variables, and matrices.

References

1. Le, T.N., Pegatoquet, A., Berder, O., Sentieys, O.: Energy-efficient power manager and MAC protocol for multi-hop wireless sensor networks powered by periodic energy harvesting sources. IEEE Sens. J. **15**(12), 7208–7220 (2015)
2. Ray, A., De, D.: Energy efficient clustering protocol based on K-means (EECPK-means)-midpoint algorithm for enhanced network lifetime in wireless sensor network. IET Wirel. Sens. Syst. **6**(6), 181–191 (2016)
3. Cengiz, K., Dag, T.: Energy aware multi-hop routing protocol for WSNs. IEEE Access **6**, 2622–2633 (2018)
4. Fawzy, A.E., Shokair, M., Saad, W.: Balanced and energy-efficient multi-hop techniques for routing in wireless sensor networks. IET Netw. **7**(1), 33–43 (2018)
5. Ari, D., Cibuk, M., Aggun, F.: The comparison of energy consumption of different topologies in multi-hop wireless sensor networks. In: 2018 International Conference on Artificial Intelligence and Data Processing, pp. 1–5. IEEE, Malatya (2018)

6. Chattopadhyay, A., Mitra, U.: Active sensing for Markov chain tracking. In: 2018 IEEE Global Conference on Signal and Information Processing, pp. 1050–1054. IEEE, Anaheim (2018)
7. Yang, X., Liu, T., Deng, D.: Inter-cluster multi-hop routing algorithm based on K-means. In: 2018 IEEE 4th Information Technology and Mechatronics Engineering Conference, pp. 1296–1301. IEEE, Chongqing (2018)
8. Upadhyay, D., Dubey, A.K., Santhi Thilagam, P.: An energy-efficient static multi-hop (ESM) routing protocol for wireless sensor network in agriculture. In: 2018 2nd International Conference on Micro-Electronics and Telecommunication Engineering, pp. 277–280. IEEE, Ghaziabad (2018)
9. Tao, L., Zhang, X., Dai, Z.: A frame prioritization based on classified contentions in multi-hop wireless Ad hoc networks. In: 2018 IEEE 4th International Conference on Computer and Communications, pp. 435–439. IEEE, Chengdu (2018)
10. Huang, H., Huang, F., Li, C., Yuan, X., Zhai, X., Hao, J.: A perturbed compressed sensing based authentication mechanism in multi-hop wireless sensor networks. In: 2018 IEEE Symposium on Product Compliance Engineering-Asia (ISPCE-CN), pp. 1–5. IEEE, Shenzhen (2018)
11. Gao, F., Wen, H., Zhao, L., Chen, Y.: Design and optimization of a cross-layer routing protocol for multi-hop wireless sensor networks. In: 2013 International Conference on Sensor Network Security Technology and Privacy Communication System, pp. 5–8. IEEE, Nangang (2013)
12. Al Rasyid, M.U.H., Saputra, F.A., Ismar, M.R.: Performance of multi-hop networks using beacon and non-beacon scheduling in wireless sensor network (WSN). In: 2015 International Electronics Symposium (IES), pp. 195–199. IEEE, Surabaya (2015)
13. Choi, H., Park, S., Cho, H.: Enhancement of technologies of GTS utilization for QoS guarantee in multi-hop wireless sensor networks based on IEEE 802.15.4. In: 2015 International SoC Design Conference (ISOCC), pp. 269–270. IEEE, Gyungju (2015)
14. Buranapanichkit, D.: Study of expected delay of multi-hop desynchronization for wireless sensor networks. In: 2016 IEEE Region 10 Conference (TENCON), pp. 1334–1337. IEEE, Singapore (2016)
15. Sethu Lakshmi, P., Jibukumar, M.G., Neenu, V.S.: Network lifetime enhancement of multi-hop wireless sensor network by RF energy harvesting. In: 2018 International Conference on Information Networking (ICOIN), pp. 738–743. IEEE, Chiang Mai (2018)
16. Bestavros, A.: An adaptive information dispersal algorithm for time-critical reliable communication. Netw. Manage. Control **2**, 423–438 (1995)

A Combined Routing Path and Node Importance Network Invulnerability Evaluating Method for Ad Hoc Network

Weiling Zhou, Bo Li, Zhongjiang Yan$^{(\boxtimes)}$, and Mao Yang

School of Electronics and Information,
Northwestern Polytechnical University, Xi'an, China
2018261692@mail.nwpu.edu.cn, {libo.npu,zhjyan,yangmao}@nwpu.edu.cn

Abstract. In this paper, a new network invulnerability evaluation model based on routing path and node importance is proposed. The core of the invulnerability algorithm lies in two levels, comprehensive consideration of the influencing factors of network to point-to-line network invulnerability. The algorithm considers the influence of the proportion of important nodes of the network on the invulnerability of the network, and considers the influence of the number of paths between the communication nodes on the invulnerability of the path. Through simulation comparison, it is found that this algorithm improves the sensitivity of network invulnerability to the number of paths, and is suitable for communication networks in the case of multiple routing paths.

Keywords: Network invulnerability · Routing path · Node importance · Ad hoc network

1 Introduction

Ad hoc network is a network system that is interconnected or organized by a communication node in a system through a distributed protocol without a backbone network. As a distributed, temporary autonomous multi-hop network, the ad hoc network itself does not have a fixed infrastructure. In the network, each user terminal can generate and process some business data for other users like a host. The terminal can also be like a router, establish and maintain a network topology, and implement some routing protocols [1,2]. Since wireless communication is limited by distance, if two user equipments that are far apart from each other want to communicate with each other, they must use some intermediate users located between their geographical locations to forward information for them, thereby realizing user communication [3].

Ad hoc networks are characterized by topological dynamics [4,5], limited link bandwidth, time-varying capacity, limited node energy, short network lifetime, and limited physical security [6,7]. Ad hoc networks are often used to secure information in harsh environments such as battlefields and natural disasters.

D.-J. Deng et al. (Eds.): WiCON 2019, LNICST 317, pp. 20–33, 2020.
https://doi.org/10.1007/978-3-030-52988-8_3

The transmission task, therefore, puts high demands on the invulnerability of the network structure [8].

The study of network invulnerability is extremely important for complex networks [9,10]. In a broad sense, it refers to the ability of a network to maintain its normal operating state after encountering a fault or being attacked [11]. In a narrow sense, network invulnerability means that after a network encounters a random failure or an external attack, there is also a connected area in the network that is proportional to the total node of the network [12,13]. There are three types of attacks in the network: one is man-made destruction, with a strong purpose, and priority attacks on important nodes. The second is natural disasters, large-scale node damage in an area [14,15]. The third is a random failure.

Invulnerability is the ability of a network to continue its function when a node [16,17] or edge in the network fails due to its own cause or by intentional attacks from the outside world. Node connectivity, network communication efficiency, and network average node degree are usually used as measures to measure network invulnerability. Based on these network invulnerability measures, Feng H, Li C and Xu Y proposed an invulnerability assessment algorithm based on temporal networks [18]. However, the algorithm can not reflect the impact of routing path resistance. In view of its failure to comprehensively evaluate the network invulnerability measure and node importance, this paper proposes an invulnerability algorithm based on link and node importance. The algorithm can well reflect the impact of the proportion of important nodes and the number of routing paths.

This article will first introduce and analyze some important measures of network system model and network invulnerability in the second section, and briefly describe the existing methods of invulnerability assessment. Then the third section details the principle and definition of the invulnerability algorithm based on link and node importance. The fourth section carries out simulation results and performance analysis and the fifth section summarizes the full text.

2   System Model

2.1   Network Model and Invulnerability Measure

There are two common network models: random networks and scale-free networks. In a random network, each pair of nodes in the network is always connected with a certain probability. Therefore, the number of nodes that each node can communicate in a random network is roughly the same, but the network topology constructed at this time is very complicated. As the number of nodes in the network increases, the number of connections that can exist increases, and the probability of node connections decreases exponentially. Therefore, random networks are also called index networks. In most real-world application networks, not all nodes are completely in the same state. There will always be some nodes that have a large degree of connectivity, while others have a small degree of connectivity, and usually they account for 2:8. A network with this characteristic is called a scale-free network.

The invulnerability measures are divided into non-topological measures and topological measures. The core idea of non-topological measures is to select network simple attributes that are independent of the network topology as a measure of the network's ability to resist damage. Common network attributes include the number of remaining available nodes, coverage area, network lifetime, and so on. These network attributes are simple and easy to obtain. In many literatures, one or several network attributes are often used as indicators of the measure of invulnerability. However, network attributes are difficult to fully and accurately reflect the network's anti-destructive performance. When designing the invulnerability algorithm, the most used is the topological measure of invulnerability.

The network topology can be mathematically represented by graph theory, that is, graph $G = (V, E)$. Suppose the graph is an undirected weightless graph, where $V = (v_1, v_2, v_3, ..., v_n)$ is a set of all nodes, $E = (e_1, e_2, e_3, ..., e_n)$ is a collection of all edges (network links) of the network topology. Here are a few important topological measures for analyzing invulnerability [19]:

The Importance of the Node. In the network model, especially the scale-free network model, the importance of the node in the network topology is often evaluated by the degree and the median, and the greater the degree and the medium, the more important the node is. The importance of a node reflects the importance of the node in the overall network topology and is an assessment of the importance of the nodes in the network topology. The impact of a critical node being destroyed on network invulnerability is much greater than that of a normal node.

The Degree of the Node. In the network, the number of edges k_i of the node v_i is called the degree of the node v_i. The greater the degree of a node, the more important it is in the network. The average of the network is:

$$k = \frac{1}{N} \sum_{j=1}^{N} k_i \tag{1}$$

The Median of Nodes. The median B_i of the node v_i is the sum of the proportion of the number of nodes passing through the shortest path in the network. If the minimum distance between a pair of nodes N_{jk}, and $N_{jk}(i)$ paths pass through node v_i, then v_i contributes to $N_{jk}(i)/N_{jk}$ for the pair of nodes, and node v_i The contributions to all pairs of nodes are added together to get the median B_i of the node v_i, namely:

$$B_i = \sum_{j,k \in V j \neq k} \frac{N_{jk}(i)}{N_{jk}} \tag{2}$$

The Critical Point Removal Ratio f_c. When a node in the network is attacked and the network is at the edge of the crash, the number of nodes attacked on the network as a percentage of the total number of nodes is called the critical point removal ratio, which is recorded as f_c.

Maximum Connectivity S. The ratio of the number of nodes in the largest connected branch in the network to the total number of nodes in the network is called the maximum connectivity, namely:

$$S = \frac{m(G)}{N} \tag{3}$$

It can be seen from the above equation that $0 \leq S \leq 1$, and if and only if the network is fully connected, there is $S = 1$; If and only if the network completely crashes, there is $S \approx 0$, that is, all nodes in the network are isolated nodes after being attacked.

Global Efficiency E. First use d_{ij} as the shortest distance between any two nodes v_i and node v_j in the network. Define the average value of the network global efficiency as the sum of the reciprocal of the shortest distance between any two nodes in the network topology, as follows:

$$E = \frac{1}{N(N-1)} \sum_{j,k \in V j \neq k} \frac{1}{d_{ij}} \tag{4}$$

This paper will focus on the scale-free network model, especially in the case of some network routes supporting multiple paths, to carry out research on network invulnerability.

2.2   Existing Invulnerability Assessment Method

In this section, an existing network invulnerability assessment method based on dynamic network model will be introduced. First explain some basic indicators of the temporal network, then describe how to use these measures to quantitatively define the non-destructibility of the temporal network [18].

Temporal Network Model. At time t, the network topology is modeled as $G(t) = (V(t), E(t))$. The network topology consists of two important factors, where $V(t)$ represents the set of vertices and $E(t)$ represents Edge set. $E(t) = e_{ij}(t)$, if the distance $d_{ij}(t)$ between the two nodes is less than the shortest communication distance, then $e_{ij}(t)$ exists.

Temporal Distance. The shortest time distance $d_{ij}(t_1, t_2)$ can be defined as the minimum time distance among the lengths of all time paths between the nodes v_i and v_j in the time window $[t_1, t_2]$. During the time window $[t_1, t_2]$, the average time distance $L(t_1, t_2)$ of a given topology model G is defined as:

$$L(t_1, t_2) = \frac{1}{N(N-1)} \sum_{j,k \in V j \neq k} d_{ij}(t_1, t_2) \tag{5}$$

Time Global Efficiency. Time efficiency means that there is a lack of path between a longer time path and a node that is simultaneously disconnected in time. The time global efficiency $E(t_1, t_2)$ of a given topology model G is:

$$E(t_1, t_2) = \frac{1}{N(N-1)} \sum_{j,k \in V j \neq k} \frac{1}{d_{ij}(t_1, t_2)} \tag{6}$$

Invulnerability Algorithm Definition. Use $\Delta E(G, D)$ to indicate that the efficiency loss on the time graph G caused by the node damage D is $\Delta E(G, D) = E_G - E_{G_D}$, then the network invulnerability R_G of the topology map G against the node damage D is defined as:

$$R_G = \frac{\Delta E(G, D)}{E_G} = 1 - \frac{E_{G_D}}{E_G} \tag{7}$$

It is easy to know from the above analysis that the invulnerability algorithm introduced in this section mainly depends on the shortest distance between two communication nodes, but does not fully consider the impact of other network invulnerability measures against destructiveness. It can be known from the definition of invulnerability that the network can still maintain the communication function when the node or edge of the network is damaged due to its own or external factors. The shortest distance of the communication link involved in the above-mentioned invulnerability algorithm can be regarded as the invulnerability of the network, but it does not reflect the invulnerability of the nodes in the network. Therefore, this invulnerability algorithm is not comprehensive.

3 Invulnerability Algorithm Based on Link and Node Importance

In the network invulnerability assessment, the analysis of the importance of the node is a very important part. The existing network invulnerability evaluation model fails to comprehensively evaluate the network invulnerability measure and the importance of the node. In this section, A new invulnerability algorithm is proposed based on the multi-index evaluation method of link invulnerability and node importance, considering the influence of the invulnerability R of the invulnerability data link network in the network. The following network invulnerability R is defined as:

$$R = k \times R_{side} + (1 - k) \times R_{node}, 0 \leq k \leq 1 \tag{8}$$

It can be seen from the above equation that the network invulnerability is determined by two aspects: one is the invulnerability of the end-to-end routing path; the other is the influence of the nature of the nodes in the network on the network invulnerability. The influence factor k is used to determine the degree of influence of these two parameters against destructiveness. The following will specifically analyze the invulnerability of the end-to-end routing path and the impact of network node resistance.

3.1   Invulnerability Calculation Method

Path Invulnerability Calculation. R_{side} is used to indicate the invulnerability of the end-to-end routing path, which is the average value of end-to-end communication invulnerability between all two nodes s and t in the network topology, as follows:

$$R_{side} = \frac{\sum_{s=1}^{M} \sum_{t=1, t \neq s}^{M} R(s,t)}{\sum_{s=1}^{M} \sum_{t=1, t \neq s}^{M} 1} \tag{9}$$

Where M represents the total number of nodes in the network. $R(s,t)$ is the end-to-end communication invulnerability measure between two nodes s, t. When there are multiple routing paths between two nodes, the path with the highest invulnerability in the path is selected to represent the current two. End-to-end communication intrusion between communication nodes, namely:

$$R(s,t) = max(r_1, r_2, r_3, ..., r_N)\frac{N}{N+C}, 0 \leq C \leq 1 \tag{10}$$

N indicates the total number of routing paths between the specified nodes s and t, and C is a parameter indicating the degree of influence of the number of paths against the destructiveness, and takes values between 0 and 1. r_n represents the invulnerability of the n-th routing path between the node s and the node t, which is a function of the path hop count α, the probability of the intermediate node being damaged β, and the intermediate link interruption probability γ, ie

$$r_n = f(\alpha, \beta, \gamma) \tag{11}$$

And r_n is negatively related to these three factors. For example, the invulnerability is negatively correlated with the number of hops of the path. When the number of hops of the path is increased, the probability that the intermediate node is damaged or the intermediate path is interrupted will be larger, and the invulnerability of the path will be lower. In the process of network communication, nodes are generally transmitted with a shortest path. The more hops, the worse the reliability of the path, and the worse its invulnerability. Because the link or node may be invalid due to external factors, if there are multiple shortest paths between the nodes, the data may be transmitted by other shortest paths after a shortest path fails.

After considering these influencing factors, define the invulnerability of a single path:

$$r_n = \prod_{i=0}^{K}(1 - P_i) \tag{12}$$

Where K is the hop count of the routing path and P_i is the probability of the interruption of the i-th intermediate link (i-th hop) in the routing path. It is easy to see that in this definition, when the K value is larger, the more hops of a single routing path, the lower the invulnerability of the path will be, so the path invulnerability and the hop count of the path have a negative correlation.

In the communication network, the outage probability of the link is proportional to the packet loss rate of the link. The packet loss rate is used to indicate the outage probability of the intermediate link:

$$P_i = P_{max} \frac{d_i}{D_{max}} \tag{13}$$

Where d_i represents the distance length of the i-th intermediate link in the current routing path, and D_{max} represents the longest link distance between two nodes that can communicate. P_{max} represents the packet loss rate when the two nodes are apart from D_{max}, and theoretically takes the parameter $P_{max} = 0.1$.

In summary, the average end-to-end invulnerability in the network topology is:

$$R_{side} = \frac{\sum_{s=1}^{M}\sum_{t=1,t\neq s}^{M} max(r_1, r_2, r_3, ..., r_N)\frac{N}{N+C}}{\sum_{s=1}^{M}\sum_{t=1,t\neq s}^{M} 1}, N \geq 1, N \in Z, M \in Z \tag{14}$$

$$r_n = \prod_{i=0}^{K}(1 - P_{max}\frac{d_i}{D_{max}}), K \geq 1, K \in Z \tag{15}$$

Node Invulnerability Calculation. At the same time, for the scale-free network model, the "importance" of a node is related to its position in the network path. A few nodes often have a large number of connections. These nodes with high degrees and median are important nodes in the network. For example, the cluster head in the clustering topology, the multi-hop relay node (MPR) in the OLSR protocol, and the like. From the perspective of the overall topology of the network, the stability of the network structure also depends on the proportion of important nodes in the network.

$$R_{node} = \frac{Number\ of\ important\ nodes}{Total\ number\ of\ network\ nodes} \tag{16}$$

The destruction of important nodes has a greater impact on the network topology than the destruction of general nodes. When there are redundant important nodes, the destroyed path will make it easier to find alternative paths, thus improving the overall network invulnerability.

3.2 Algorithm Innovation

Consider Multiple Paths. The target algorithm only considers the shortest distance between two nodes, which is equivalent to considering a single routing path for communication between two nodes. The newly defined invulnerability algorithm fully considers the invulnerability of multiple paths.

$$R(s,t) = max(r_1, r_2, r_3, ..., r_N)\frac{N}{N+C}, 0 \leq C \leq 1 \tag{17}$$

In the definition of the above formula, the parameter C is used to adjust the degree of influence of the number of paths against the damage. When the value of C is larger, the influence of the change of the number of paths on the network invulnerability is greater.

Network invulnerability is defined as "the ability of the entire network to complete the transmission of business information after the destruction of some nodes in the network." The network completes the transmission of service information, mainly relying on the routing path between the source end node and the destination end node. Therefore, analyzing the impact of node destruction on the number of network routing paths can be found to include the following two cases:

All routing paths are lost: If some of the critical nodes in the network are damaged, the routing path between the source node and the destination node is completely disconnected and does not exist, it can be considered that "the network is damaged by this part of the node" And a network crash occurs;

The number of routing paths is reduced: some links are disconnected and the path through the link is lost due to node destruction, thereby reducing network invulnerability; for example, two paths are required to transmit the same information before the node is damaged (thus Reduce the impact of the node due to packet loss), but now due to the destruction of a node, only one path can be used to transmit the message, so the network invulnerability is reduced.

The new invulnerability formula shows that the invulnerability is positively correlated with the number of paths between the two nodes. When there are more alternative paths between the two nodes, the invulnerability is higher.

Consider All Nodes. The target algorithm only considers the nodes that can communicate with each other, and does not consider nodes that are isolated and cannot communicate. The newly defined invulnerability algorithm takes into account not only all nodes in the network.

$$R_{side} = \frac{\sum_{s=1}^{M} \sum_{t=1, t \neq s}^{M} R(s,t)}{\sum_{s=1}^{M} \sum_{t=1, t \neq s}^{M} 1} \tag{18}$$

It also considers the impact of the nature of the nodes in the network on the overall network invulnerability:

$$R_{node} = \frac{Number\ of\ important\ nodes}{Total\ number\ of\ network\ nodes} \tag{19}$$

In this algorithm, the degree of the node, that is, the number of edges associated with the node, is used to determine whether the node is an important node. In the case of a known network topology, the number of important nodes in the network can be determined, thereby obtaining the influence of the nature of the nodes in the network on the network invulnerability.

4   Performance Analysis of Invulnerability Algorithm

4.1   Performance Trends for Different Link Distances

When the original algorithm calculates invulnerability, only the shortest distance between two nodes is considered, which is equivalent to considering a single routing path for communication between two nodes. The newly defined invulnerability algorithm fully considers the invulnerability of multiple paths. The following simulation graph abscissa is the number of routing paths that can exist between two communication nodes set in the routing protocol, and the ordinate is the invulnerability R of the network. It can be seen that the original algorithm calculates the network invulnerability without the routing path. The number of bars affects, while the new invulnerability formula shows that the

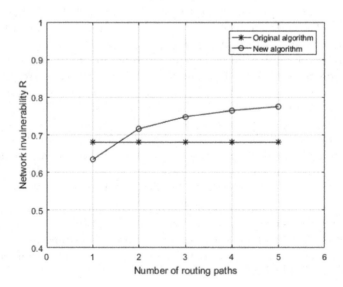

Fig. 1. Comparison between original algorithm and new algorithm when path number changes

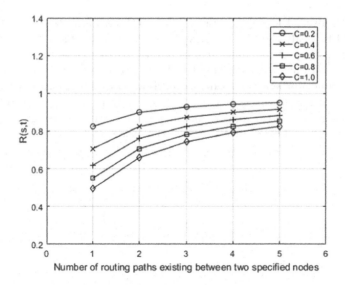

Fig. 2. The relationship between the new algorithm and the number of routing paths

invulnerability is positively related to the number of paths between two nodes, that is, when there are more alternative paths between the two nodes, the higher the invulnerability. This performance is also in line with actual communication.

In order to study the relationship between the newly proposed network invulnerability measurement algorithm and the number of routing paths, the impact of the number of routing paths on the end-to-end communication invulnerability can be analyzed.

The horizontal coordinate of the above figure is the number of routing paths existing between two communication nodes, and the ordinate is the end-to-end path invulnerability $R(s, t)$ between the two communication nodes. The parameter C is used to indicate the degree of influence of the number of paths against the damage, and the value is between 0 and 1. It can be found from the above figure that when the fixed parameter C is constant, as the number of communication routing paths between two nodes increases, the invulnerability becomes larger. With the increase of C value, the influence of the number of paths on the path invulnerability is more and more obvious, and the curvature of the curve is larger (Figs. 1 and 2).

It can be proved that the newly proposed invulnerability algorithm is applicable to multipath routing networks. Because in the routing protocol, when two designated nodes communicate with each other, the more recorded paths, when the network link is damaged, other alternative links can be found for information transmission without causing two nodes. Inter-communication is interrupted, and the path invulnerability will be relatively large. This is consistent with our simulation results of invulnerability analysis.

The path invariance algorithm is applied to the dynamic source routing protocol (DSR) to study the effectiveness of the network invulnerability algorithm. DSR is a routing protocol used in the Mobile Ad Hoc Network (MANET). It works in the Internet layer of the TCP/IP protocol suite and is a simple and efficient routing protocol designed for multi-hop wireless Ad Hoc networks. In the DSR routing protocol, a specified number of routing paths can be set and recorded. Therefore, in this paper, the number of different routing paths can be set under the DSR routing protocol, and the following figure can be simulated (Fig. 3).

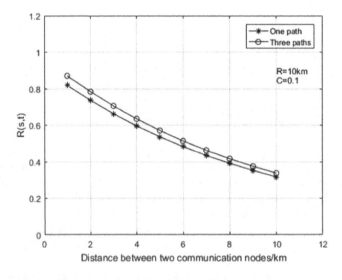

Fig. 3. Invulnerability of the same route under different path number settings, $C = 0.1$

The abscissa of the above figure is the physical distance between two communication nodes, and the ordinate is the end-to-end path invulnerability $R(s, t)$ between the two communication nodes. First, we can see that as the physical distance between two communication nodes increases, the path invulnerability continues to decrease. Moreover, a DSR routing protocol with three routing paths is always more invulnerable than an DSR routing protocol with only one path. However, the sensitivity of the two routing protocols to the number of paths is controlled by parameter C.

Study the effect of the distance between two communication nodes and the maximum transmission distance against destruction (Figs. 4 and 5):

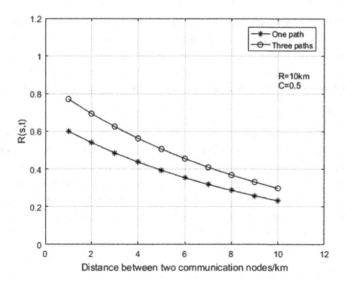

Fig. 4. Invulnerability of the same route under different path number settings, $C = 0.5$

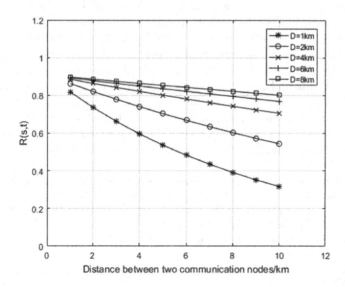

Fig. 5. Relationship between invulnerability and node distance and maximum communication distance

The abscissa of the above figure is the physical distance between two communication nodes, and the ordinate is the end-to-end path invulnerability $R(s, t)$ between the two communication nodes. Analysis shows that when the maximum transmission distance between two communication nodes is fixed, such as when $D = 1$ km, as the distance between two communication nodes increases, the path invulnerability is continuously reduced, which is related to the actual situation. It is consistent. As the communication path increases, the link is more likely to be damaged due to its own or external elements. The increased probability of the link being destroyed will increase the probability of the interruption of the routing path, which in turn will lead to a decrease in the path invulnerability of the network.

The maximum transmission distance between two communication nodes also has an impact on the destructiveness. The smaller the maximum transmission distance, the lower the path resistance of the network. This is because the maximum transmission distance becomes smaller, which may lead to an increase in the number of hops of the node communication path, and more intermediate nodes, so that the probability of the node being damaged on the communication link increases, and the probability of interruption of the sub-link increases. Thus, the path of the mentor network is reduced.

5   Conclusion

This paper focuses on the research of self-organizing network invulnerability. Firstly, it introduces two common network topology models: random network and scale-free network, and analyzes some important topological network invulnerability measures. Aiming at the problem that the existing network invulnerability evaluation model fails to comprehensively evaluate the network invulnerability measure and node importance, a new network invulnerability evaluation algorithm based on link and node importance is proposed. The algorithm can reflect the influence of the number of routing paths and the degree of importance of network nodes. Through simulation verification, it is also found that the algorithm can correctly and effectively reflect the influence of node communication distance and maximum transmission distance on network invulnerability.

Acknowledgement. This work was supported in part by the National Natural Science Foundations of CHINA (Grant No.61771392, 61771390, 61871322, 61501373 and 61271279), the National Science and Technology Major Project (Grant No. 2015ZX03002006-004 and 2016ZX03001018-004), and Science and Technology on Avionics Integration Laboratory (Grant No. 20185553035).

References

1. Li, K., Wang, H.: Research on invulnerability of scale-free network with a unified method. Int. J. Arts Technol. **11**(3), 266–284 (2019)
2. He, S., Jin, C., Wei, H., Liu, Q.: A measure method for network invulnerability based on improved albert algorithm. In: International Conference on Instrumentation (2011)
3. Albert, R., Jeong, H., Barabasi, A.L.: Error and attack tolerance of complex networks. Nature **340**(1), 378–382 (2000)
4. Fu, X., Yao, H., Yang, Y.: Exploring the invulnerability of wireless sensor networks against cascading failures. Inf. Sci. (2019)

5. Wen, C., Zhang, X.: The invulnerability of robust communication network. In: IEEE International Conference on Communication Software & Networks (2016)
6. Luo, J.-J., Feng, Y.-H., Zuo, C.: Analysis on the invulnerability of network based on scale-free network, pp. 1519–1522 (2018)
7. Rao, Y.P., Lin, J.Y., Hou, D.T.: Evaluation method for network invulnerability based on shortest route number. J. Commun. **30**(4), 113–117 (2009)
8. Yun, F., Hong, L.Z., Hai, T.Y.: Research of new certain metrics of network invulnerability. Adv. Mater. Res. **301–303**, 1322–1326 (2011)
9. Li, E., Gong, J., Huang, J.: Analysis about functional invulnerability of convergent network based on function chain. Binggong Xuebao/Acta Armamentarii **40**(7), 1450–1459 (2019)
10. Zhao, D.J., Yang, H.T., Jian, J., Yu, H.: Modeling and simulation of the invulnerability of space information network. In: International Conference on Internet Technology & Applications (2010)
11. Peng, K., Huang, B.: The invulnerability studies on data center network. Int. J. Secur. Appl. **9**(11), 167–186 (2015)
12. Tian, X.W., Liu, S.Y., Zhang, Z.H., Dong, H.J.: A topology optimal algorithm for improving the invulnerability of scale-free networks. In: International Conference on Information System & Artificial Intelligence (2017)
13. Bao, X.-C., Dai, F.-S., Han, W.-Z.: Evaluation method of network invulnerability based on disjoint paths in topology. Xi Tong Gong Cheng Yu Dian Zi Ji Shu/Syst. Eng. Electron. **34**(1), 168–174 (2012)
14. Chen, H.-H., Lin, A.-M.: Complex network characteristics and invulnerability simulating analysis of supply chain. J. Netw. **7**(3), 591–597 (2012)
15. Wu, J., Tan, S.-Y., Tan, Y.-J., Deng, H.-Z.: Analysis of invulnerability in complex networks based on natural connectivity. Complex Syst. Complex. Sci. **11**(1), 77–86 (2014)
16. Jiang, L., Zhang, F., Yang, R., Xu, K.: Influence of sensor nodes on the invulnerability of tree network. Telkomnika (Telecommun. Comput. Electron. Control) **13**(4), 1242–1250 (2015)
17. Fu, X., Li, W., Fortino, G.: Empowering the invulnerability of wireless sensor networks through super wires and super nodes, pp. 561–568 (2013)
18. Feng, H., Li, C., Xu, Y.: Invulnerability analysis of vehicular ad hoc networks based on temporal networks. In: IEEE International Conference on Computer & Communications (2017)
19. Feng, H.-F., Li, C.-H.: Invulnerability analysis of vehicle self-organizing network based on complex network. Comput. Appl. **36**(7), 1789–1792 (2016)

An OFDMA-Based Neighbor Discovery and Tracking Protocol for Directional Ad-Hoc Network

Xiaojiao Hu, Yang Qi, Bo Li, Zhongjiang Yan[(✉)], and Mao Yang

School of Electronics and Information, Northwestern Polytechnical University,
Xi'an, China
18392990273@mail.nwpu.edu.cn,
{yangqi,libo.npu,zhjyan,yangmao}@nwpu.edu.cn

Abstract. In order to implement an effective directed medium access control and routing protocol in a directed ad hoc network, the node in the network should know the state of the neighboring nodes. However, it is difficult to sense signals in other directions, due to the strong directivity of the directional antenna. It will result in problems such as link collision. In order to solve the above problems, this paper proposes an orthogonal frequency division multiple access (OFDMA) based neighbor discover and tracking protocol for directional ad-hoc network. Then this paper discusses the neighboring state partitioning method based on discovery time and multiple resource unit access and frame format design based on OFDMA. The simulation results show that compared with the directional transmission and reception algorithms protocol, the protocol proposed in this paper increases the number of neighbor discovered nodes by 200% when the number of neighbor nodes is about 30. The nodes can connect neighbor nodes frequently, and it improves accuracy of neighbor nodes position.

Keywords: OFDMA · Directional wireless ad hoc networks · Link collision · Neighbor node discovery and tracking

1 Introduction

Wireless ad hoc networks is formed by a group of autonomous wireless nodes or terminals cooperating with each other [1]. And the wireless ad hoc network has better stability. Because of the self-healing and self-regulating characteristics, the wireless ad hoc network does not depend on a single node, and the normality of the operation of a single node does not affect the normality of the entire network. Therefore, wireless ad hoc network applications are becoming more widespread.

Wireless ad hoc networks can be divided into omnidirectional ad hoc networks and directed ad hoc networks [2]. The technology of the access and transmission phase of the omni-directional ad hoc network is very mature, but since the antennas for receiving and transmitting are omnidirectional, it will bring great

© ICST Institute for Computer Sciences, Social Informatics and Telecommunications Engineering 2020
Published by Springer Nature Switzerland AG 2020. All Rights Reserved
D.-J. Deng et al. (Eds.): WiCON 2019, LNICST 317, pp. 34–47, 2020.
https://doi.org/10.1007/978-3-030-52988-8_4

interference to other nodes, and the power attenuation is faster, and the range of communication is reduced sharply. The capacity of the network has reached the bottleneck. Due to the ultra-long transmission distance brought by directional antennas, directional ad hoc networks have large network capacity [3]. In recent years, directed ad hoc networks have received more and more attention from scholars at home and abroad [4].

The directionality of the directional network brings great challenges to network communication. Since the widespread application of directional antenna technology, scholars at home and abroad have proposed a large number of directed medium access control protocol (DMAC). The literature [5] divides the channel access time into time slots, and the channel connection according to the time slots effectively mitigates the packet collision, but does not help the dynamic changes brought by the node movement. Based on the feedback confirmation mechanism, the literature [6] improves the interaction rules of the handshake process by adding multiple sub-nodes, shortens the discovery delay, and avoids unnecessary packet collisions. Although it can overcome the communication of the large-node density network, it still cannot improve. The problem caused by the movement of nodes in the network. Reference [7] is mainly for the master node to maintain information about the location of the neighbor node, which performs a topology control scheme on the discovered neighbors to select and maintain the neighbor subsets that are already connected. Although the scheme maintains the connectivity of the network. Sexuality, low path expansion is achieved, but it is based on the degree of limiting nodes, and is not applicable when the network node density is large. In [8], distributed antennas are used in directional antenna networks, and new nodes obtain their own neighbor information by querying a subset of other neighbors. In summary, these studies can not solve the problem of link conflict and node movement, especially when the node density increases and the node movement probability is high, the performance of the network will be greatly affected.

It is worth noting that IEEE 802.11ax will soon introduce official standards. OFDMA allows users to share band resources and is one of the key technologies of IEEE 802.11ax [9]. OFDMA can reach the transmission requirements of multiple users in a single transmission, which can greatly increase the capacity of the network [10]. Therefore, the introduction of OFDMA technology into directed ad hoc networks can further improve the performance of DMAC.

Based on the DTRA protocol, this paper proposes an OFDMA-based neighbor discovery and tracking protocol (ONDT). Specifically, based on the IEEE 802.11ax OFDMA as the next-generation WLAN standard, the multi-RU access mode is implemented, and the problem of high link collision caused by a single channel in the traditional DTRA protocol is solved, and the idea of "scheduling" is added to avoid The problem of node location "unreliable" due to node movement [11].

OFDMA is an evolution of Orthogonal Frequency Division Multiple technology (OFDM) that combines OFDM and FDMA technologies [12]. After the parent carrier is channelized by OFDM, the transmission technology of the transmission data is loaded on a part of the subcarriers. First, the resources of the entire channel are divided into a small fixed-size time-frequency resource block, which is also a Resource Unit (RU). In this mode, the user's data is carried on each RU, so from the perspective of the total time-frequency resources, there may be multiple users on each time slice.

The main contributions of this paper are as follows:

(1) The combination of OFDMA and neighbor discovery and tracking is proposed. This is a work to combine OFDMA with DMAC.
(2) Effectively solves problems such as link conflicts and node movements.
(3) The simulation platform evaluates the performance of the protocol. The simulation results show that ONDT effectively improves the number of neighbor discovery and ensures the reliability of the node location.

The rest of this paper is organized as follows. In Sect. 2, the system model of communication between the primary node and multiple neighbor nodes is introduced. And in Sect. 3, the details of the multi-RU neighbor discovery and tracking are described. In Sect. 4, the simulation platform is built to verify the protocol performance. This paper is summarized in Sect. 5.

2 System Model

In the directed ad hoc network, N nodes are randomly distributed in a circular area as shown in Fig. 1, each node is equipped with a directional antenna, and the communication area is divided into B sectors, each sector is covered by one beam. In this paper, the sector and beam are considered equivalent. At the same time, the model of the antenna is simplified, and the radiation intensity in the radiation range of the antenna is considered to be the same, that is, as long as the beam is radiated to the node, the received power of the node can be considered to reach the receiving threshold.

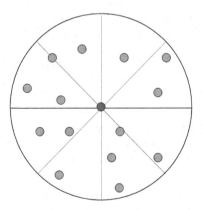

Fig. 1. Wireless ad hoc network node distribution.

Before introducing the protocol, the paper also makes the following assumptions: each node is distinguished by the number of $0{\sim}N{-}1$, and all nodes are randomly distributed in each sector; each node can quickly switch to the next sector. The switching time is ignored; the transmit power of each node is the same; of course, all nodes can communicate successfully only within the first transmit beam. Since this protocol is designed based on OFDMA, each user can only transmit data on a single RU. If multiple users select the same RU, the RU transmission is considered to have failed.

This protocol is based on the three-way handshake protocol of the DTRA scanning phase. We assume that there is one scan initiating node and several scanning receiving nodes in the wireless ad hoc network. All nodes communicate on the same channel. The scanning phase consists of $X{\times}Y$ time slots, where X is the number of scanning rounds, and Y is the number of sectors, that is, the number of directional beams.

In the traditional DTRA scanning phase, each node needs to perform beam switching in each time slot, and communication can be successfully performed only when the beams are aligned between the two nodes [13]. In our system model, each node can switch to the next sector quickly, and the switching time is ignored. This protocol focuses on how to resolve link collisions and problems caused by node movements, improve the efficiency of the scanning phase, and optimize the entire DMAC protocol to improve network performance. This assumption is made because, on the one hand, beam switching is not the focus of this article. On the other hand, beam switching does not significantly improve the above problems.

3 Directional Neighbor Discovery and Tracking Protocol Design

3.1 The Background and Motivation

Literature [14] proposed a TDMA (Time-division multiple access)-based DMAC protocol DTRA. Divide a superframe into three subframes in DTRA: neighbor discovery frame, reservation frame, and data transmission frame. In the neighbor discovery frame, the node performs a three-step handshake in a competitive manner to discover the neighbor nodes. In the scanning phase, because DTRA adopts a single channel, when there are many nodes in the network, there will be a large number of link conflicts. Node A is the receiving node, node B, and C are the transmitting nodes in the Fig. 2. Due to a single channel, Node A will receive the data of Node B and C at the same time, which will cause link AB and AC to fail at the same time. When the number of nodes communicating increases, the efficiency of the scanning phase will be greatly reduced.

One of the most serious problems in the access phase of the existing DMAC protocol is the "unreliable" problem of nodes due to node movement [15]. In reality, each node is not fixed. Conversely, in an environment where a military, an unmanned vehicle, or the like uses a wireless ad hoc network, the node address is

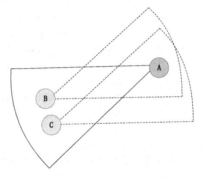

Fig. 2. An example of link conflict.

constantly changing [16]. During the scanning phase, the discovered nodes deviate from their original positions due to movement, resulting in a large number of "invalid" nodes, which would seriously affect the efficiency of the reservation and data transmission phases, thereby affecting the performance of the entire DMAC. As shown in Fig. 3, Node B has been discovered by Node A in the previous number of scan rounds, but at this moment, Node B moved to another sector and was not re-discovered by Node A in subsequent scans. Node A will mistakenly believe that Node B still exists in its original location. When there are more nodes in the network, such "invalid" nodes will increase in a large amount.

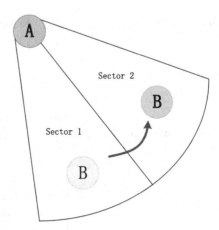

Fig. 3. An example of node movement.

This paper proposes an adjacent node discovery and tracking protocol based on OFDMA for the two problems of "link collision" [17] and node movement [18].

3.2 Protocol Description

The scanning phase is composed of X×Y time slots, X is the number of scanning rounds, Y is the number of sectors, and each time slot is composed of three mini-slots, corresponding to the three-way handshake of DTRA. The specific process is shown in Fig. 4

(1) Channel access phase: The AP monitors the channel state according to the carrier sense program of the IEEE 802.11 standard. When the channel is detected as idle, the scan initiating node starts performing binary backoff.
(2) Scheduling phase: After the retreat procedure is completed, the scan initiating node sends a scan request frame (SREQ) on the main channel, and the SREQ includes the user information field. According to the scheduling result, the AID12 field is set to scan the number S of the corresponding node or 0, and fill in the location of the RU in the resource allocation field.
(3) Data transmission phase: The scanning response node receives the SREQ, performs the Scanning Response (SRES) transmission on the assigned RU or randomly selects the RU.
(4) Confirm transmission phase: The scanning initiator node replies with Scanning Acknowledgement (SACK) on the primary channel.

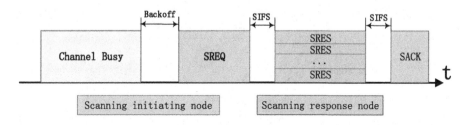

Fig. 4. The procedure of neighbor scan.

3.3 Neighbor Discovering and Tracking

Before introducing the specific meaning of neighbor discovery and tracking, we first divide the state of the nodes into four categories during the scanning process

α: The status of all nodes before the start of the scan phase.

β: It means that the current time slot node is scanned by the freely competitive way to initiate the node discovery.

γ: The node that has been discovered before the current time slot needs to be discovered again by tracking.

λ: Refers to the node that failed to track and needs to compete again freely.

In order to better introduce our proposed protocol, the following data structures are defined. There will Maintain a collection $X = [X_i]$ on the scan originating node, This is a three-dimensional array $X_i = (a, b, s)$ ndicating that the node s was found in the b-th sector of scan in round a.

Neighbor Discovering: At the beginning of the scanning phase, all nodes are in the state, the scanning phase sends SREQ, and the AID field of the user information field in SREQ is set to 0, indicating that this RU is used for free competition. The scan response node will reply SRES with probability ζ and randomly select one RU for transmission in the RU for free contention. Compared with the single channel of the traditional DTRA, the OFDMA approach can significantly reduce the link collision, and the number of nodes capable of establishing communication in a single time slot will be greatly increased. As shown in the Fig. 5, nodes B, C, and D simultaneously send SREQ to node A. In the case of a single channel, all three links will collide. In the access mode of OFDMA, the probability of all three links failing is only 1.2% (select 20M channel). After receiving the SRES, the scan initiating node updates the node set X, and the status of these nodes is updated to β.

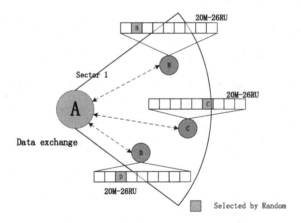

Fig. 5. RU choice in free competition.

Neighbor Tracking: The scan initiating node checks the nodes in the current scan sector in the node set X before sending the SREQ. If the difference between the current number of scan rounds and the number of rounds stored in the set X is greater than or equal to a certain fixed value, This node status is updated to γ and these nodes are tracked in this time slot. This fixed value is also called the tracking threshold μ.

The steps of node tracking are as shown in Fig. 6:

- The scanning initiator node writes the nodes B, C, and D to be tracked into the AID field in the SREQ, and assigns the RU location of the node in the corresponding resource allocation field.
- Node B, C, D, E Query in the user information field of SREQ whether the current transmission has been assigned to the node, that is, whether there is a node number of the node in the AID field. If it exists, SRES is sent on the assigned RU, otherwise it is accessed through free competition.
- The scan initiating node updates the node set X after receiving the SRES. If the tracking node fails to reply to the SRES, the node is deleted from the X table, and the status of these nodes is updated to λ.

In summary, neighbor tracking can effectively avoid the problem of "unreliable" nodes caused by node movement [19]. When a node is not in contact with the scanning initiating node for a long time, on the one hand, it is because the node is No successful links have been established in the free competition. On the other hand, due to the movement of the node, the node is deviated from the original position and cannot be contacted with the scanning initiating node. Through neighbor node tracking, the scanning initiating node establishes communication with the nodes that are not in contact for a long time, and by assigning non-interfering RUs to these nodes, the reliability of data transmission is ensured, and interference of other factors is excluded.

The moving node has a certain probability to leave the original sector or leave the communication range. Tracking the nodes in this case will definitely cause the tracking to fail. The scanning initiating node deletes these nodes from the X table, ensuring reliable scanning results. Sex, laying a good foundation for the appointment and data transfer phases [20].

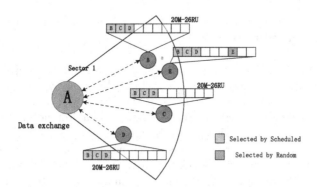

Fig. 6. RU choice in neighbor tracing.

3.4   Frame Format

Based on the three-way handshake protocol in the DTRA scanning phase, the packet interaction of this protocol is completed in three parts as shown in Fig. 7, we mainly define the data frame format of SREQ, but there is no clear requirement for SRES and SACK. There is a format field for each packet to indicate what type of packet the current packet is. For SREQ, the source address field is the scan originating node address and Destination address is broadcast address. According to the scheduling result of the scan initiating node, several user information fields are filled in the SREQ, and the single user information field is 4 bytes. Specifically, the AID field indicates which node the RU is assigned to or for free contention, and the resource allocation field indicates the RU location of the node. SRES and SACK only make the simplest requirements, including source address domain and destination address domain.

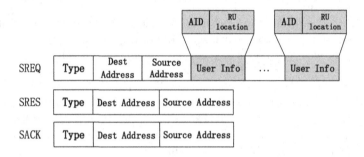

Fig. 7. Frame format.

4   Simulation and Results

In order to evaluate the performance of ONDT proposed in this paper, the physical layer simulation of the proposed algorithm is built on the integrated system level and link level simulation platform of the IEEE 802.11ax key technology supporting UL OFDMA function. In the simulation environment, a scan initiating node and a number of randomly distributed scanning response nodes, namely one AP and several STAs, are set. It is worth noting that we assume that only the scan initiating node performs beam switching, and The corresponding node beam direction always points to the scan originating node. That is, when the beam of the scanning initiating node is switched to the corresponding sector, all the scanning response nodes in the sector have the right to communicate with the scanning initiating node.

The scan-in node competition window has a backoff value of at least 15, and a maximum of 63. In this paper, the 20M channel 26 tone-RU is used, that is, the channel is divided into 9 time-frequency resource blocks for selection by several STAs. The three scenarios of the simulation are as follows:

- Scenario I: The total number of nodes is increased from 5 to 65, which is intended to compare the protocol and DTRA performance comparisons.
- Scenario II: The number of scan rounds is increased from 1 round to 10 rounds, the tracking threshold is infinite, and the moving probability is 0.
- Scenario III: The total number of nodes is fixed at 60, and the tracking threshold is 2/3/4 rounds.

4.1 The Simulation Results in Scene I

Compared with DTRA and ONDT, the simulation results of the number of neighbor nodes increasing with the total number of nodes are shown in Fig. 8. Since a single channel is used in the DTRA protocol, when all nodes is large, the probability of collision increases, and the efficiency of neighboring nodes is reduced. For the neighbor discovery and tracking algorithm that joins the OFDMA subchannel division, multiple time-frequency resource blocks improve the efficiency and number of neighbor discovery, and there is a neighbor tracking mechanism. When the number of discovered nodes is greater than the tracking threshold, the scan originating node will assign the RU to the scan response node. As the density of network nodes increases, the neighbor discovery and tracking mechanism is more efficient than the DTRA protocol. The parameter table used in the simulation is shown in Table 1.

Table 1. Node configuration parameter table

Parameter	Value
Scan round	10
Number of sectors	6
Tracking threshold/Round	3
Transmission probability	0.5
Moving probability	0.2

4.2 The Simulation Results in Scene II

The simulation result of the number of nodes found under different number of nodes as the number of scanning rounds increases is shown in Fig. 9, and the ordinate is the number of nodes around the scan initiating node. As the number of scan rounds increases, the efficiency of the number of neighbor nodes found in different total nodes is different. The more the total number of nodes, the higher the scanning efficiency, because the time-frequency resource blocks are more fully utilized.

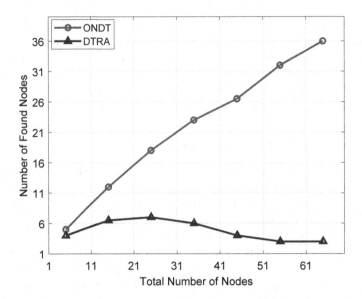

Fig. 8. ONDT vs. DTRA.

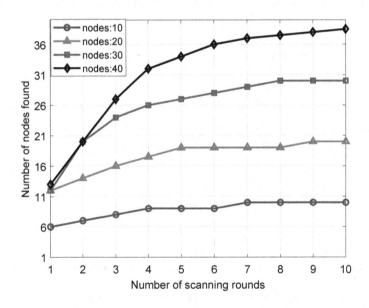

Fig. 9. Number of nodes vs. Number of rounds.

4.3   The Simulation Results in Scene III

The number of nodes that successfully tracked under different tracking thresholds changes with the change of the moving probability as shown in Fig. 10. When the tracking threshold is getting higher and higher, the neighbor nodes have already reached the threshold and have been discovered through free competition, so the number of nodes successfully tracked gradually decreases. As the probability of movement increases, the change in the position of the node causes the tracking to fail, thereby reducing the amount of successful nodes.

The number of unrecorded nodes caused by different moving probabilities is shown in Fig. 11. The number of unrecorded nodes includes the number of undiscovered nodes and the total number of failed nodes. When the tracking threshold is too low, as the probability of moving increases, the node reaching the tracking threshold occupies more frequency band resources, but the movement of the position causes the tracking to fail, so the tracking threshold is not easily too high or too low.

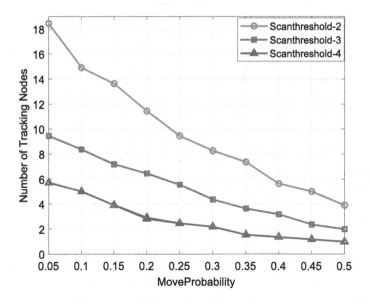

Fig. 10. MoveProbability vs. number of tracking nodes.

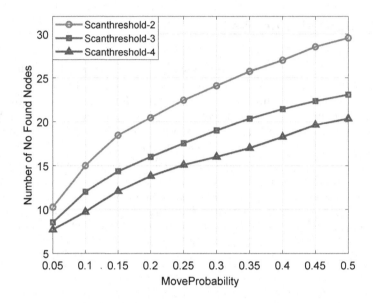

Fig. 11. MoveProbability vs. number of no found nodes.

5   Conclusion and Future Works

This paper proposes a new protocol called ONDT, which introduces the system model and design principle of the protocol. And this is a work to design a neighbor discovery protocol in a directed ad hoc network using OFDMA. Simulation results show that ONDT can significantly improves the number of neighbor discovered. The nodes can connect neighbor nodes frequently, and it improves accuracy of neighbor nodes position. In the future, the problem of beam switching and sidelobe interference in neighbor discovery and tracking needs to be further studied.

Acknowledgement. This work was supported in part by the National Natural Science Foundations of CHINA (Grant No. 61771392, 61771390, 61871322, 61501373 and 61271279), the National Science and Technology Major Project (Grant No. 2015ZX03002006-004 and 2016ZX03001018-004), and Science and Technology on Avionics Integration Laboratory (Grant No. 20185553035).

References

1. Montero, S., Gozalvez, J., Sepulcre, M.: Neighbor discovery for industrial wireless sensor networks with mobile nodes. Comput. Commun. **111**, 41–55 (2017)
2. Haas, Z.J., Deng, J., Liang, B., Papadimitratos, P., Sajama, S.: Wireless ad hoc Networks (2003)
3. Basagni, S., Conti, M., Giordano, S., Stojmenovic, I.: Mobile ad hoc networking. In: Hawaii International Conference on System Sciences (2017)

4. Djukic, P., Valaee, S.: Delay aware link scheduling for multi-hop tdma wireless networks. IEEE/ACM Trans. Networking **17**(3), 870–883 (2009)
5. Singh, H., Singh, S.: Smart-aloha for multi-hop wireless networks. Mob. Netw. Appl. **10**(5), 651–662 (2005)
6. Zhao, S., Liu, Y., Yang, T., Feng, Z., Zhang, Q., Chao, G.: 3-way multi-carrier asynchronous neighbor discovery algorithm using directional antennas. In: IEEE Wireless Communications & Networking Conference (2016)
7. Gelal, E., Jakllari, G., Krishnamurthy, S.V., Young, N.E.: An integrated scheme for fully-directional neighbor discovery and topology management in mobile ad hoc networks. In: IEEE International Conference on Mobile Adhoc & Sensor Systems (2006)
8. Santosa, R.A., Lee, B.S., Chai, K.Y., Lim, T.M.: Distributed neighbor discovery in ad hoc networks using directional antennas. In: IEEE International Conference on Computer & Information Technology (2006)
9. Qiao, Q., Bo, L., Mao, Y., Yan, Z.: An OFDMA based concurrent multiuser mac for upcoming IEEE 802.11ax. In: Wireless Communications & Networking Conference Workshops (2015)
10. Xu, C., Guo, D., Wornell, G.W.: Sparse OFDM: a compressive sensing approach to asynchronous neighbor discovery (2017)
11. Burghal, D., Tehrani, A., Molisch, A.: On expected neighbor discovery time with prior information: modeling, bounds and optimization. IEEE Trans. Wirel. Commun. **PP**(99), 1 (2017)
12. Fernando, X.N., Srikanth, S., Pandian, P.A.M.: Orthogonal frequency division multiple access in WiMAX and LTE a comparison. IEEE Commun. Mag. **50**(9), 153–161 (2010)
13. Stahlbuhk, T.B., Shrader, B.E., Modiano, E.H.: Topology control for wireless networks with highly-directional antennas. In: International Symposium on Modeling & Optimization in Mobile (2016)
14. Zhang, Z.: DTRA: Directional transmission and reception algorithms in WLANS with directional antennas for QoS support. IEEE Netw. **19**(3), 27–32 (2005)
15. Luo, T., Motani, M., Srinivasan, V.: Cooperative asynchronous multichannel MAC: design, analysis, and implementation. IEEE Trans. Mob. Comput. **8**(3), 338–352 (2009)
16. Hsu, J.L., Rubin, I.: Performance analysis of directional random access scheme for multiple access mobile ad-hoc wireless networks. In: Military Communications Conference (2006)
17. Nasipuri, A., Ye, S., You, J., Hiromoto, R.E.: A MAC protocol for mobile ad hoc networks using directional antennas. In: Wireless Communications & Networking Confernce, WCNC (2002)
18. Mcglynn, M.J., Borbash, S.A.: Birthday protocols for low energy deployment and flexible neighbor discovery in ad hoc wireless networks. In: ACM International Symposium on Mobile Ad Hoc Networking & Computing (2001)
19. An, X., Hekmat, R.: Self-adaptive neighbor discovery in ad hoc networks with directional antennas. In: Mobile & Wireless Communications Summit (2007)
20. Wang, Z., Peng, L., Xu, R., Lei, Z., Zhu, J.: Neighbor discovery in three-dimensional mobile ad hoc networks with directional antennas. In: Wireless & Optical Communication Conference (2016)

Artificial Intelligence

Understanding Mobile User Intent Using Attentive Sequence-to-Sequence RNNs

Che-Hsuan Yu[1](✉), Hung-Yuan Chen[2], Fang-Yie Leu[3], and Yao-Chung Fan[4]

[1] Chunghwa Telecom Research Institute, Taipei, Taiwan
shaneyu07@gmail.com
[2] TungHai University, Taichung, Taiwan
hychen@itri.org.tw
[3] Industrial Technology Research Institute, Zhudong, Taiwan
leufy@thu.edu.tw
[4] National Chung Hsing University, Taichung, Taiwan
yfan@nchu.edu.tw

Abstract. Smartphones have become an indispensable part of our lives. Understanding user behaviors based on smartphone usage data is therefore critical to many applications. In this paper, we propose to address a novel task called *Intention2Text* which attempts to capture user intents based on smartphone usage log. The goal of Intention2Text is to learn a deep learning model taking mobile context logs as input and generate sentences as output for describing mobile user intentions. So far, we have developed an attentive sequence-to-sequence recurrent neural network for the Intention2Text task as a fundamental model. Also, various model encoding/decoding strategies are introduced and considered. The experiments based on a real community question dataset are conducted to verify the effectiveness of the proposed framework.

1 Introduction

Smartphones have become a necessity in our lives. As smartphones are usually carried around by their owner the whole day, it became a close observer of the owner's behaviors. From this point of view, mining data generated from smartphones has become active research. Substantial research results on various smartphone data such as GPS trajectories [1–4], accelerometer readings [5–9], or Wi-Fi logs [10,11] have been reported in recent literature.

While significant research efforts have been made on mining various smartphone data, we found that a new type of smartphone usage data, which are generated from the I/O interaction between a user and the apps on his/her smartphone, is not well-explored in previous studies. Existing smartphone operating systems all provide built-in APIs[1] to support accessibility, e.g. reading the text on the screen to enable the visually impaired to use smartphones. Such

---

[1] VoiceOver API for iOS and Accessibility Service API for Android.

© ICST Institute for Computer Sciences, Social Informatics and Telecommunications Engineering 2020
Published by Springer Nature Switzerland AG 2020. All Rights Reserved
D.-J. Deng et al. (Eds.): WiCON 2019, LNICST 317, pp. 51–61, 2020.
https://doi.org/10.1007/978-3-030-52988-8_5

APIs provide rich contextual information about the user's activities. More specifically, when a user interacts with his/her smartphone, operations such as screen scrolling or screen touching trigger I/O context events. Consequently, information associated with the events, such as time, app, behavior type, and associated contents, are recorded into *context log*. Figure 2 shows the screenshot when the user is browsing some contents in MoPTT[2] and the Android Accessibility API[3] is executing. The I/O context logs provide rich signals and contain rich information about the behaviors of a smartphone user. Such information is particularly useful for mobile data mining applications.

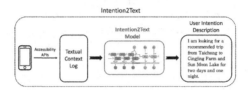

Fig. 1. An illustration of the Intention2Text task.

1.1 Research Goal

In this study, we propose a task called *Intention2Text* with the goal of generating descriptions about a mobile user's intention based attentive RNN models. Specifically, our Intention2Text model takes the textual context logs (within which the text on the user's screen is recorded) as an input, and outputs a meaningful and grammatical sentence that describes the user's intention, as illustrated in Fig. 1. The Intention2Text task is inspired by the image caption task [12] where a neural network model is first used for capturing image feature representation and then a recurrent neural network (RNN) is employed to generate a sequence of words as a description of a given image.

2 Method

In this section, we present how we use the sequence-to-sequence RNNs to implement our Intention2Text model.

2.1 Intention2Text with Sequence-to-Sequence RNNs

We use a sequence-to-sequence learning framework to tackle our Intention2Text task. The sequence-to-sequence learning is performed by an encoder-decoder RNN which learns to encode user mobile context log into a fix-length vector and decode the encoded vector back into a sentence that describes the user's intention. Figure 3 illustrates our proposed model.

---

2 https://play.google.com/store/apps/details?id=mong.moptt&hl=zh_TW.
3 https://developer.android.com/reference/android/view/accessibility/package-summary.

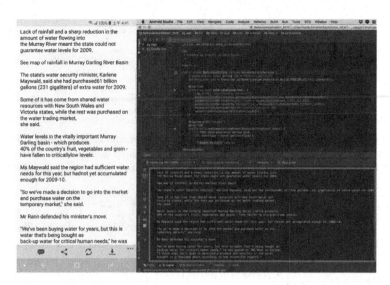

Fig. 2. A screenshot while the Android Accessibility API is executing. The left part is a screenshot of a user browsing contents in MoPTT on an Android device. The right part is a screenshot when the Android Accessibility API is executing. The context log is shown in the logcat section of the Android Studio. Each behavior event consists of four entries: 1) the time the event is generated 2) the sourcing app 3) the text on the screen of the device 4) the event type with respect to the interaction.

From a probabilistic perspective, the encoder-decoder RNN learns the conditional probability distribution over the desired user intention description given the user behavior context log

$$P(o_1, ..., o_{t'} \mid w_1, ..., w_t),$$

where $(w_1, ..., w_t)$ is the context log with the length of t and $(o_1, ..., o_{t'})$ is the intention description with the length of t'. Note that the length of the context log t and the length of the intention description t' can be different.

In our model, we convert each word w_i in the context log into a 1-of-N encoded vector x_i, and these vectors are integrated into an input sequence X, where

$$X = (x_1, ..., x_t), \forall x_i \in \mathbb{R}^V,$$

and the Intention2Text model generates a sequence of 1-of-N encoded word vectors as output

$$O = (o_1, ..., o_{t'}), \forall o_i \in \mathbb{R}^V,$$

where V is the vocabulary size. For the Intention2Text model, we use the same vocabulary for both input and output.

Encoder. The encoder's job is to encode the context log into a fixed-length vector. To do so, we use a bi-directional Long Short-Term Memory (bi-directional

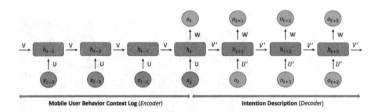

Fig. 3. The proposed model implemented via encoder-decoder RNN architecture. Each blue circle here indicates one word of the context log. Each green circle indicates one word of the intention description that the model generates. (Color figure online)

LSTM) [13] that reads one word from the context log $X = (x_1, ..., x_t)$ sequentially at each time step. First, for the forward direction of the bi-directional LSTM of the encoder, the hidden state $h_{(t)}$ at every timestep t is updated by

$$\begin{cases} h_{(t)} = tanh(c_{(t)}o_{(t)}) \text{ , if } i > 0 \\ \qquad 0 \qquad\qquad \text{ , if } i = 0 \end{cases},$$

where

$$
\begin{aligned}
c_{(t)} &= f_{(t)}c_{(t-1)} + i_{(t)}g_{(t)} \\
o_{(t)} &= \sigma(U_o Ex_{(t)} + V_o h_{(t-1)} + b_o) \\
g_{(t)} &= tanh(U_g Ex_{(t)} + V_g h_{(t-1)} + b_g) \\
i_{(t)} &= \sigma(U_i Ex_{(t)} + V_i h_{(t-1)} + b_i) \\
f_{(t)} &= \sigma(U_f Ex_{(t)} + V_f h_{(t-1)} + b_f).
\end{aligned}
$$

$i_{(t)}$, $o_{(t)}$ and $f_{(t)}$ denote the **input gate**, **output gate** and **forget gate** in the LSTM respectively. $g_{(t)}$ computes the candidate information that's possibly going into the memory state. $c_{(t)}$ serves as the new memory state at timestep t. $E \in \mathbb{R}^{m \times V}$ is the word embedding matrix which converts a V-dimension 1-of-N encoded word vector of the context log into a lower-dimension representation. $U_o, U_g, U_i, U_f \in \mathbb{R}^{n \times m}$ and $V_o, V_g, V_i, V_f \in \mathbb{R}^{n \times n}$ are weight matrices. $b_o, b_g, b_i, b_f \in \mathbb{R}^{n \times 1}$ are bias terms. m is the word embedding dimensionality. n is the number of hidden units. σ is as normal as a logistic sigmoid function. One should note that all the parameters including the word embedding matrix are jointly learned during the training.

The backward direction of the bi-directional LSTM is operated similarly. We share the word embedding matrix for both forward and backward LSTMs. We concatenate the forward and backward directions to obtain a sequence of hidden states $(h_1, ..., h_{(t)_x})$ with the same length as the input context log, where

$$h_i = \begin{bmatrix} h_{i_{forward}} \\ h_{i_{backward}} \end{bmatrix}.$$

When the forward direction of the bi-directional LSTM reaches the end of the context log(an end-of-sentence (EOS) token which denotes the end of input is appended to the context log), the hidden state $h_{(t)_x}$ will be a summary s that contains all the information from the context log. It's also the feature representation of the context log.

Decoder. The decoder's job is to decode the final hidden states of the encoder, that is, the summary s that summarizes the context log, and generate the user intention description. We use an uni-directional LSTM for the decoder. The hidden states $d_{(i)}$ of the decoder is computed by

$$d_{(t)}' = tanh(c_{(t)}' y_{(t)}') ,$$

where

$$
\begin{aligned}
c_{(t)}' &= f_{(t)}' c_{(t-1)}' + i_{(t)}' g_{(t)}' \\
y_{(t)}' &= \sigma(U_{y'} Eo_{(t-1)} + V_{y'} d_{(t-1)}' + b_{y'}) \\
g_{(t)}' &= tanh(U_{g'} Eo_{(t-1)} + V_{g'} d_{(t-1)}' + b_{g'}) \\
i_{(t)}' &= \sigma(U_{i'} Eo_{(t-1)} + V_{i'} d_{(t-1)}' + b_{i'}) \\
f_{(t)}' &= \sigma(U_{f'} Eo_{(t-1)} + V_{f'} d_{(t-1)}' + b_{f'}) .
\end{aligned}
$$

E is the shared word embedding matrix for both encoder and decoder. $y_{(t)}$ here denotes the output gate and $o_{(t-1)}$ denotes the output word from last timestep due to the repeated use of symbols. $U_{y'}, U_{g'}, U_{i'}, U_{f'} \in \mathbb{R}^{n \times m}$ and $V_{y'}, V_{g'}, V_{i'}, V_{f'} \in \mathbb{R}^{n \times n}$ are weights and $b_{y'}, b_{g'}, b_{i'}, b_{f'} \in \mathbb{R}^{n \times 1}$ are the biases. Again, m and n are the word embedding dimensionality and the number of hidden units respectively. The initial hidden state $d_{(0)}$ at the beginning of the decoding is the summary vector s that we've mentioned above. We take the output $o_{(t-1)}$ from last timestep as the input at the current timestep, which lets the machine knows what it has outputted so that it can decode with more accurate results.

The decoder outputs a 1-of-N encoded vector of dimension V at every timestep by computing the conditional probability distribution with a softmax activation function

$$P(o_{t,i} = 1 | o_{t-1}, o_{t-2}, ..., o_1) = \frac{exp(w_i h_{(t)})}{\sum_{k=1}^{V} exp(w_k h_{(t)})} ,$$

where i is the i-th candidate word, V is the size of the vocabulary and w_i is the i-th row of the weight matrix $\mathbf{W}$.

The decoder finishes decoding when the end-of-sentence token is generated. We can compute the conditional probability of our complete user intention description O by computing the joint probability of all predicted words from every timestep

$$p(O) = \prod p(o_t | o_{t-1}, ..., o_1) .$$

Figure 4 illustrates the model we've described so far.

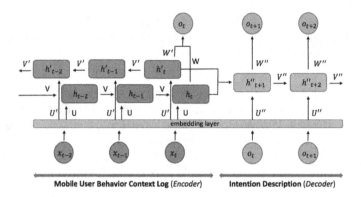

Fig. 4. The encoder-decoder RNN architecture. Note that the three hidden states colored differently are LSTM cells, we simplify them for better readability. The encoder is composed of a bi-directional LSTM while the decoder is an uni-directional LSTM. Both inputs and outputs at every timestep are 1-of-N encoded vector. In the decoder, the output o_{t-1} from the last timestep will be fed in as input at the current timestep. All the parameters including the embedding layer will be jointly learned during the training.

The encoder and decoder are jointly trained to maximize the log-likelihood

$$max_{\theta} \frac{1}{N} \sum_{n=1}^{N} logp_{\theta}(O_n|X_n),$$

where θ is the set of the parameters in the model, and each (X_n, O_n) pair is a pair of context log and intention description from the training set. In this study, we use stochastic gradient decent (SGD) [14] to update the parameters.

2.2 Attentive Encoder-Decoder RNN Architecture

The potential issue of the encoder-decoder architecture above is that it suffers from the problem of processing long mobile context logs. As reported by [15], the performance of the traditional encoder-decoder RNNs degrades rapidly when the length of the input sequence increases. Thus, we address this issue by adding the attention mechanism [16] to the original encoder-decoder RNN architecture. We extend the encoder-decoder RNNs with a trainable context vector **c** which connects to the hidden units of both the encoder and the decoder. When the new attentive model predicts a word at every time step, it takes each word of the context log into consideration and tries to concentrate on the most relevant information. In this way, the model does not attempt to encode the whole context log into a fixed-length vector. Instead, it encodes each word of the context log into a sequence of vector, and adaptively choose a subset of these vectors during the output decoding.

In the new attentive encoder-decoder RNN architecture, we learn an extra context vector c_i, which is computed as a weighted sum of the encoder's hidden states $h_{(j)}$ at every timestep j by

$$c_i = \sum_j^X \alpha_{ij} h_j \, .$$

The weights α_{ij} of the encoder's hidden states h_j is computed by

$$\alpha_{ij} = \frac{exp(a_{ij})}{\sum_{k=1}^{X} exp(a_{ik})} \, ,$$

where

$$a_{ij} = score(d_{i-1}, h_j) \, .$$

At time i where the decoder wants to generate the i-th word, a_{ij} computes a score between the last decoder hidden state d_{i-1} and every encoder hidden state h_j. The scoring can be as complicated as a neural network, or as simple as a dot product which is used in this study. The score represents how relevant the word we want to output is to a certain word in the context log. These scores a_{ij} (a sequence of scalar) will then be normalized by a softmax function to produce a probability distribution α_{ij}. Eventually, the context vector c_i is computed as a weighted sum of the encoder hidden states h_j.

3   Experiments

3.1   Training Data Sets

For training the Intention2Text model, we need to pair a user mobile context log to an intention description sentence. However, it is impossible and impractical of doing so. As a result, in our study, we propose to leverage community questions and their web search results as alternative data sets for training our model. The idea of using this alternative is that if the user is using a mobile phone with a certain intent, the user might browse the web and searching result for the intent. Therefore, we crawled 40,532 questions from the tourism category in Quora, and use the Google search engine to obtain top-10 web search results for each question. There are 523,430 question-description, and by further filtering out ads, spams, and duplicate question-description pairs, 476,107 records are retained for training.

3.2   Implementation Details

The model has been implemented with Tensorflow. Below we provide some details of our model's implementation (Table 1).

– We use a 2-layer Bi-directional LSTM network for encoder and 2-layer uni-directional LSTM for decoder. The number of hidden units is 128. All biases are initialized to 0. All weights are initialized with a truncated normal distribution with the standard deviation set to 0.0001.

Table 1. Sample outputs of the Intention2Text model.

User Behavior Context Log

Europe is a favored destination for many world travelers, but it isn't always the cheapest getaway. Here are # easy ways to plan a future euro trip

Real User Intention Description

How can I plan to visit most of the places in Europe cheaply?

Machine-Generated User Intention Description

What is a cheap itinerary for a # day trip to Europe?

User Behavior Context Log

June is a great time to visit Goa if you enjoy the rains. The unpleasant heat of the summer is gone, it's green everywhere because of the rain

Real User Intention Description

Is there any group of girls visiting Goa in June

Machine-Generated User Intention Description

What are the best places to visit in Goa in June?

User Behavior Context Log

Wondering where to travel this new year. Here are the best places to visit in southeast Asia in January that one never should miss. Check out

Real User Intention Description

What is the best place to visit in Asia in January?

Machine-Generated User Intention Description

What are the best places to visit in Asia in January?

- We use an embedding layer of dimensionality 128 to convert the input 1-of-N encoded vector to a lower-dimensional representation.
- The input context log's length is limited to 120, and the output description's length is limited to 30. An *EOS* token is appended at the end of every sentence to represent the end of sentence token.
- At training, we use **Teacher Forcing** technique. When training traditional encoder-decoder RNNs, the prediction at the current timestep depends on the output from the previous timestep. With Teacher Forcing, we feed in the ground truth word to the decoder, forcing the model to learn to decode the correct words. One should note that Teacher Forcing is only used at training.
- We use a sampled softmax loss instead of a full softmax loss where we need to compute the complete probability distribution and the total cross entropy loss. Since computing the full softmax loss for a huge number of classes is where the expensive computing exists, we use sampled softmax loss to speed up the loss computing by only considering a small randomly-chosen subset of candidates for each batch of training examples. We restrict the number of classes to randomly sample per batch to 4,096.
- We trained the model with SGD with batch size 4. We split the data to 70% training (333,274 training), 30% validation (142,833 validation). With single NVIDIA GeForce 1080Ti, it takes 6 days and 15 h to train 2.408M steps.

Table 2. Sample outputs of the Intention2Text model.

User Behavior Context Log

With a citypass you can get access to # of New York's top attractions for # of art deco design, and perhaps the most famous office building in the world. The united states is a must-see for anyone interested in the personal stories

Real User Intention Description

What are the most exciting places to visit things to do in New York state?

Machine-Generated User Intention Description

What is there to do in the northeastern United States

User Behavior Context Log

Monsoon destinations in India that will make you dance in the rain. UNK and mountains get UNK with lush greenery, the lakes UNK with. It's the perfect place to get soaked in the rains and enjoy

Real User Intention Description

What are some of the best places to visit in India where there are more greenery and less population to enjoy time?

Machine-Generated User Intention Description

What is the best place in south India to visit?

User Behavior Context Log

Compare book from more than # hotels. Best deals guaranteed. Product offering makemytrip about the site partner programs more links follow

Real User Intention Description

What is best site to book hotels

Machine-Generated User Intention Description

What is the best hotel booking site.

User Behavior Context Log

We have a # day driving itinerary for Norway on UNK link in my bio. What would be a great # week itinerary to get the best out of a backpacking trip?

Real User Intention Description

What would be a great # week itinerary to get the best out of a backpacking trip to Norway?

Machine-Generated User Intention Description

How much money do I need to take to Norway trip somewhere by hitchhiking?

User Behavior Context Log

Honeymoon packages yatra.com offers honeymoon holiday tour and travel packages. Find best honeymoon vacation packages for top honeymoon

Real User Intention Description

Which travel agents should I choose to book a honeymoon holiday

Machine-Generated User Intention Description

Which is the best honeymoon package provider company

---

4   Results

We show the sample outputs of our Intention2Text model in Table 2. In the sample outputs, all the numbers including date, time, price etc have been converted to # and all the words that are out-of-vocabulary have been converted to *UNK*. In the table, **User Behavior Context Log** indicates the context log that was recorded by the Accessibility API, i.e. the text on the user's screen at the moment. **Real User Intention Description** is the ground-truth user intention. **Machine-Generated User Intention Description** is the intention description that our Intention2Text model generates.

5 Conclusion

In this study, we attempted to apply the attentive sequence-to-sequence recurrent neural network to the context logs, and manage to implement the Intention2Text model that understands the user behavior and describes the user's intent with a properly formed sentence. We show that the attention-based encoder-decoder RNN is also one of the approaches to solve the problem of mobile user intent understanding. We would like to explore this task further by collecting a multi-domain dataset of large size in the future.

References

1. Zheng, Y., Zhang, L., Xie, X., Ma, W.-Y.: Mining interesting locations and travel sequences from GPS trajectories. In: Proceedings of the 18th International Conference on World Wide Web, pp. 791–800. ACM (2009)
2. Siła-Nowicka, K., Vandrol, J., Oshan, T., Long, J.A., Demšar, U., Fotheringham, A.S.: Analysis of human mobility patterns from GPS trajectories and contextual information. Int. J. Geogr. Inf. Sci. **30**(5), 881–906 (2016)
3. Zheng, Y., Li, Q., Chen, Y., Xie, X., Ma, W.-Y.: Understanding mobility based on GPS data. In: Proceedings of the 10th International Conference on Ubiquitous Computing, pp. 312–321. ACM (2008)
4. Zheng, V.W., Zheng, Y., Xie, X., Yang, Q.: Towards mobile intelligence: learning from GPS history data for collaborative recommendation. Artif. Intell. **184**, 17–37 (2012)
5. Khan, A.M., Lee, Y.-K., Lee, S., Kim, T.-S.: Human activity recognition via an accelerometer-enabled-smartphone using kernel discriminant analysis. In: 2010 5th International Conference on Future Information Technology (FutureTech), pp. 1–6. IEEE (2010)
6. Khan, A.M., Lee, Y.-K., Lee, S.Y., Kim, T.-S.: A triaxial accelerometer-based physical-activity recognition via augmented-signal features and a hierarchical recognizer. IEEE Trans. Inf Technol. Biomed. **14**(5), 1166–1172 (2010)
7. Zhang, S., McCullagh, P., Nugent, C., Zheng, H.: Activity monitoring using a smart phone's accelerometer with hierarchical classification. In: 2010 Sixth International Conference on Intelligent Environments (IE), pp. 158–163. IEEE (2010)
8. Sun, L., Zhang, D., Li, B., Guo, B., Li, S.: Activity recognition on an accelerometer embedded mobile phone with varying positions and orientations. In: Yu, Z., Liscano, R., Chen, G., Zhang, D., Zhou, X. (eds.) UIC 2010. LNCS, vol. 6406, pp. 548–562. Springer, Heidelberg (2010). https://doi.org/10.1007/978-3-642-16355-5_42

9. Yang, J.: Toward physical activity diary: motion recognition using simple acceleration features with mobile phones. In: Proceedings of the 1st International Workshop on Interactive Multimedia for Consumer Electronics, pp. 1–10. ACM (2009)
10. Fan, Y.-C., Chen, Y.-C., Tung, K.-C., Wu, K.-C., Chen, A.L.: A framework for enabling user preference profiling through wi-fi logs. IEEE Trans. Knowl. Data Eng. **28**(3), 592–603 (2016)
11. Rekimoto, J., Miyaki, T., Ishizawa, T.: LifeTag: WiFi-based continuous location logging for life pattern analysis. In: Hightower, J., Schiele, B., Strang, T. (eds.) LoCA 2007. LNCS, vol. 4718, pp. 35–49. Springer, Heidelberg (2007). https://doi.org/10.1007/978-3-540-75160-1_3
12. Vinyals, O., Toshev, A., Bengio, S., Erhan, D.: Show and tell: a neural image caption generator. In: Proceedings of the IEEE Conference on Computer Vision and Pattern Recognition, pp. 3156–3164 (2015)
13. Graves, A., Schmidhuber, J.: Framewise phoneme classification with bidirectional lstm and other neural network architectures. Neural Networks **18**(5–6), 602–610 (2005)
14. Kiefer, J., Wolfowitz, J.: Stochastic estimation of the maximum of a regression function. Ann. Math. Stat. **23**(3), 462–466 (1952)
15. Cho, K., Van Merriënboer, B., Bahdanau, D., Bengio, Y.: On the properties of neural machine translation: encoder-decoder approaches. arXiv preprint arXiv:1409.1259 (2014)
16. Bahdanau, D., Cho, K., Bengio, Y.: Neural machine translation by jointly learning to align and translate. arXiv preprint arXiv:1409.0473 (2014)

Relay Selection Exploiting Genetic Algorithms for Multi-hop Device-to-Device Communication

Toha Ardi Nugraha$^{(\boxtimes)}$, Zdenek Becvar, and Pavel Mach

Department of Telecommunication Engineering,
Czech Technical University in Prague, Prague, Czech Republic
{nugratoh,zdenek.becvar,machp2}@fel.cvut.cz

Abstract. Device-to-device (D2D) communication allows a direct transmission between two devices. In this way, cellular user equipment's are not always obliged to route the data conventionally through a cellular base station. This paper focuses on multi-hop D2D communication, where D2D relays are exploited to delivery of data from a source to a destination. We propose a novel algorithm that finds the most suitable path between the D2D source and destination so that the capacity of multi-hop communication is maximized. The appropriate route is found via Genetic Algorithm (GA) with an ordered crossover. The simulation results show that the proposed algorithm improves the capacity of multi-hop D2D communication from a source to a destination compared to an existing relay selection algorithm by 20–61%. We also show that the proposed solution converges fast enough to be beneficial even in realistic mobile networks.

Keywords: D2D communication · Genetic Algorithm · Relay selection

1 Introduction

New generation of cellular networks introduces a plethora of technological advancements with respect to 4G, such as ultra-dense (heterogeneous) networks, mobile edge computing, Internet of Things, vehicular networks, drones (UAVs), intelligent transportation systems, or device-to-device (D2D) communication. Contrary to conventional cellular networks, the D2D communication allows a direct communication between two or more devices without intervention of a base station (BS) [1]. The benefits of D2D communication can be fully exploited in the relay-based communication scenario, where two devices may communicate with each other through one or several relays [2,3].

The relay(s) exploited by the D2D communication can be either a fixed relay station, which is part of the network infrastructure, or other User Equipment (UE). Fixed relay is considered, for example, in [4] where the authors propose a full-duplex scenario for D2D system in two-hop networks. The paper assumes

D.-J. Deng et al. (Eds.): WiCON 2019, LNICST 317, pp. 62–72, 2020.
https://doi.org/10.1007/978-3-030-52988-8_6

multiple potential full-duplex decode-and-forward relays can assist the transmission between two D2D UEs. The UE acting as a relay between two D2D UEs is considered, e.g., in [5]. The authors apply a relay to D2D communication in order improve cellular downlink throughput. Most of the works, however, focus on the one-hop or two-hop scenarios, i.e., only UE within the one-hop or two-hop range can communicate with each other. The use of multi-hop communication can overcome extend communication range and/or enhance the capacity of the whole network [6]. In this respect, enabling the multi-hop D2D communication can significantly expand opportunities of the D2D communication in cellular networks, especially for UE that are relatively far from each other and cannot communicate directly or through just one relay.

The fundamental challenge in multi-hop enabled D2D communications is to find a suitable set of D2D relay UEs between the D2D UE acting as a source and the D2D UE acting as a destination while maximizing the overall capacity. The multi-hop D2D communication is considered in, e.g., [7–9]. The paper [7] proposes a multi-hop D2D communication in order to extend the coverage of BS. In this case, the D2D relays retransmit data between the BS and the UEs out of BS coverage. The multi-hop D2D communication also can be used to offload data from network backhaul, as investigated in [8]. The authors analyze the problem of relaying data through multiple relay UEs and also sharing resources allocation from cellular UEs. For each D2D communication pair, the algorithm finds the optimal shortest path using Dijkstra's algorithm based the distance. However, the Dijkstra's algorithm often cannot be used, because it is too computationally demanding for practical implementations.

Several optimization algorithms based on the machine learning, such as Genetic Algorithm (GA), have been developed in order to reduce computation complexity of the relaying algorithms. In [9], the GA is used to find shortest path from the source to the destination and to reduce complexity. The authors exploit standard single-point crossover to determine new routing options. Since the standard crossover leads to the creation of loops between source and destination, the authors propose a loop elimination algorithm. In [10], a multi-population GA with immigrant's scheme is proposed to solve the dynamic shortest path routing. The GA is also exploited in wireless networks to find a suitable path from cluster head to the base station, as suggested in [11]. The GA with spanning tree topology is implemented to maximize the usage of the network [12]. In [13], the GA is used to solve the shortest path routing problem with an adaptive routing. Nevertheless, this method needs a routing table to find a link communication between the source and destination.

The GA can be also exploited in the area of D2D communication. For example, the GA-based resource allocation and power control for the network optimization is proposed in [14]. The scheme is designed to mitigate the intra-cell interference and to enhance the system throughput by means of proper resource allocation. A relay-aided D2D with the single-point crossover is implemented in [15]. The paper proposes joint resource allocation for relay aided underlay D2D communication in cellular networks. Nevertheless, none of these papers consider the multi-hop D2D communication, which extend the coverage area and opportunities related to optimizing the capacity.

In this paper, we target to maximize the overall network throughput via multi-hop D2D communication. We propose an algorithm based on the GA to enhance the capacity for multi-hop D2D communication in the presence of co-channel interference, where the D2D relays use the same radio resources. As the conventional GA would lead to redundant use of relays, we exploit ordered crossover to reduce interference, and, thus, increase the communication capacity. We show that the proposed D2D relay selection based on the ordered crossover scheme overcomes the existing solutions in terms of capacity between D2D source and destination.

The rest of this paper is organized as follow. System model and problem formulation is defined in Sect. 2. The proposed relay selection scheme exploiting genetic algorithms with the ordered crossover is described in Sect. 3. Section 4 presents the simulation scenario and results. Last, major conclusions and findings are summarized in Sect. 4.3.

2   System Model and Problem Formulation

This section describes first the system model and then, we formulate the problem of relay selection for D2D communication.

2.1   System Model

In this section, we introduce a general system model for multi-hop D2D communication. We assume that the D2D communications is carried in dedicated resources. Therefore, there is no interference to conventional cellular UEs. We assume one D2D source (S) is sending data to one D2D destination (D). We assume R relay UEs deployed between the S and the D as shown in Fig. 1. The capacity between the S and D without any relays is calculated as:

$$C_{sd} = B\log_2\left(1 + \frac{P_s g_{sd}}{BN_o}\right) \tag{1}$$

where P_s is the transmission power of S, g_{sd} is the channel gain between the S and D UEs, N_o is the thermal noise with a spectral density of $-174\,\mathrm{dBm/Hz}$, and B is the channel bandwidth used for the communication. Notice that for the direct communication, there is no interference to the D, since only the S is transmitting while all potential relays are idle.

To calculate the capacity of each link in the multi-hop D2D communication from any i-th D2D source to any j-th D2D destination is calculated as:

$$C_{ij} = B\log_2\left(1 + \frac{P_i g_{ij}}{BN_o + I_j}\right) \tag{2}$$

where P_i is the transmission power of the i-th UE, g_{ij} is the channel gain between the i-th and the j-th UE, and I_j is the interference to the j-th UE (i.e., the one who receives data from the i-th UE) expressed as:

$$I_j = \sum_{i \in N, j \in N, i \neq j} P_i g_{i,j} \qquad (3)$$

where N is the number of UEs, P_i is the transmission power of the i-th UE while interference from the i-th UE is not considered as this UE transmits data to the j-th UE. The interference from an idle mode (i.e., potential relays that are not used for relaying) is not included as these do not transmit any data.

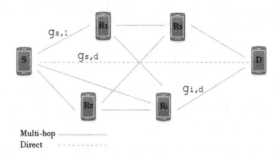

Fig. 1. System model with D2D source (S), destination (D), and relays (R)

2.2   Problem Formulation

This section is focused on problem formulation. Our objective is to maximize capacity in multi-hop D2D communication from the source UE (S) to the destination UE (D) by incorporation of the relays. Since the capacity of multi-hop communication is determined as a minimum capacity on all involved hops, the objective can be formulated as:

$$C^* = \arg\max_{y \in R}(\min\{C_y\})$$

$$s.t \qquad\qquad\qquad\qquad\qquad\qquad\qquad (4)$$

$4a. \quad h_{\max} - 1 \leq R$

$4b. \quad \forall y_{s,R_i,d}, y_{s,R_j,d} : i \neq j : R_i \neq R_j : i, j \in \{1 \cdots n\}$

where y the set sequences of multi hop communication from S to D, h_{max} is the maximum number of hops and R is the number of all relays. Note that in the sequence of combination, S is always in the first and D is in the end of communication chain. The constrain (4a) ensures that the number of hops is less or equal than the number of relays. The constrain (4b) ensures that the relay UE cannot be used more than once in the whole communication chain.

3 Proposed Relay Selection

In this section, we present the proposed solution for selection of relays to increase the capacity of the link between the S and the D. We exploit the genetic algorithm with the ordered crossover as used in [16] to select the most suitable relays. In the common genetic algorithm, the relays are selected completely randomly. Then, such solution allows to choose any arbitrary set of relays including those with repeating relays (loops). Avoidance of loops is straightforward and can be solved by a simple removal of relays that appears twice or more. However, still, the order of relays in the communication chain is crucial a common genetic algorithm cannot guarantee a right order of the relays. Reordering of the relays after each randomly generated set would lead to confusion in fitness function, in our case represented by capacity achieved for give ordered set of relays.

The fitness function (f) is formulated as:

$$f = \max \left\{ C_{s,R_{(i,j)},d}^h \right\} \tag{5}$$

Thus, we propose to use ordered cross-over instead of the common one. The process of the proposed genetic algorithm for the relay selection is described as follows.

- Step 1. We start with an initial population constituted of only a direct communication between the S and the D. For this case, the capacity $C_{s,d}^1$ is estimated from the known channel quality. If the capacity using direct communication from S to D results in the highest capacity compared to all possible relay UEs $C_{s,j}^1, C_{s,d}^1 > C_{s,j}^1$, then relay selection process is finished. We do not need to follow the next step because the direct communication is always the option with the maximum capacity from S to D.
- Step 2. If there is at least one relay that leads to solution that is better than the direct communication,

$$C_{s,d}^1 < C_{s,j}^1 \tag{6}$$

the ordered crossover operation is initialized. The ordered crossover operation combines two members of the populations (denoted as parents) to create a new path from the S to the D. In other words, the path via relay(s) represented by the Parent $P1$ (one possible and good performing combination of relays between S and D) and the Parent $P2$ (another good performing set of relays from S to D) is randomly generate. The new, can be expressed as follow:

$$
\begin{aligned}
P1 &= y_{s,Ri,d}^h \\
P2 &= y_{s,Rj,d}^h \\
&\downarrow \\
O1 &= y_{s,R_{(i,j)},d}^h : i \neq j : R_{(i,j)} \neq R_{(j,i)} \\
O2 &= y_{s,R_{(j,i)},d}^h : j \neq i : R_{(j,i)} \neq R_{(i,j)}
\end{aligned} \tag{7}
$$

where y is the set sequences of relay UEs in the communication link between S and D, $O1$ and $O2$ are the offspring of the new communication link,

i and j denote the relays based on the ordered crossover process by choosing the high capacity (2).

To preserve diversity in the population, a mutation m is exploited besides the crossover operation. The mutation $M1$ is used to get a new set of the relays from the S to the D. The mutation is expressed as:

$$O1 = y^h_{(s,R_j,d)} \rightarrow M1 = y^h_{(s,R_m,d)} : m \neq j \tag{8}$$

where m is any UEs except the relay j included in the communication link from the S to the D.

- Step 3. The process of ordered crossover starts from single hop to h relay hops so with each new population, one more relay is added to the communication chain between the S and the D. New population is generated based on the previous population (following ordered cross-over explained in previous step), but a random new relay (out of these not used so far) is integrated into the communication chains. Note that each parent can integrate any random new relay not used so far.

  If an inclusion of one more relay into the communication chain improves performance, the whole process is repeated, but one more relay is added (i.e., the number of hops is increased by one). Of course, if all the of UEs have already been used for relaying, the process is stopped. If the inclusion of the new relay does not lead to any improvement in the capacity, the process is stopped. The final communication path is selected as the one leading to the highest estimated capacity out of all members of the previous population (i.e. with one less relay).

  Note that each new generation is determined based on channels estimation, so the time duration required for the whole process is negligible (in order of milli or microseconds).

The pseudo code of the algorithm is shown in Algorithm 1.

4   Performance Evaluation

In this section, the simulation scenarios and main simulation parameters are described, then, the simulation result are presented and discussed.

4.1   Simulation Scenario

The multi-hop relay D2D communication scenario is evaluated by simulation in MATLAB software. We consider simulation distance from S to D from 100–1000 m. Within the distance, R relay UEs are randomly distributed. We consider two deployment scenarios assuming either 5 or 10 relay UEs. Note that the number of relays used between S and D is usually less than maximum number of relays in the area. Thus, we also evaluate the impact of number of relays, we investigate the capacity and number of relays actually used for multi-hop D2D communication. In order to see the impact of distance on the number of

Algorithm 1. Relay Selection for Multi-hop D2D Communication with GA

1: Choose initial population
2: Calculate capacity (C) acc. to (6)
3: Determine $y \leftarrow 1 < i < j < n$;
4: Apply ordered crossover via (7) and acc. to (2),
5: $t_1 = t_2 = v = j + 1$
6: **for** $h = 1, ..., h_{max}$
7:    **for** $w = 1, ..., n$
8:      **if** $P_{1,w} \notin \{P_{2,i} ... P_{2,j}\}$ **then** $O_{1,t_1} = P_{1,v}; t_1 + +$;
9:      **if** $P_{2,w} \notin \{P_{1,i} ... P_{1,j}\}$ **then** $O_{2,t_1} = P_{2,v}; t_2 + +$;
10:      $v = v + 1$
11:      $O_1 = [O_{1,1} ... O_{1,i-1} P_{2,i} \cdots P_{2,j-1} O_{2,i} ... O_{1,i-1}]$
12:      $O_2 = [O_{2,1} ... O_{2,i-1} P_{1,i} \cdots P_{1,j-1} O_{2,i} ... O_{2,i-1}]$
13:      Apply mutation M via (8)
14:      Calculate capacity (C) via (2)
15:    **end for**
16:    Select highest capacity (f) via (5).
17: **end for**

relays, we also investigate the difference range distance from D2D source and D2D destination. The simulation results are investigated and averaged out over 100 simulation drops in each scenario.

The transmission power of all UEs is set to the same level equal to $23dBm$. All UEs (S, and all active relays) also use the same channel frequency and bandwidth. Thus, the interference can have a significant impact on the quality of the relay links. The path loss between all communicating UEs is calculated according the indoor propagation models defined by ITU standards [17].

The simulation compares the proposed ordered crossover with the others previous solutions. To be more specific, we simulate the proposed ordered crossover in Genetic Algorithm (OGA) with SGA in [15], IGA in [9], and Dijkstra based distance in [8]. The SGA method uses the random one- and two-point crossover. The crossover method that is implemented in IGA is the same as in SGA methods, but the methods can mutate the relay UEs with the same number. Consequently, IGA method is able to remove the looping problem of the D2D links. We also compare our proposed algorithm with the conventional shortest path method, i.e., Dijkstra based distance and direct communication (no relays in communication route). Table 1 shows the list of major parameter scenario that is used in this paper.

4.2   Simulation Result and Discussion

Figure 2 illustrates the capacity performance of the proposed method for different sizes of the distance. Note that the S and D are positioned at the same place and, thus, distance between them is always fixed over all drops. Figure 2 shows that the capacity is gradually decreased with increasing of the distance between S and D is increased as well. First, we investigate the proposed OGA methods

Table 1. Simulation parameter

Parameter	Value
UE transmit power	23 dBm
Bandwidth	100 MHz
Distance	100–1000 m
Number of relay/ D2D link	5 and 10 Relays
Carrier frequency	2000 MHz
Noise power spectral density	−174 dBm/Hz
Path-loss model	ITU indoor propagation [17]

with 5 relay UEs in the network between S and D. If the distance is 100–1000 m, the OGA method achieves an average capacity gain between 10%–20%, 20%–36%, and 40%–54% in comparison to the IGA, SGA, and Dijkstra based distance, respectively. In 10 relay cases, the OGA still outperforms the IGA, SGA, and Dijkstra based distance, by up to 20%–30%, 40%–61%, and 50%–57% respectively. In this case, SGA gives the worst performance because all relay UEs are used in D2D communication and significant interference among transmitters occur.

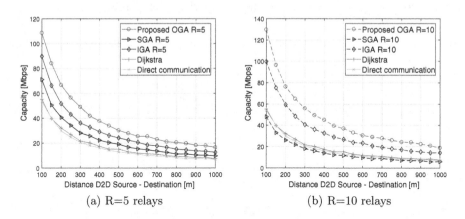

(a) R=5 relays   (b) R=10 relays

Fig. 2. Capacity over distance between S and D for scenario with $R = 5$ (a) and $R = 10$ (b) relays

Figure 3 investigate how many relays are exploited on average, if the distance increases proportionally with the distance between S and D similarly as in Fig. 2. Since the SGA method uses the same length of communication link (i.e., the same number of relays) in the crossover methods, the number of relays used is always the maximum number deployed in the simulation (i.e., 5 or 10). In the previous IGA method, there is a difference in the number of relay uses at each distance

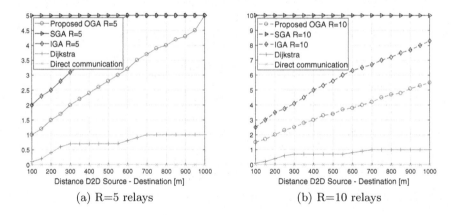

Fig. 3. Probability of relay usage

compare to SGA, because IGA methods removes the looping where there is a same relay UE in the link, but it does not consider the relay selection. Since our proposed OGA method selects the relays from the first hop, therefore the number of relays in the multi-hop D2D networks can be minimized and the capacity can be maximized. Figure 3 also demonstrates that Dijkstra achieves the lowest number of relays on average since only up to one relay is always used. This is, however at the cost of low capacity as shown in Fig. 2.

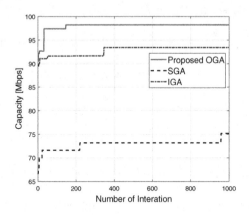

Fig. 4. Evolution of the communication capacity over iterations of the algorithm, $R = 5$

Figure 4 shows a sample of the capacity performance characteristic for a designated number of generations. In this case, the OGA not only converges fast to get its best solution (i.e. only roughly 150 iterations are needed) but also outperforms IGA and SGA method by almost 6% and 22%, respectively. Still, it is worth mentioning that already after first generation is created, the OGA outperforms both SGA and IGA.

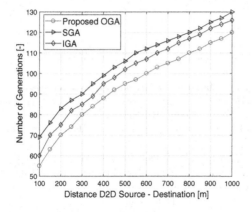

Fig. 5. Number of generations to reach the highest capacity, R = 5

Figure 5 takes a closer look at how many generations are needed if distance is changing. We can see that the all methods can reach the high capacity in fewer generations if there is a short distance between S and D. With increase of distance, more crossover operations need to be performed to achieve satisfactory results. In other words, more relays should be in communication path between S and D to obtain good performance. Nevertheless, disregarding the distance the proposed ordered crossover still outperforms both the SGA and IGA methods.

4.3 Conclusion

In this paper, we have presented a novel algorithm for relay selection to improve capacity between the D2D source and the D2D destination in multi-hop D2D communication. The objective is to find the communication path via relays by choosing suitable relaying UEs between the source and the destination UEs. The proposed solution is based on the genetic algorithm with ordered crossover. The simulation results show that the proposed algorithm improves the communication capacity up to 57%, 61%, and 30% in the distance up to 1000 m with respect to the Dijkstra based distance, SGA, and IGA, respectively. At the same time, the OGA converges faster than IGA and SGA and outperforms existing solutions even the first iteration.

Future work should address a problem of resource allocation in scenario with multiple source UEs transmitting data to their respective destinations but sharing the relaying UEs.

Acknowledgment. This work has been supported by grant No. GA17-17538S funded by Czech Science Foundation and by the grant of Czech Technical University in Prague No. SGS17/184/OHK3/3T/13.

References

1. Tehrani, M.N., Uysal, M., Yanikomeroglu, H.: Device-to-device communication in 5g cellular networks: challenges, solutions, and future directions. IEEE Commun. Mag. **52**(5), 86–92 (2014)
2. Asadi, A., Wang, Q., Mancuso, V.: A survey on device-to-device communication in cellular networks. IEEE Commun. Surv. Tutorials **16**(4), 1801–1819 (2014)
3. Liu, T., Lui, J.C., Ma, X., Jiang, H.: Enabling relay-assisted D2D communication for cellular networks: algorithm and protocols. IEEE Internet Things J. **5**(4), 3136–3150 (2018)
4. Wang, L., Peng, T., Yang, Y., Wang, W.: Interference constrained D2D communication with relay underlaying cellular networks. In: 2013 IEEE 78th Vehicular Technology Conference (VTC Fall), pp. 1–5. IEEE, September 2013
5. Zhou, K., Gui, J., Xiong, N.: Improving cellular downlink throughput by multi-hop relay-assisted outband D2D communications. EURASIP Journal on Wireless Communications and Networking **2017**(1), 1–23 (2017). https://doi.org/10.1186/s13638-017-0998-9
6. Shaikh, F.S., Wismuller, R.: Routing in multi-hop cellular device-to-device (D2D) networks: a survey. IEEE Commun. Surv. Tutorials **20**(4), 2622–2657 (2018)
7. Dang, S., Chen, G., Coon, J.P.: Multicarrier relay selection for full-duplex relay-assisted OFDM D2D systems. IEEE Trans. Veh. Technol. **67**(8), 7204–7218 (2018)
8. Ebrahimi, D., Elbiaze, H., Ajib, W.: Device-to-device data transfer through multi-hop relay links underlaying cellular networks. IEEE Trans. Veh. Technol. **67**(10), 9669–9680 (2018)
9. Yu, Z., Ni, M., Wang, Z., Zhang, Y.: Dynamic route guidance using improved genetic algorithms. Math. Probl. Eng. **2013** (2013)
10. Zhu, X., Luo, W., Zhu, T.: An improved genetic algorithm for dynamic shortest path problems. In: 2014 IEEE Congress on Evolutionary Computation (CEC), pp. 2093–2100. IEEE, July 2014
11. Nayak, P., Vathasavai, B.: Genetic algorithm based clustering approach for wireless sensor network to optimize routing techniques. In: 2017 7th International Conference on Cloud Computing, Data Science & Engineering-Confluence, pp. 373–380. IEEE (2017)
12. Apetroaei, I., Oprea, I.-A., Proca, B.-E., Gheorghe, L.: Genetic algorithms applied in routing protocols for wireless sensor networks. In: 2011 RoEduNet International Conference 10th Edition: Networking in Education and Research, pp. 1–6. IEEE (2011)
13. Sharma, Y., Saini, S.C., Bhandhari, M.: Comparison of Dijkstra's shortest path algorithm with genetic algorithm for static and dynamic routing network. Int. J. Electr. Comput. Sci. Eng. **1**(2), 416–425 (2012)
14. Yang, C., Xu, X., Han, J., Tao, X.: GA based user matching with optimal power allocation in D2D underlaying network. In: 2014 IEEE 79th Vehicular Technology Conference (VTC Spring), pp. 1–5. IEEE (2014)
15. Vlachos, C., Elshaer, H., Chen, J., Friderikos, V., Dohler, M.: Bioinspired resource allocation for relay-aided device-to-device communications. In: 2016 IEEE 84th Vehicular Technology Conference (VTCFall), pp. 1–6. IEEE (2016)
16. Abdoun, O., Abouchabaka, J.: A comparative study of adaptive crossover operators for genetic algorithms to resolve the traveling salesman problem. arXiv preprint arXiv:1203.3097 (2012)
17. Lin, X., Andrews, J.G., Ghosh, A., Ratasuk, R.: An overview of 3GPP device-to-device proximity services. IEEE Commun. Mag. **52**(4), 40–48 (2014)

A Deep Reinforcement Learning Based Intrusion Detection System (DRL-IDS) for Securing Wireless Sensor Networks and Internet of Things

Hafsa Benaddi[1], Khalil Ibrahimi[1], Abderrahim Benslimane[2(✉)], and Junaid Qadir[3]

[1] FSK/MISC Laboratory, Ibn Tofail University, Kenitra, Morocco
{hafsa.benaddi,ibrahimi.khalil}@uit.ac.ma
[2] University of Avignon, CERI/LIA, Avignon, France
abderrahim.benslimane@univ-avignon.fr
[3] Information Technology University, Punjab, Pakistan
junaid.qadir@itu.edu.pk

Abstract. Many modern infrastructures incorporate a number of sensors and actuators interconnected via wireless links using *Wireless Sensor Network* (WSN) and *Internet of Things* (IoT) technology. With a number of mission-critical infrastructures embracing these technologies, the security of such infrastructures assumes paramount importance. A motivated malicious adversary, if not kept in check by a strong defense, can cause much damage in such settings by taking actions that compromise the availability, integrity, confidentiality of network services as well as the privacy of users. This motivates the development of a strong *Intrusion Detection System* (IDS). In this paper, we have proposed a new *Deep Reinforcement Learning* (DRL)-based IDS for WSNs and IoTs that uses the formalism of *Markov decision process* (MDP) to improve the IDS decision performance. To evaluate the performance of our scheme, we compare our scheme against the baseline benchmark of standard reinforcement learning (RL) and the supervised algorithm of machine learning K-Nearest Neighbors (KNN). Through our a thorough simulation-based performance analysis, we demonstrate that our model DRL-IDS returns superior performance in terms of improved detection rate and enhancement the production of accuracy with reduced number of false alarms compared with this current approaches.

Keywords: Wireless Sensor Network · Intrusion Detection System · Cybersecurity · Deep Reinforcement Learning · Q-learning · NSL-KDD

1 Introduction

In modern times, cyber-threats are emerging as the central challenge facing networking architectures such as *Wireless Sensor Networks* (WSN) and *Internet of*

© ICST Institute for Computer Sciences, Social Informatics and Telecommunications Engineering 2020
Published by Springer Nature Switzerland AG 2020. All Rights Reserved
D.-J. Deng et al. (Eds.): WiCON 2019, LNICST 317, pp. 73–87, 2020.
https://doi.org/10.1007/978-3-030-52988-8_7

Things (IoT), which are now deployed widely for applications in diverse settings such as smart cities, smart industry, business, and healthcare, etc. [1]. A number of security challenges arise for such networks including the presence of various security flaws in commodity IoT and WSN devices, along with the challenges coming from zero-day vulnerabilities, and the tendency of such networks to be open to a large number of users (including potential malicious adversaries). It is important to address these challenges since a motivated malicious adversary can wreak havoc on the functionality of the network as well as on the network users if it is able to access privileged services without authorization through malicious software deployment in a wide range of services [2].

Intrusion Detection System (IDS) is a primary process in network security that aims to defend and monitor the network from abnormal activities and threat of intrusions in the network traffic and differentiation of normal and anomalous network activities. At a high level, we can broadly classify IDS into two types. The first type called *misuse-based* IDS (also called *signature-based IDS*) finds the intrusion by observing activities which are similar to known methods. The ability of the first method to predict new and unknown attacks is limited. The second type (*anomaly detection based IDS*) works by creating a profile of normal network behavior and then by identifying any anomalous behavior that substantially differs from the pattern of normal traffic. Such IDS can identify previously unseen attacks [3].

In this work, we propose using *Artificial Intelligence* (AI) based algorithms for developing a sophisticated IDS that can monitor streaming big network data streams generated from WSN and IoTs [6]. In previous works, various authors have used standard *Machine Learning* (ML) techniques such as Linear Discriminant Analysis (LDA) and Principal Component Analysis (PCA) as algorithms of classification to manage the performance of the IDS by detecting with high precision normal and identifying abnormal records [7–10]. In another work [12], the authors proposed a new approach called Deep Feature Embedding occupying to reduce data dimensionality from IoT in real time by taking the edge of Deep Learning (DL) and applying the pre-trained paradigm to boost the detecting and the speediness of classical ML algorithms. The advantage of DL arises in complex large-scale settings where number of states is very large, and DL models can be used in such settings to efficiently estimate the action values by offering the ability to perform classification of an incident, object monitoring, image captioning and semantic segmentation in real-time [14]. Furthermore, by taking for example the concept Q-Learning of *Reinforcement Learning* (RL) based IDS has been comprehensively explored for auditing and defending the sensor network which is used for building decision procedures and faster control where a software agent learns an optimal policy of actions over the set of states in an studied environment [15].

The *major contributions of this paper* are summarized next:

- We propose a DRL-based IDS that is modeled by Markov Decision Process (MDP) for analyzing, monitoring, and observing the network activity in real time;
- The RL and DL are combined on IDS scheme (DRL-IDS) to enhance the quality of surveillance of critical infrastructure by detecting cyber threats

for WSN and IoT in real-time by identifying new and existing malware like Botnet, Man-In-the Middle, and Denial-of-Service (DoS) with a high precision and gaining maximum rewards;

- The Deep Q-Network is used to improve the Q-function estimation given by RL deployed by the IDS. The error target of the estimated Q-function is defined by the RL to aid Deep Q-Network decision on estimated (State, Action);
- The IDS use NSL-KDD as a traffic model of WSN and IoT to monitor the real time network streams. The performance evaluation of the proposed model is given with several tests on the proposed environment;
- Our approach can extract the attack according to the risk with high accuracy and precision with a low false alarm rate.

The rest of the paper is organized as follows: In Sect. 2, we formulate the system model and describe our DRL-IDS methodology. In Sect. 3, we provide a performance evaluation of our DRL-based IDS scheme and compare it with classical RL and supervised ML schemes. In Sect. 4, we investigate the related work that has focusing on developing ML-based IDS. Finally, we conclude our study in Sect. 5 and highlight some directions for future work.

2   Proposed Model

In this section, we provide details of the suggested Deep Q-Learning network based model deployed in critical infrastructures whose purpose is to predict and monitor cyber-attacks in big sensed data streams. Our discussion encompasses the following four aspects:

1. The different degrees of risks of attacks;
2. The details of the preprocessing engaged for filtering and cleaning data in particular, and for transforming records value and reducing the dimensionality of data;
3. The interaction strategy of the agent IDS modeled to defend against the attacks using the concept of RL (Q-Learning);
4. The results of the estimation of the Q-function (State, Action) will be affected into Deep Q-Network for taking the best decision.

Figure 1 show the architecture of the proposed model, where the data of WSN are prepared conducting them to the mechanism analytic where DRL-IDS is requested to take a decision.

2.1   Classification of Attacks

Traditional IDS proposals do not provide enough security due to its centralized architecture which is vulnerable and at position of failures bonds. Even with the appearance of new technologies, no guarantee has been shown to protect the environments as a whole. Thus, traditional IDS are still deficient in terms of

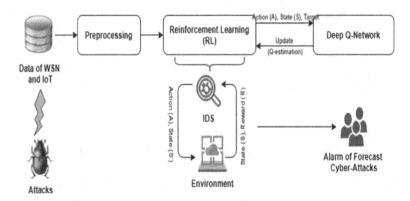

Fig. 1. Proposed scheme of improving the WSN and IoT based DRL-IDS.

security and privacy due to the massive rise in network traffic. Critical infrastructure faces both classical and unknown cyber-intrusions. Classical attacks work to collect, retrieve, and maintain access of the target data by using various techniques, the most used attacks however exploit software vulnerabilities and flaws. On the other hand, unknown attacks can be defined as newly discovered malicious. However, we classify the vulnerabilities of known attacks as described in Table 1 based on the degree of its impact on data stream, which varies from low to critical giving some examples existing in the dataset studied.

Table 1. Examples of classical attacks according to the level of risk

Degree of the risk	Example of attacks
Low	Guess-passwd, FTP-write, warezclient
Medium	nmap, satan, portsweep
High	ARP Spoofing, DNS Poisoning, Cross-Site Scripting (XSS)
Critical	Land, Apache2, Smurf, Ping of death, ICMP Flood

2.2   Preprocessing

During this step, the recording of dataset that assembly the network traffic are registered with a different type which can represent a challenge of data streaming over the IoT applications. To analyze this dataset, we first perform the preprocessing to remove the redundant and invalid records. Therefore, we do the transformation of records according to the type [9]. Firstly, we apply aggregation of the sensor data [17] to reduce the dimensionality of data and conduct them for doing the study the DRL-IDS model.

2.3   Reinforcement Learning Based IDS.

We start by defining the concept of RL, as known an another extension of ML based on a *Markov decision process* (MDP), the main idea concerning how to take an action a in order to exploit reward R environment by giving a state s to the IDS [15]. Next, we define briefly quintuple concepts of the proposed contribution-based IDS by (S, A, R, P_a, γ).

- Space of System States: The set of states captured by the IDS is denoted as $S = \{s_0 = normal, s_1 = detection, s_2 = noDetection\}$ respectively, where s_0 means the normal traffic record on the WSN record, s_1 which means detection of attacks by IDS in the traffic, and s_2 indicates that the IDS cannot detect the attacks because of these attacks do not exist in the list of known attacks or new attacks that have not yet exploited.

- Space of Actions: Set of possible actions that can be taken by the IDS, it can expressed by:

$$A = \{a_0, a_1, a_2, a_3, ..., a_m\}, \tag{1}$$

where a_k indicate the type of reaction of the IDS in the kth attacks class and $k = 0, 1, 2, 3, ...m$, e.g., according to Table 1. Moreover, the actions are ordered by the risk level of these attacks with $a_0 < a_1 < a_2 < a_3 < ... < a_m$.

- Reward Function: The objective function that will be optimized in the system which allows to represent the returns of the IDS and to feat an action immediately with the location of reward received in the state s and the action a, it can takes two forms negative value R_n when the IDS take the best action to protect the system even if the investment against the action is too expensive and positive value R_p when the IDS decides the right action. We consider the value of the reward as:

$$r_t(s_t, a_t) = \begin{cases} R_p & \text{For } s_t = s_0 \text{ and } a_t = a_0; \\ (1 - \mu_j(a_t))R_p & \text{For } s_t = s_0 \text{ and } a_t \in \{a_1, .., a_m\}; \\ R_p & \text{For } s_t = s_1 \text{ and } a_t = a_k; \\ (1 - \lambda_j(a_t))R_p & \text{For } s_t = s_1 \text{ and } a_t \in \{a_0, .., a_{k-1}\}; \\ R_n & \text{For } s_t = s_1 \text{ and } a_t \in \{a_{k+1}, .., a_m\}; \\ R_p & \text{For } s_t = s_2 \text{ and } a_t = a_m; \\ (1 - \theta_j(a_t))R_p & \text{For } s_t = s_2 \text{ and } a_t \neq a_0, \end{cases} \tag{2}$$

where $0 < \mu_j(a_t) < 1$, $0 < \lambda_j(a_t) < 1$ and $0 < \theta_j(a_t) < 1$.

The action in each state can be either a reward if detected or a cost if undetected. And so this Eq. (2) represents the gains obtained RP (which means reward positive) in each state this is when it is detected and the costs RN(reward negative) when it is undetected. We can consider the average of reward in each time step t as expressed by the following formula:

$$r_t(s_t = s, a_t = a) = \sum_{s' \in S} p(s/s', a)r_t(s', a). \tag{3}$$

- **Transition of State Probability:** Matrix of transition probabilities observing at time t for $a \in A$ is define as:

$$\mathbf{P_a} = \begin{pmatrix} \beta^a_{1,1} & \beta^a_{1,2} & \beta^a_{1,3} \\ \beta^a_{2,1} & \beta^a_{2,2} & \beta^a_{2,3} \\ \beta^a_{3,1} & \beta^a_{3,2} & \beta^a_{3,3}, \end{pmatrix} \qquad (4)$$

where $\beta^a_{i,j}$ the probability to change the state of the IDS depending on the impact of actions. Given by $\beta^a_{i,j} = p(s_{t+1}/s_t) = p(s_i|s_j, a)$ for $i, j = 1, 2, 3$ and:

$$\sum_{j=1}^{3} \beta^a_{i,j} = 1 \quad , \; i = 1, 2, 3 \; and \; a \in A. \qquad (5)$$

- **Discount Factor:** γ is between $0 < \gamma < 1$.

The IDS in our experience works to select randomly an a_t, then the environment take samples of reward $r_t(s_t, a_t)$ depending on the state of arrival s'. After that, the agent obtains the reward on the next state s_{t+1}. Furthermore, π is a given policy from s_t to s_{t+1} that specifies what a_t will be taken in each state s_t. Then, strategy will be updated in each modification of the observation of the IDS in the environment, it produces samples path (s_0, a_0, r_0), (s_1, a_1, r_1), (s_2, a_2, r_2), ... We define $\pi = (\pi_1, \pi_2, ...)$ as the vector of the optimal policies. The goal of each data stream is to obtain π_t that represents the best scheme. The state of the system s is a sufficient statistic for select the best action. Thus, to find the maximum of expected sum of rewards of the IDS at t is given by:

$$\pi^* = \underset{a \in A}{\operatorname{argmax}} \left\{ r_t(s_t, a_t) + \sum_{s' \in S} P_t(s'|s, a) V_{I-1-t}(s') \right\}. \qquad (6)$$

To choose the best state, we define the optimal value function V_{i+1} of our IDS in state s as the expected cumulative reward from the policy π^*. It can be calculated in each step i by:

$$V_{i+1}(s) = \underset{a \in A}{\operatorname{argmax}} \left\{ r_{I-1-i}(s_t, a_t) + \sum_{s' \in S} P_{I-1-i}(s'|s, a) V_i(s') \right\}. \qquad (7)$$

Using the concept of Q-Learning, we will determine a time step size in progression what will be the action a_t performed at the next time step. The Q-learning algorithm performs the updates according to the optimal policy π^* corresponding to the best action a in each state s, even if it is not these optimal actions that the IDS realizes, with the learning sample $0 < \alpha < 1$.

$$Q(s_t, a_t) = Q(s_t, a_t) + \alpha[r_t + \gamma max_{a_t \in A} \{Q(s_{t+1}, a_t) - Q(s_t, a_t)\}]. \qquad (8)$$

The IDS predicts the state value function V_{i+1} in order to update the pair (s, a) in each iteration to determine which step has the best reward. Then, Q-Learning constructs a Q-table whose lines represent the states s and the columns represents the actions a. In each s_t, the agent realizes an action a_t, observes the reward r_t of this action as well as the next state as (s_{t+1}) mentioned in [18], and updates the estimated value of $\hat{Q}$ satisfies Bellman equation:

$$\hat{Q}(s_{t+1}, a_{t+1}) = (1 - \alpha)Q(s_t, a_t) + \alpha[r_t + \gamma max_{a' \in A} \{Q(s', a')\}]. \tag{9}$$

2.4 Deep Q-Network

We included the *Deep Q-Network* (DQN) to our model the Q-function that we estimated before so that we can find the best decision of attack prediction and also improve the effectiveness in estimating the action values over the set of states by the non-linear function $Q(s_t, a_t; \theta) \approx \hat{Q}(s_{t+1}, a_{t+1})$. In fact, the parameter θ refers to the weights of the neuron which is updated in each iteration step i to train the Q-Network mentioned in [16, 17]. We have indicated the improvement of the implementation taken:

1. Use a feedforward pass for the current state s to get predict Q-values for all actions;
2. Apply the experiences replay like an historical of the interaction process of the IDS in over-time t as $f_t = (s_t, a_t, r_t, s_{t+1})$ into the replay dataset $H_t = \{h(1), h(2), ..., h(t)\}$ which can help the network to learn the various transitions of the ancient experiences.
3. Update Deep Q-Network on the records from the training data (s, a, r, s') around the target Q-value by optimizing the loss function at each iteration i denoted as following:

$$L_i(\theta_i) = E[(x_i - Q(s, a; \theta_i))^2], \tag{10}$$

which $x_i = r_t + \gamma argmax_{a'} Q(s', a'; \theta_{i-1})$. Where θ_{i-1} network parameters of the previous network.
4. Update the weights using back-propagation using the gradient of the loss function with respect to the parameters θ as shown above:

$$\nabla_{\theta_i} L_i(\theta_i) = E[(x_i - Q(s, a; \theta_i))\nabla_{\theta_i} Q(s, a; \theta_i)]. \tag{11}$$

2.5 Performance Evaluation Metrics

In this work, we calculate the performance of suggested model efficiency to predict each state of data and to estimate the quality of detection attacks, we evaluate and analyze our described approach based on the following metrics : *Tp* (True positives), *Tn* (True negatives), *Fp* (False positives), *Fn* (False negatives) their meaning indicated in [13]. To estimate it we can use the following measures:

- **Accuracy:** The aptness to predict accurately and to detect all known and newly malicious activities notated in terms of metrics performance:

$$A = \frac{Tp + Tn}{Tp + Tn + Fp + Fn} * 100\%. \tag{12}$$

- **Detection rate:** Configurable hyper-parameter used to detect correctly the behaviour manners that are showing an intrusive actions, expressed as follow:

$$DR = \frac{Tp}{Tp + Fp} * 100\%. \tag{13}$$

- **False negative rate:** The abnormal behaviors that are detected as normal sensor behaviors, it is written in the formula:

$$FR = \frac{Fn}{Fn + Fp + Tp + Tn} * 100\%. \tag{14}$$

The system performance metrics are based on the Algorithm 1:

3   Performance Evaluation and Results

3.1   Simulation Environment Description

In this section, a description of our simulation environment is provided. We used a device with Intel(R) Core(TM) i5-5200U CPU with 8 GB memory, and Python 3.7 with TensorFlow 1.13.1 on 64-bit Windows 10 operating system. For evaluating the performance, our model is compared with two other approaches: Reinforcement Learning based IDS (RL) and another classical approach of machine learning (KNN). In order to check the performance of our proposed solution, we use the popular NSL-KDD dataset that is frequently used in analyzing attacks based on IDS. This dataset represents a reduced version of the KDDCUP 99 dataset, proposed in 2010 by experts in the field of network intrusion detection to solve some problems existing in the KDD'99 database [19]. The dataset has a reasonable number of training records 125973 and testing records 22544 and also possesses TCP/IP connection records (each record consist of 41 attributes characterizing the connection (each attribute can be normal or abnormal records) [18].

Algorithm 1. Pseudo code of WSN and IoT-based DRL-IDS.

Data: Dataset of Sensor Data Y
Input: Initialize State, Action, environment, parameters θ
Initialize the target Q-network
Initialize Replay memory H space
Output: return vector $Q(s_t, a_t; \theta))$

1 **while** $|\hat{Q}_{i+1} - \hat{Q}_i| < \sigma$ **do**
2   **for** *each feature X=1,2,3...N* **do**
3           $s_0 =$ starting of State s
         for *t=0,2,3...T-1* **do**
4   - Select a random action a_t with the random probability p based on ϵ-strategy as:
             $a_t = \text{argmax}_a \, Q(s, a_k; \theta)$
             - Apply a_t and the IDS observe the reward r_t and the next state - Observe chosen reward r_t and Store the tuple (s_t, a_t, r_t, s_{t+1}) in H
             - Choose a Mini Batch arbitrary with this selected features (s_l, a_l, r_l, s_{l+1}) from H
             if s_{l+1} *terminal State* **then**
5                   $\mu_l = r_l$
6   **end**
7   **else**
8                   $\mu_l = r_l + \delta \text{argmax}_{a'} \, Q(s', a'; \theta)$
9   **end**
10   - Calculate the gradient of the loss function based on (11).
11   **end**
12   **end**
13 **end**

Before dataset analysis, we start by the preprocessing where we aim to convert the discrete recorded dataset to continuous. To this end, we categorize 41 features that describe the connection protocol. Three bytes are used to identify those protocols. As example, we take three scenarios of TCP, UDP, ICMP such as $(1, 0, 0)$, $(0, 1, 0)$ and $(0, 0, 1)$ respectively. Through this study, we have the detection of data streams cover three states: normal, detection and noDetection. We consider the transition probability matrix between states P_{a1} which is the probability symmetric, then we have the same of P_{a2} and P_{a3} as:

$$\mathbf{P_{a1}} = \begin{pmatrix} 0.4 & 0.3 & 0.3 \\ 0.3 & 0.4 & 0.3 \\ 0.3 & 0.3 & 0.4 \end{pmatrix} \tag{15}$$

To find the best optimal actions that can improve the performance of the proposed scheme, we adopted the technique of deep Q-network in the convolution neural network (CNN). The complexity of the Q-learning algorithm depends on many possible aspects such as the high number of actions and the state transition probability. Hence, the deep Q-learning uses DL to approximate the Q-function, the convergence time is affected by many factors including the learning rate, the

Table 2. Parameters values taken in this contribution

Parameters	Value
Training steps	10,000
Learning rate α	0.00001
Mini-batch	16
Convolution layers	2
Max pooling layers	2
Number of layer	2
Target network	0.001
Discount factor	0.999
Frequency	5
Epochs	100
Type of features	Normal, DoS, R2L, U2L, PROBE

mini-batch size, the number of convolutional layers, etc. However, the evaluation of the target Q-network is the only one trained relying on the gradient descent method, and we substitute the target Q-network for every mini-batch size by the updated trained Q-value. The parameters values used in our contribution are listed in Table 2.

3.2 Learning Performance

Among the tests we performed for our implementation, we focused on calculating the convergence of the model. Initially, we choose a learning rate of $\alpha = 0.00001$ that gives the best result. We can notice that the average of actions estimated

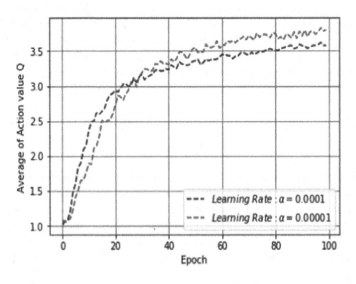

Fig. 2. Convergence of DRL-IDS with various learning rates.

in the DRL-IDS is very low at the beginning of the learning process due to the limited historic of previous actions employed in this process. By increasing the epochs count the average of action value Q increases until it reaches a stable value in Fig. 2. The epoch count is limited to 100 due to the calculation complexity. This Fig. 3 shows the impact of the epoch count on the reward received by the IDS agent. It's shown that increasing the epoch count the average reward allowed by the proposed scheme variate and decrease randomly whiting min and max value.

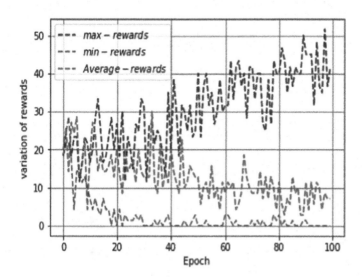

Fig. 3. Received reward by the IDS agent in function of epochs count.

3.3   Impact of Proposed IDS Metrics

In this section, we will analyze and discuss the impact of DRL-IDS as well its performance compared to reinforcement learning based IDS (RL) and K-Nearest Neighbor (KNN) given in Fig. 4, 5 and 6. A summary of simulation results is presented next.

Figure 4 illustrates the accuracy performance for our proposed model compared to the existing approaches, where high accuracy is shown at begging of the simulation due to the use of Q-learning concept with deep Q-Network. This combination that our model contains provides more accuracy to the estimated attacks by the IDS agent providing the ability to identify normal and abnormal activities and reduce the no detection activities. However, our results start to deteriorate after a while due to the complexity of calculations that increase with the epoch. From the results shown in Fig. 5, we conclude that the agent in our model is successful at predicting detection rate (Rp) (Reward positive) compared to RL and KNN approaches. Also, with the high detection accuracy we obtained before Fig. 4, we proved that the IDS agent reduces the false alarm

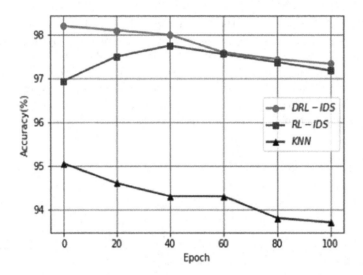

Fig. 4. Performance evaluation of DRL-IDS with the existing approaches in term of accuracy.

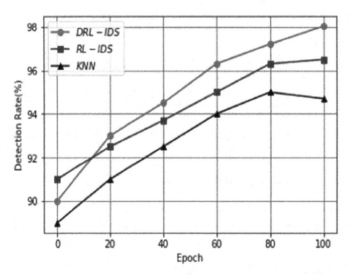

Fig. 5. Detection rate of DRL comparing to RL and KNN.

detection and consequently improves the detection rate. Figure 6 goes in the same way as Figs. 4 and 5 which shows the false rate of miss detected threats by IDS agent. As mentioned above the combination of deep Q-Network by the RL, first proposed by our paper, allows the increase of detection rate, accuracy and consequently reduces the FNR to 0.4% of the IDS agent.

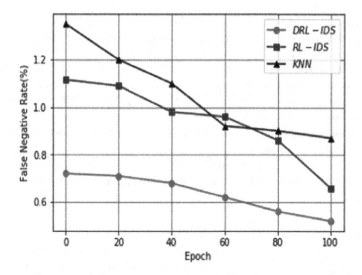

Fig. 6. Computation of false negative rates of the proposed scheme with the existing approaches.

4   Related Work

In this section, we provide a brief summary of the related work covering only the most relevant works. For a more elaborate discussion on the state of the art in intrusion detection and open research problems in the area, the interested readers are referred to the various detailed works published in literature [3–5]. In [7–10], classical ML techniques for anomaly detection have been extensively investigated to evaluate the performance metrics by reducing the false alarm and increasing detection rate and producing highly accuracy. In [11], another approach of detecting the change point of cardinalities of network data stream in time series aims to detect the various malicious activities and to calculate time, space, and trace to find this phenomenon. In [2], the authors combined supervised and unsupervised learning for vulnerability of attacks by specifying a new feature to the unknown behaviors before they are considered as attacks by using tree-based feature transformation for extracting the features. In [13], the authors established a model for IoT based on fuzzy clustering for classifying data into (high risk, low risk) then detecting this risk into (high frequency, low frequency) by ordinary. In [14,17], the authors recommended DL for network IDS to solve the classification of the high dimensional of complex features by classifying the critical examples and giving the optimal activation function to get best performance of the model.

In [15], an extension of ML (RL) is used in WSN to learn big sensed data by exploring and analyzing it by detecting malicious reaction of the hackers. However, it assumes an agent that can modeled by the process of MDP that can take the best actions in order to maximize the rewards based on the concept of

Q-Learning [20]. In another work [16], the authors addressed a DRL in cache-enabled opportunistic IA WSN by giving more effectiveness and improvement to the classical RL which can approximate and estimate reward in a large scale. In [21,22], the authors employed a stochastic game for solving the problem of detecting malicious nodes in WSN and suggested fuzzy logic theory to empowering the performance evaluation metrics during the network lifetime by respecting the critical challenge the security.

Our proposal is different from these approaches in that we focus on extracting several types of attacks in WSN and IoT with high precision, by modeling the agent IDS using the concept of MDP. The IDS is able to choose according to this formalism the best action-state witch can maximize the reward function successfully.

5   Conclusion

In this paper, we proposed a Deep Reinforcement Learning (DRL)-based Intrusion Detection System (IDS) to protect the critical infrastructures as Wireless Sensor Network (WSN) and Internet of Things (IoT) technologies. The malicious activities are detected in data streaming. The proposed DRL approach has shown efficient performance compared to Reinforcement Learning (RL) and the classical ML techniques (such as KNN) in term of detection rate, accuracy and false alarms. Otherwise, the model suffer from serious drawback which is the high calculation complexity when we took large number of samples for simulation. As future work, this later motivate us to consider the use of the proposed model to defend the network against large-scale intrusions and show if there is an impact of the heterogeneity on the IDS performance.

References

1. Ghosh, A., Khalid, O., Rais, R.N.B., Rehman, A., Malik, S.U.R., Khan, I.A.: Data offloading in IoT environment: modeling, analysis, and verification. EURASIP J. Wireless Commun. Networking **2019**, 53 (2019)
2. Mandayam, P., Liu, L., Saha, S., Tan, P., Nucci, A.: Combining supervised and unsupervised learning for zero-day malware detection. In: Proceedings of IEEE INFOCOM, pp. 2070–2078 (2013)
3. Liao, H.J., Lin, C.H.R., Lin, Y.C., Tung, K.Y.: Intrusion detection system: a comprehensive review. J. Network Comput. Appl. **36**(1), 16–24 (2013)
4. Axelsson, S.: Intrusion Detection Systems: A Survey and Taxonomy. Chalmers University of Technology, pp. 1–27 (2000)
5. Hamid, Y., Sugumaran, M., Balasaraswathi, V.: IDS using machine learning - current state of art and future directions. Br. J. Appl. Sci. Technol. **15**(3), 1–22 (2016)
6. Mitchell, R., Chen, I.-R.: A survey of intrusion detection techniques for cyber-physical systems. ACM Comput. Surv. (CSUR) **46**(4), 1–29 (2014). 55
7. Ibrahimi, K., Ouaddane, M.: Management of intrusion detection systems based-KDD99: analysis with LDA and PCA. In: International Conference on Wireless Networks and Mobile Communications (WINCOM), pp. 1–6 (2017)

8. Wang, W., Battiti, R.: Identifying intrusions in computer networks with principal component analysis. In: Proceedings of the First International Conference on Availability Reliability and Security (ARES 2006), pp. 270–279 (2006)
9. Benaddi, H., Ibrahimi, K., Benslimane, A.: Improving the intrusion detection system for NSL-KDD dataset based on PCA-fuzzy clustering-KNN. In: Conference on Wireless Networks and Mobile Communications (WINCOM), pp. 1–6 (2018)
10. Siddiqui, M.K., Naahid, S.: Analysis of KDD CUP 99 dataset using clustering based data mining. Int. J. Database Theory Appl. 6(5), 23–34 (2013)
11. Chen, W., Liu, Y., Guan, Y.: Cardinality change-based early detection of large-scale cyber-attacks. In: Proceedings of IEEE INFOCOM, pp. 1836–1844 (2013)
12. Zhou, Y., Han, M., Liu, L., He, J., Wang, Y.: Deep learning approach for cyber-attack detection. In: Conference on Computer Communications Workshops (INFOCOM WKSHPS): IEEE Infocom MiseNet Workshop, pp. 262–267 (2018)
13. Liu, L., Xu, B., Zhang, X., Wu, X.: An intrusion detection method for internet of things based on suppressed fuzzy clustering. EURASIP J. Wireless Commun. Networking **2018**(1), 1–7 (2018). https://doi.org/10.1186/s13638-018-1128-z
14. Al-Zewairi, M., Almajali, S., Awajan, A.: Experimental evaluation of a multi-layer feed-forward artificial neural network classifier for network intrusion detection system. In: International Conference on New Trends in Computing Sciences (ICTCS), pp. 167–172 (2017)
15. Otoum, S., Kantarci, B., Mouftah, H.: Empowering reinforcement learning on big sensed data for intrusion detection. In: International Conference on Communications (2019)
16. Yu, F.R., He, Y.: Deep Reinforcement Learning for Wireless Networks. SECE. Springer, Cham (2019). https://doi.org/10.1007/978-3-030-10546-4
17. Mohammadi, M., Al-Fuqaha, A., Guizani, M., Oh, J.-S.: Semi supervised deep reinforcement learning in support of IoT and smart city services. IEEE Internet Things J. **PP**(99), 1–12 (2017)
18. Xu, X., Xie, T.: A reinforcement learning approach for host-based intrusion detection using sequences of system calls. In: Huang, D.-S., Zhang, X.-P., Huang, G.-B. (eds.) ICIC 2005. LNCS, vol. 3644, pp. 995–1003. Springer, Heidelberg (2005). https://doi.org/10.1007/11538059_103
19. Servin, A., Kudenko, D.: Multi-agent reinforcement learning for intrusion detection. In: Tuyls, K., Nowe, A., Guessoum, Z., Kudenko, D. (eds.) AAMAS/ALAMAS 2005-2007. LNCS (LNAI), vol. 4865, pp. 211–223. Springer, Heidelberg (2008). https://doi.org/10.1007/978-3-540-77949-0_15
20. Alpcan, T., Basar, T.: An intrusion detection game with limited observations. In: Proceedings of the 12th International Symposium on Dynamic Games and Applications. Citeseer (2006)
21. Shen, S., Han, R., Guo, L., Li, W., Cao, Q.: Survivability evaluation towards attacked WSNs based on stochastic game and continuous-time Markov chain. Appl. Soft Comput. **12**(5), 1467–1476 (2012)
22. Liu, J., Yue, G., Shen, S., Shang, H., Li, H.: A game-theoretic response strategy for coordinator attack in wireless sensor networks. Sci. World J. **2014**, Article ID 950618, 10 pages (2014). https://doi.org/10.1155/2014/950618

A Coin Recognition System Towards Unmanned Stores Using Convolutional Neural Networks

Chi Han Chen, Bo Han Chen, and Anthony Y. Chang[✉]

Department of Information Technology, Overseas Chinese University, Taichung, Taiwan, R.O.C.
achang@ocu.edu.tw

Abstract. In unmanned stores, automated checkout is an integral part of the process, and the checkout is usually completed by expensive identification machines. Some unmanned stores lacking banknotes and coins only provide credit cards, EasyCard, or QR code payment methods, sometimes that cause the difficulty of payment when they check out. This research is aimed at the coin recognition for images. It processes the images using OpenCV, and substitutes into the trained convolutional neural network (CNN) for identification. The result of the research shows that the accuracy of the model identification is 94%, and it can be used to identify more than one coin.

Keywords: Coin recognition system · Embedded systems · Convolutional neural networks (CNN) · Unmanned stores

1 Introduction

Coin Recognition is a hot research topic, common techniques for calculating coins are (1) Traditional coin-operated machine using lasers and electromagnets to identify coins, (2) cash registers. This research used Canny edge detection, Hough transform, Gaussian blur, Convolution Neural Network, combined with all the techniques to detect and identify coins.

There are many factors in real life that hinder coin recognition, such as light, shape, size, and coin design. If the experiment only uses edge detection, when the environmental factors are changed, the originally parameters may be invalid, that will force the experiment to adjust the parameters often and results in poor experimental results.

Alex proved that convolutional neural networks can be good at identifying and classifying images [1]. The research proposed that OpenCV and CNN can be combined to identify coin images with various environmental factors by image recognition training of different attributes.

2 Related Works

Unmanned stores are a hot topic in recent years, it opened up new consumption models, which bring advantages such as saving labor costs, 24-h business, and technology-based systems. In the future consumption pattern, Dhruv Grewal et al. mentioned that

© ICST Institute for Computer Sciences, Social Informatics and Telecommunications Engineering 2020
Published by Springer Nature Switzerland AG 2020. All Rights Reserved
D.-J. Deng et al. (Eds.): WiCON 2019, LNICST 317, pp. 88–98, 2020.
https://doi.org/10.1007/978-3-030-52988-8_8

retailers have embraced a variety of technologies to attract customers, with a focus on five key areas that are moving the field forward: (1) technology and tools to facilitate decision making, (2) visual display and merchandise offer decisions, (3) consumption and engagement, (4) big data collection and usage, and (5) analytics and profitability. Consumers offer a variety of different messages to retailers when they trade, such as transaction data, consumer information, and environmental data, that enable retailers to effectively predict consumer behavior from these data, to design products that are more appealing to consumers, and to improve profitability [2]. Although the consumption pattern is gradually digitized from early coin and banknote transactions to modern credit cards, mobile phone digital payment, etc., it still requires traditional cash transactions. If it is combined with computer vision to complete the action through the machine, it could reduce the cost of processing.

Mohamed Roushdy used Canny edge detection in conjunction with Hough transform to detect coins with different radii, Hough transform can detect Gaussian blur and noise effectively, and successfully detect coins, where the threshold is a significant and deter-minant factor in coin detection [3]. Velu C M proposes a multi-stage back-propagation neural network with combination of Robert's edge detection, Gaussian edge detection, and Canny edge detection. It has been identified for implementation using Matlab and the simulation results are tested. The recognition rate of ML-CPNN method is 99.47% [4]. This method is tested in the virtual environment, but it is not executed on the actual hardware.

Alex Krizhevsky et al. used a large number of deep convolutional neural networks to classify 1.2 million images in the ImageNet competition. The top-1 and top-5 error rates were 37.5% and 17.0% respectively, which was significantly better than the previous technology [1], but AlexNet is a huge neural network, it is not suitable for edge comput-ing. Suchika Malik et al. proposed a combination of Hough transform and Canny edge detection, and used in the coin recognition system of neural network. The difference between Sobel edge detection and Canny edge detection is that Sobel edge detection can't effectively remove the noise, and Canny edge detection can detect the complete edge [5]. Sandeep Kaur and Mandeep Kaur proposed using polar harmonic transform to find the horizontal and vertical coordinates of the coin, eliminating the need to place the coin in a specific position [6]. S. Mohamed Mansoor Roomi et al. proposed the use of neural networks for coin detection, the algorithm is robust and invariant to rota-tion, translation and scaling. Using Fourier transform can reduce the effect from surface reflection of coins [7].

The purpose of this paper is to identify the edge and cut it into a picture containing coins by OpenCV, and substitute the pictures into a trained CNN model for identification to solve the problem that the coin recognition can only identify one. A small convolutional neural network speeds up the identification and maintains a certain degree of recognition. This study can be applied to unmanned stores to identify the number and amount of coins.

3   Technical Use

3.1   Neural Network - Convolutional Neural Network

The Convolutional Neural Network (CNN) is similar to the traditional artificial neural network (ANN). CNN is self-optimized by neuron learning, and each neuron will receive input and execute. From the original picture inputs to the last class outputs, the whole network represents the weight of a single perceptron. The last layer contains the loss function associated with the class. The only difference between CNN and ANN is that CNN is mainly used in the field of image recognition, so that we can encode specific images into the architecture and complete the neural network architecture [8]. The common CNN architecture is shown in Fig. 1.

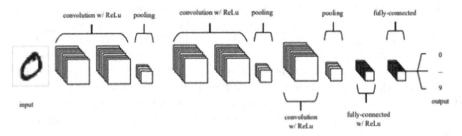

Fig. 1. Common CNN architecture.

3.2   OpenCV

Canny Edge Detection. Canny edge detection is already one of the standard detection algorithms of images. The main target of image processing is the message features in the image. The image is composed of different messages of the scene, for example: the size, color and direction of different objects in the scene [9].

Convolution with a linear edge detection function aligned perpendicular to the edge direction and a projection function parallel to the edge direction, and create a 2D template for this direction [10]. Equations (1) and (2) use Gn convolutional images. Gn is the first derivative n of a two-dimensional Gaussian G direction.

$$G = \exp\left(-\frac{x^2 + y^2}{2\sigma^2}\right) \tag{1}$$

and

$$G_n = \frac{\partial G}{\partial n} = n \cdot \nabla G \tag{2}$$

Ideally, n should be perpendicular to the direction of edge detection, although this direction is unknown, but a good prediction can be made from the smooth gradient direction (3).

$$n = \frac{\nabla(G * I)}{|\nabla(G * I)|} \tag{3}$$

In the formula * indicates convolution. This proved to be a very good step of detecting the edge direction because the smoothing step has a strong gradient of vertical edges. When there is no noise, it is accurate for straight edges and Gaussian smoothing makes it insensitive to noise. The edge point is defined as the maximum value of the image I local (in the n direction), and the local maximum is (4):

$$\frac{\partial}{\partial n} Gn * I = 0 \tag{4}$$

Substituting Gn with Gaussian convolution, as the Eq. (5):

$$\frac{\partial^2}{\partial n^2} G * I = 0 \tag{5}$$

The edge point size of Eq. (6) is the edge strength:

$$|G_n * I| = |\nabla(G * I)| \tag{6}$$

Hough Transform. Paul Hough proposed a method for efficiently detecting binary image segments in 1962 [11]. Hough transform (HT) converts the global detection problem in image space into a simpler local space peak detection problem [12].

The curve is resolved according to the generalized shape parameters S, x, y, θ. Shape parameter table as shown in (Table 1)

Table 1. General shape parameters.

Analytic form	Parameters	Equation
Line	S, θ	$x\cos\theta + y\sin\theta = S$
Circle	x_r, y_r, S	$(x - x_r)^2 + (y - y_r)^2 = S^2$
Parabola	x_r, y_r, S_x, θ	$(y - y_r)^2 = 4S_x(x - x_r)^*$
Ellipse	$x_r, y_r, S_x, S_y, \theta$	$\frac{(y-y_r)^2}{S_r^2} + \frac{(x-x_r)^2}{S_x^2} = 1^*$

*Plus rotation by θ.

Equation (7) Defines the representation parameters of arbitrary shape.

$$a = \{y, s, \theta\} \tag{7}$$

where y = (xr, yr,) is a reference origin for the shape, 0 is its orientation, and s = (sx, sy) describes two orthogonal (x-axis and y-axis) scale factors [13].

· **Gaussian Blur.** Gaussian blur operations are used in many image processing applications. The execution times of these operations can be rather long, when large kernels are involved. Proper use of two properties of Gaussian blurs can help to reduce long execution times:

1. Large kernels can be decomposed into the sequential application of small kernels.
2. Gaussian blurs are separable into row and column operations [14].

The optimal image smoothing filter is located in the spatial and frequency domains and is defined in the two-dimensional space as (8):

$$g(x, y) = \frac{1}{2\pi\sigma^2} e^{-(x^2+y^2/2\sigma^2)} \tag{8}$$

Operating Environment. The system uses Raspberry pi3 b+ based on the Linux operating system, with an ARM architecture processor with a single core clock of up to 1.4 GHz. Supports 2.4 GHz and 5 GHz dual-band and supports Bluetooth 4.2. The Linux system uses raspberrypi 4.19.42-v7+, and the programming language uses Python 3.5.3 and OpenCV 4.2.0.

We use the 5MP Raspberry Pi Camera Module for image capture. The transmission interface uses CSI-2 to connect to Raspberry Pi. The resolution is 5 million pixels, and the static image resolution is 2592 * 1944. The maximum image transmission rate is 1080p, 30 fps.

4   Dataset

4.1   Collecting Images

The image is taken by the Raspberry Pi camera. After the computer vision processing, the coin contained in the image is found and cut. The image is 100 * 100 pixels. The coin image is as follows (Fig. 2).

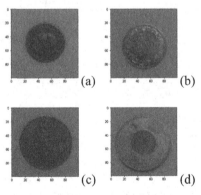

Fig. 2. The coins (a) one NT dollar (b) five NT dollars (c) ten NT dollars (d) fifty NT dollars.

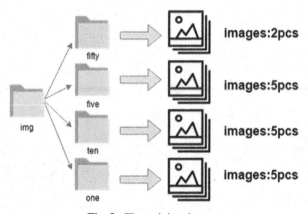

Fig. 3. The training dataset.

4.2 Training Dataset

This study uses ImageDatagenerator to generate training data. First, the images collected in (Fig. 1) are merged into folders of various categories. ImageDatagenerator uses the folder name as the category label. For example, the coin category labels used in (Fig. 3) are divided into one dollar, five dollars, ten dollars and fifty dollars. A total of seventeen photos in four categories constitute a training data set.

4.3 Training Images

The model learns the images of different attributes according to the set rotation, width offset, height offset, crop, zoom and horizontal flip. The image to be learned is 100 * 100 grayscale. The sample image is as Fig. 4.

4.4 Test Model Dataset

The test model data set is the same as the training data set architecture. The only difference is the difference numbers of photos used to test the model accuracy. The architecture of test model data set is as shown in Fig. 5.

(a)

(b)

(c)

Fig. 4. After the data set is learned by the model, images with different attributes are generated.

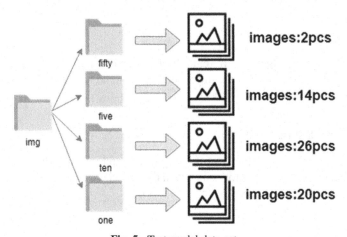

Fig. 5. Test model data set.

5 Methods

See Fig. 6.

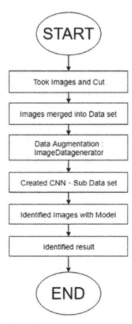

Fig. 6. Process chart.

5.1 Get Coin Images

Based on OpenCV, use the camera to capture images for identification, and to find and cut the center of the coin in the image. The image pixel size is 100 * 100, and the images are organized into data sets.

5.2 Create CNN

This study does not use a large convolutional neural network since it does not benefit edge computing. For embedded systems with limited performance, a simple neural network architecture can improve recognition speed. We have built a small convolutional neural network that reduces computation and recognition time. It can also get proper weights to maintain good recognition.

5.3 Data Augmentation

In the case of a small number of data sets, use the ImageDatagenerator in the Keras library to augment the data, increase the strength of the training data, and generate data with different attributes according to the parameter range.

5.4 Training Model

The paper proposed control group and experimental test group to compare with the original test data and augmented data. The learning curve is as Fig. 7.

(a)

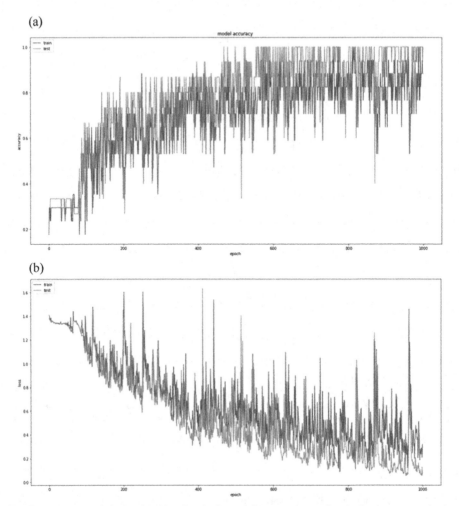

(b)

Fig. 7. The result of the model, blue line is the training set, orange line is the test set, (a) is the accuracy, and (b) is the loss rate. (Color figure online)

Control Group. Control group uses ImageDatagenerator to increase the strength of the data set and the batch data is a learning cycle every 4 times for total 1000 learning times. The experimental results show that the accuracy of the learning model is gradually improved, and the accuracy is improved from 23.5% to 94%.

Test Group. Test Group uses ImageDatagenerator to convert image dimensions only, without increasing the data strength, and the rest of the codes remain the same. The experimental results show that the model is over-fitting. When the model has been learned 600 times, the model accuracy is often maintained at 1, it indicates that the model over-fitting the data set, and it is difficult to identify other coin data sets.

5.5 Test Model

The trained model is inputted into the test model data set to predicate, and the predicted result is selected from the four class labels as the identification result. The test method is to compare the predicted result of the model with the class label of the coins. If the two are the same, the identification is successful, otherwise the identification is failure.

6 Conclusions

In summary, we believe that the system achieved sufficient commercial accuracy and the results of the model training reached 94%. Our works have shown that using Image-Datagenertor to augment the data allows the model to maintain good learning results and the data is not over-fitting. Compared with the previous research, the adaptability to environmental factors is effectively improved, and the parameters have not to be adjusted with environmental factors, and it can be practically applied to real hardware. The research combines the technologies of OpenCV and CNN to identify and predict coins. At present, the coins at the time of stacking have not been identified however. In the future, we hope that a method of identifying stacked coins can be developed to meet the needs of unmanned stores through this research.

References

1. Krizhevsky, A., Sutskever, I., Hinton, G.E.: ImageNet classification with deep convolutional neural networks. In: Neural Information Processing Systems (NIPS 2012), vol. 2 (2012)
2. Grewal, D., Roggeveen, A.L., Nordfält, J.: The future of retailing. J. Retail. **93**, 1–6 (2017)
3. Roushdy, M.: Detecting coins with different radii based on hough transform in noisy and deformed image. GVIP J. **7**(1), 25–29 (2007)
4. Velu, C.M., Vivekanadan, P., Kashwan, K.R.: Indian coin recognition and sum counting system of image data mining using artificial neural networks. Int. J. Adv. Sci. Technol. **31**, 67–80 (2011)
5. Malik, S., Bajaj, P., Kaur, M.: Sample coin recognition system using artificial neural network on static image dataset. IJARCSSE **4**(1) (2014)
6. Kaur, S., Kaur, M.: Review on the coin recognition system with rotation invariant. IJCSMC **3**(9), 259–262 (2014)
7. Roomi, S.M.M., Rajee, R.B.J.: Coin detection and recognition using neural networks. In: 2015 International Conference on Circuits, Power and Computing Technologies (ICCPCT 2015) (2015)
8. O'Shea, K., Nash, R.: An Introduction to convolutional neural networks. arXiv:1511.08458v2 [cs.NE] (2015)
9. Kabade, A.L., Sangam, V.G.: Canny edge detection algorithm. IJARECE **5**(5), 1292–1295 (2016)
10. Canny, J.: A computational approach to edge detection. IEEE Trans. Pattern Anal. Mach. Intell **PAMI-8**(6), 679–698 (1986)
11. Hough, P.V.C.: Method and Means for Recognizing Complex Patterns. United States Patent Office, Ann Arbor, Mich (1962)
12. Hassanein, A.S., Mohammad, S., Sameer, M., Ragab, M.E.: A survey on hough transform, theory, techniques and applications. IJCSI **12**(1), (2015)

13. Ballard, D.H.: Generalizing the hough transform to detect arbitrary shapes. Pattern Recogn. **13**(2), 111–122 (1981)
14. Waltz, F.M., Miller, J.W.V.: An efficient algorithm for Gaussian blur using finite-state machines. In: Machine Vision Systems for Inspection and Metrology VII (1998)

Towards the Implementation of Movie Recommender System by Using Unsupervised Machine Learning Schemes

Debby Cintia Ganesha Putri[(⊠)] and Jenq-Shiou Leu

Electronic
and Computer Engineering Department, National Taiwan University of Science and Technology,
Taipei City 106, Taiwan
{M10602822,jsleu}@mail.ntust.edu.tw

Abstract. This study aimed at finding out the similarity to create a movie recommendation system and grouping based on the user. The purpose of the recommendation system as information for customers in selecting films according to features. The recommendation system can be performed with several algorithms as a grouping such as K-Means, K-Means Mini Batch, Birch Algorithm, Affinity Propagation Algorithm and Mean Shift Algorithm. We recommend methods to optimize K as a precaution in increasing variance. We use clustering based on Movie ratings, Tags, and Genre. This study would find a better method and way to evaluate the clustering algorithm. To check the recommendation system, we utilize social network analysis and mean squared error to explore the relationships between clusters. We also utilize average similarity, computation time, and clustering performance evaluation in getting an evaluation as a comparison of the recommendation system. Clustering Performance Evaluation with Silhouette Coefficient, Calinski-Harabasz, Davies-Bouldin.

Keywords: Recommendations system · Birch Algorithm · K-Means · Mini Batch K-Means · Affinity Propagation, and Mean shift · Social Network Analysis (SNA) · Mean Squared Error (MSE) · Average similarity · Computation time · Clustering performance evaluation

1 Introduction

The progress of technology has made the growth of information that is synonymous. The recommendation system is an algorithm as a feature processing in the software in getting accurate information based on the needs of the user. The purpose of using the Recommendation system is to provide information to users as suggestions that can be used such as films or books based on historical references. Some examples of websites that apply to the recommendation system are yahoo, eBay, amazon [1], and others. A recommendation system is needed because there are too many types and amounts of data on the internet. The recommendation system can analyze so much data about users and

© ICST Institute for Computer Sciences, Social Informatics and Telecommunications Engineering 2020
Published by Springer Nature Switzerland AG 2020. All Rights Reserved
D.-J. Deng et al. (Eds.): WiCON 2019, LNICST 317, pp. 99–113, 2020.
https://doi.org/10.1007/978-3-030-52988-8_9

available films and analyze information for other users. The algorithm used evaluates items and shows the user which items are high-level and appropriate content for film recommendations are used based on individuals who "think alike" with the same tastes and preferences in the reference.

However, the recommendation system is vulnerable to scalability and poor capacity [2]. Several studies have proven the benefits of the recommendation system. From the literature, there is the development of models that discuss partition algorithms, such as self-organizing maps (SOM) and K-means [3]. Other methods such as the clarification method or grouping data. The goal is as a grouping to divide users who are "like-minded" (closest) as an increase in system scalability [4]. Getting films that can be recommended in the system recommendations is part of the challenge. The feature used as a recommendation is as a behavior analysis on the user as a personalized recommendation [5].

To address the challenges aforementioned, there are several methods to proposed the clustering performance comparison for recommendation systems on a movie, such as Birch, K-Means, Affinity Propagation, Mini Batch K-Means, and Mean shift. In this article, we developed to optimized the groupings with several algorithms, after that compared to get better algorithms in grouping similarity users by tags, genre, and rating on the movie with MovieLens dataset. When we talk about variance, we are referring to the error. To ensure the quality for recommendation system we will use MSE and SNA. We also use the similarities in average, computational time, and grouping in performance evaluation as a measurement of system performance recommendations.

In this research, we will make a comparison of algorithm performance to get quality in the recommendation system. The contributions of this study include the following,

1. identify the quality of the method which is better than several methods in grouping to get a recommendation system on the film.
2. to get the optimal K value in the Mini Batch-Kmeans, Birch, and Kmeans methods.
3. to analyze the recommendation system, we will use social network analysis. We also use the similarity of averages for the system performance recommendation method.

The following papers are organized as follows: Sect. 2, we explain the design for the recommending system. We detailed algorithm designs with Birch, K-Means, K-Means Mini Batches, Affinity Propagation, and Mean shift. We optimize K in several methods. Experiments and results can be described in Sects. 3. Then evaluate the algorithm with several methods in Sect. 4. Section 5 will give the conclusions to this work.

2 System Design and Clustering Algorithm

In this section, system design to defining the process to satisfy specified requirements and clustering algorithm is an algorithm used in this study.

2.1 System Design

In designing a recommendation system, we used Birch Algorithm, K-Means Algorithm, Mini Batch K-Means Algorithm, Affinity Propagation Algorithm, and Mean shift Algorithm to find out the best performing algorithm in recommendation movie, assisted by optimizing K value. Then after applying some of the existing algorithms, find the closest neighbor to the user's similarity in the common cluster and get Top-N for the list of recommended films. Figure 1 showing the overview of the application of five existing algorithms. The module is represented by a flow chart that starts from select datasets to find the Top-N list of movie recommendations for user similarity. We explain the following details.

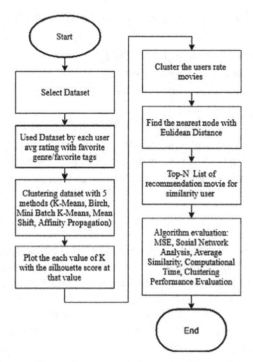

Fig. 1. Flowchart configure a recommendation system for movie recommendations

2.2 Clustering Algorithm

Following the algorithm used in this learning,

K-Means Clustering and Optimizing K Number Cluster

K-means clustering (MacQueen 1967) is part of the method which is automatic partitioned datasets to become k groups [6]. It starts with selecting the initial central cluster k and the closest central cluster. Each center in the Cj cluster is used to sample the average constituents. K-means is an approach by grouping the most commonly used flexibility, and efficiency in several data. K-means takes into account the center of the cluster to assign objects to the closest cluster. Selecting a seed randomly produces a locally optimal solution which is quite low in finding direct K values. Given a set of objects (x1, x2, . . . , xn). The following Table 1 explains the K-means process.

Table 1. K-mean Algorithm and optimize K number cluster

1. Choose the dataset to use and process the dataset by each average user with favorite genre / tag
2. Choose k for the initial cluster center for Cj, j= 1,2,3 ..., k;
3. each xi will be assigned to the nearest cluster center depends on the distance metric
4. Then calculate the number of distances by squared on all members in one cluster

$$J = \sum_{j=1}^{k} \sum_{i \in C_{temp}} ||Xi - Mj||^2 \qquad (1)$$

where Mj will give average data points on C_{temp};
5. Determine for K in the number of Clusters
6. Classifying film rates to users
7. The nearest node to determine the similarity in the user as Euclidean distance
8. The algorithm will merge and the task of grouping ends, after that it will recalculate Mj from the k cluster as the center of the new cluster
9. Then, the result will be obtained Top-N movie as User Similarity

Optimize K Number of Cluster

We optimized the K for choosing the right K number of clusters. Took the right number of clusters is one of the key points of the K-means clustering. To find out K, we calculated the clustering error used mean squared error. First, selecting our dataset to choosing the range of the k values to test. Then, defining the function can calculate the clustering errors and calculating error values for the k values. Last, plotting each value of k with the silhouette score. The following is an explanation of the silhouette score and mean squared error,

1. Silhouette score is to find out K in a number cluster
    The silhouette was described by Peter J. Rousseeuw in 1986 [7]. Silhouette is a method of validation or interpretation of data clusters. The silhouette value for the given attribute is in the equation below

$$s(i) = \frac{a(i)b(i)}{\max\{a(i), b(i)\}} \qquad (2)$$

where $a(i)$ is the average dissimilarity of i the data point with all other data within the same cluster.
2. Mean squared Error to find out K number cluster

$$\frac{1}{n} \sum_{i=1}^{n} [\min_{j} d^2(x_i, m_j)] \qquad (3)$$

where $d(x_i, m_j)$ denoted with Euclidean distance between x_i and m_j. The points $\{m_j\}$ (j = 1, 2, ..., k) were known as the cluster centroids [8].

Birch Clustering Algorithm
Reduced Iterative Reducing and Clustering uses a Hierarchies (Birch clustering) that uses data structures with a CF-tree hierarchy in a dynamic grouping as data points [9]. The first phase in the CF tree from the data point is the high balanced tree data structure. This can be defined with N d-dimensional data points, the *clustering feature* (CF) of the set is defined the triple CF = (N, LS, SS), where

$$\overrightarrow{LS} = \sum_{i=1}^{N} \overrightarrow{xi} \quad \text{is the linear sum and,} \tag{4}$$

$$\overrightarrow{SS} = \sum_{i=1}^{N} \overrightarrow{(xi)^2} \quad \text{sum of data points.} \tag{5}$$

Mini Batch K-Means Clustering
The mini-batch k-means clustering algorithm is a renewal of the k-means algorithm, with the advantage of reducing time with large-scale dataset calculations. Mini Batch K-means are faster than k-means and can usually be used for large-scale datasets. For dataset $T = \{x_1, x_2, \ldots, x_n\}$, $xi \in R^{m*n}$ xi represents a network record with an n-dimensional real vector [10]. For cluster centers, note K will be chosen randomly. Mini Batch K-Means reduce overall convergence time. The following is a calculation of the sum of squares in all members of one cluster.

$$min \sum_{x \in T} ||f(C, x) - x||^2 \tag{6}$$

where, f (C, x) returned for closest cluster center $c \in C$ to record x.

Mean Shift Clustering
Shift algorithm is one of method in analysis the cluster [11]. Intuition is shifted to determine gradient increments, process convergence requires verification, and its relationship with the same algorithm needs clarification. The algorithm will automatically set the number of clusters, rather than using bandwidth parameters. Calculate the mean vector with the variance of each cluster (the basis of attraction), update it from centroid as the sample mean,

$$m(xi) = \frac{\sum_{xj \in N(xi)} K(xj - xi)xj}{\sum_{xj \in N(xi)} K(xj - xi)} \tag{7}$$

Affinity Propagation Clustering
Affinity propagation is one of the method considers data points for possible examples. Affinity propaganda exchanges messages between them as a series of high-quality copies and cluster adjustments. Messages based on a simple formula as the number of products that reflect an affinity with one point to choose another point, this is called "affinity propagation" [12].

Availability of a (i, k), as proof of sample accumulation k. Sample k becomes the sample given by formula below,

$$r(i, k) \leftarrow s(i, k) - \max\left[a(i, k') + s(i, k') \forall k' \neq k\right] \tag{8}$$

The similarity between sample i and k, s (i, k). Availability with sample k will be an example as the sample i is given by,

$$a(i, k) \leftarrow \min[0, r(k, k) + \sum_{i' s.t.i' \notin \{i,k\}} r(i', k)] \tag{9}$$

And define cluster with update r (i, k) and a (i, k),

The values for r and a will be set to zero and the calculation is iterated until convergence is found to avoid numerical oscillations in the message update, the iteration process with the damping factor γ,

$$r_{t+1}(i, k) = \lambda . r_t(i, k) + (1 - \lambda) . r_{t+1}(i, k) \tag{10}$$

$$a_{t+1}(i, k) = \lambda . a_t(i, k) + (1 - \lambda) . a_{t+1}(i, k) \tag{11}$$

3 Experiments and Results

In this section, we describe the experimental design. In addition, investigating the film recommendation algorithm proposed through K-Means, Birch, K-Means Mini Batch, Shift mean, and Affinity Propagation techniques. Then we will evaluate in several ways. Experiments were carried out with Intel (R) Core (TM) i5-2400 CPU @ 3.10 GHz, 8.0 GB RAM computer and Python 3 with a version of Jupyter Notebook 5.7.8 that simulate the algorithms.

3.1 Dataset

We consider the dataset with the famous Movielens in conducting experiments, which are available online, the dataset to be a stable benchmark with datasets in 20 million ratings and 465,000 application tags then applied to 27,000 films, supported by 138,000 users, and 19 film genres. The dataset uses a discrete scale of 1–5. We do restrictions based on 3 genres and 3 tags to analyze how the algorithm works and get good visualization, high dimensions produce visualizations that are not good enough when using more than 3 tags and genres. Then the dataset is randomly divided through training and test data, each data with a ratio of 80%/20%. The aim is to group people into developing film recommendation systems for users. Then, this system generates a list of films based on user similarity.

3.2 Experiment Result

Algorithm Clustering Result
In this section grouping different algorithms with kmeans, Affinity Propagation, Mini-Batch K-Means, and Meanshift to group users based on similarities and get the right film recommendations. We limit research based on 3 genres and 3 tags as analyzing and getting the best visualization. After that, sort by film ranking from high to low with a

dataset to a discrete scale of 1–5. Then optimize K in choosing the right number of K clusters. Looking for cluster neighbors can be done with euclidean distance. Visualization on k, the genre is better than tags because the data on tags tends to be small. Then an N-list from the movie list will be obtained based on the user's similarity. The following are the results in visualizing grouping of five algorithms (Figs. 2 and 3).

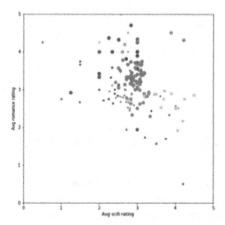

Fig. 2. Visualization of Kmeans clustering algorithms

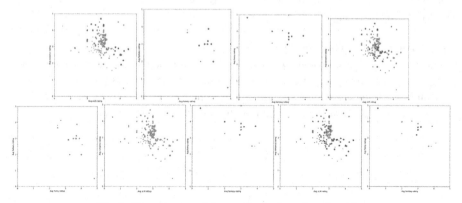

Fig. 3. Visualization of five methods clustering algorithm

In order to have a more delimited for a subset of people to study, we were going to bias our grouping to only get ratings from those users that like either romance or science fiction movies. We used the x and y axes of the romance and sci-fi ratings. In addition, the bigger the dot the higher the adventure rating. We can see that with the addition of the adventure genre the clustering very significantly. Kmeans genre n cluster = 12, Kmeans tag n cluster = 7, Birch tags n cluster = 12, Birch genre n cluster = 12, Mean shift genre, Mean shift tags, MiniBatch-Kmeans genre n cluster = 12, MiniBatch-Kmeans tags (n_clusters = 7), Affinity Propagation genre, Affinity Propagation tags (Fig. 4).

```
Amelie (Fabuleux destin d'Amélie Poulain, Le) (2001)    4.800000
Snow White and the Seven Dwarfs (1937)                  4.750000
Casino (1995)                                           4.700000
Godfather, The (1972)                                   4.700000
American History X (1998)                               4.666667
Good Will Hunting (1997)                                4.642857
Swingers (1996)                                         4.625000
Memento (2000)                                          4.600000
Princess Bride, The (1987)                              4.600000
Usual Suspects, The (1995)                              4.500000
Batman Begins (2005)                                    4.500000
O Brother, Where Art Thou? (2000)                       4.500000
Pinocchio (1940)                                        4.500000
Rear Window (1954)                                      4.500000
E.T. the Extra-Terrestrial (1982)                       4.500000
There's Something About Mary (1998)                     4.500000
Godfather: Part II, The (1974)                          4.500000
Schindler's List (1993)                                 4.458333
Goodfellas (1990)                                       4.450000
Braveheart (1995)                                       4.423077
Name: 0, dtype: float64
```

Fig. 4. Example for Genre Kmeans visualization for Top list-N of Movies

We get ratings from users who tend to like romantic films or science fiction. The x and y-axis of romance and science fiction ranks. After that the point size will represent the adventure film ranking, the bigger the point, the higher the adventure film ranking. Kmeans genre n cluster = 12, Kmeans tag n cluster = 7, Birch tag n cluster = 12, Birch genre n cluster = 12, Average shift genre, Tag shift average, MiniBatch-Genre genre n cluster = 12, tags MiniBatch-Kmeans (n_clusters = 7), Affinity Propagation genre, Affinity Propagation tags.

Optimize K Number Cluster
The results of the algorithm can show a better choice for the K value. The exact number of clusters is crucial in using the K-means algorithm, and also the Birch Algorithm and the Mini Batch K-means Algorithm, this is not applied to Affinity propagation and Mean shift due to the algorithm. This is based on the Silhouette Score (Fig. 5).

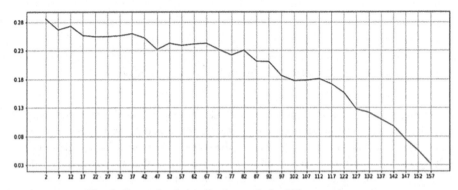

Fig. 5. Example of visualization optimize K in genre kmeans.

4 Evaluation and Discussion

This section explains about evaluation and discussion in research,

4.1 Evaluation Criteria

Training data is used for the offline model, and the remainder of the tada is used to analyze the film recommendations. As a system verification, we use mean squared error and social network analysis. Then use computational time, average similarity, and evaluation of clustering performance. The following is verification and evaluation.

Mean Squared Errors (MSE)
MSE will facilitate training, some measure of the error in the whole which is used as an objective function [13].

$$MSE = \frac{1}{M}\frac{1}{N}\sum_{m=1}^{M}\sum_{j=1}^{N}(d_{mj} - y_{mj})^2 \tag{12}$$

where d_{mj} and y_{mj} represent the desired (target) value.

Social Network Analysis (SNA)
In analyzing the relationship between one user and another user for grouping social network analysis will be used. Social Network Analysis is a collection of relational methods that can be used to understand and identify the relationships between actors [14] User relationships for grouping through centrality with three measurements as general centrality, namely [15]:

Degree
The degree to which the number of relationships is a very important actor relationship. In finding densities in the most varied groupings using similarities in one cluster. Calculation with Equation,

$$C_D = d(n_i) = \sum_{j} X_{ij} \tag{13}$$

with C_D = centrality degree, $d(n_i)$ = degree of node i, and X_{ij} = edge $i - j$.

Closeness
Closeness is part of the closeness of the actor with other actors. This is related to the high relationship regarding clusters. The following is calculated by Equation:

$$C_C(n_i) = \left[\sum_{j=1}^{g} d(n_i, n_j)\right]^{-1} \tag{14}$$

with $C_c(n_i)$ = centrality closeness of node I and $d(n_i, n_j)$ = edge $i - j$

$$C'_C = (n_i) = (C_C(n_i))(g - 1) \tag{15}$$

Betweenness
Betweenness as the shortest path between actor a and b where actor c is located. The shortest distance will have the highest relationship between clusters. This can be calculated using Equation as follows:

$$C_B(n_i) = \sum_{j<k} \frac{g_{jk}(n_i)}{g_{jk}} \tag{16}$$

with CHF (ni) = number of actors path where c is, C_B (n_i) = betweenness actor centrality (node) I, and
CHF = number of the path that connects actors a and b.

Average Similarity
The average similarity is the result of the similarity between one cluster with other existing clusters and the similarity will be a benchmark for many clusters to be grouped. Cosine equality measures similarity are two vectors that take the cosine of the angles of two vectors and will give two points [16]. If the result of the angle is zero, the similarity is one, the greater the angle, the smaller the similarity. The cosine with formula:

$$A \cdot B = \|A\| \|B\| \cos \theta \tag{17}$$

$$similarity = \cos(\theta) = \frac{A \cdot B}{\|A\| \|B\|} = \frac{\sum_{i=1}^{n} A_i B_i}{\sqrt{\sum_{i=1}^{n} A_i^2} \sqrt{\sum_{i=1}^{n} B_1^2}} \tag{18}$$

Computation Time
Computational time is the running time as the length of time for program calculations. In this case, the computational time (CT) will be calculated by the end time (e) and early time (s). The time is calculated using the following formula,

$$CT = e - s \tag{19}$$

Clustering Performance Evaluation
This section explains, five algorithms as a grouping are used to evaluate partitions and are obtained with three techniques that are used as different index values [17].

Silhouette Coefficient
If in an experiment the basic truth label cannot be known, then the evaluation can be done using the model itself.

Silhouette coefficients are part of this evaluation, better groups can be produced with higher silhouette coefficient values. The silhouette coefficient is a sample consisting of two scores: a is the average distance between samples and the distance between points on the same class and b is the average distance between the sample and other points in the closest cluster. The Silhouette Coefficient in one sample will then be given as follows,

$$s = \frac{b-a}{\max(a,b)} \tag{20}$$

Calinski-Harabasz Index

The Calinski-Harabasz index can be used if the basic truth labels cannot be known. Calinski-Harabasz which has a higher score then relates to the model in the form of a cluster group for a better definition. The ration for k cluster that average inter-cluster dispersions and in-cluster dispersions,

$$s(k) = \frac{Tr(B_k)}{Tr(w_k)} \times \frac{N-k}{k-1} \tag{21}$$

where B_K is part of the group dispersion matrix and W_K as the dispersion matrix of the in-cluster defined by,

$$W_k = \sum_{q=1}^{k} \sum_{x \in C_q} (x - c_q)(x - c_q)^T \tag{22}$$

$$B_k = \sum_q n_q (c_q - c)(c_q - c)^T \tag{23}$$

where N is the number of points in the data, Cq is the set of points from cluster q, cq is the center of cluster q, c becomes the center of E, nq as the number of points from cluster q.

Davies-Bouldin Index

The Davies-Bouldin index is used when the basic truth values are unknown, to evaluate a model, the lower Davies-Bouldin index is related to the model according to separation between clusters. Simple choice in non-negative Rijis and symmetrical with,

$$R_{ij} = \frac{S_i + S_j}{d_{ij}} \tag{24}$$

$$DB = \frac{1}{k} \sum_{i=n}^{k} \max_{i \neq j} R_{ij} \tag{25}$$

4.2 Evaluation Results

The following result of verifying and evaluation,

Mean Squared Error (MSE)
MSE for birch methods from five clustering algorithm (Fig. 6).

Social Network Analysis Result (SNA)
Mean shift example results as five clustering for methods from SNA result (Table 2).

Average Similarity
See Table 3

Clustering Performance Evaluation
See Table 4.

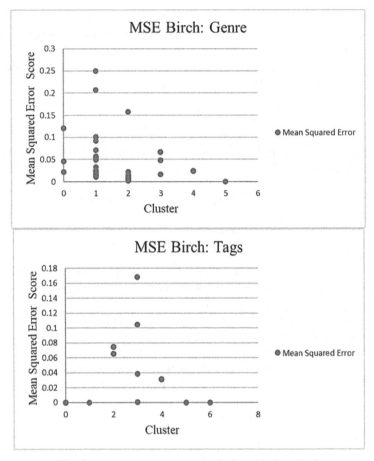

Fig. 6. Mean squared error example from birch methods

4.3 Discussion

A detailed explanation of experiment for evaluation from the five clustering methods that revealed the following,

1) The best MSE is relatively small by the birch method for squared error score in the rating genre and the rating tags.
2) The closest distance to the SNA is the mean shift method which means that between clusters had a high linkage relationship the invariance.
3) The Birch method had a relatively high average similarly.
4) The best computation time is declared by the mini-batch method with 13.75 ms.
5) Clustering visualization and optimizing k that movie genre in algorithms is better than movie tags cause fewer data in movie tags.
6) Clustering the performance evaluation perform that the kmeans method is a good performance used Calinski-Harabasz with a score of 59.418329661475276 and on the Birch with the score of 1.2409779860630252 on Davies-Bouldin.

Table 2. Mean shift example result of SNA

Methods	Cluster	SNA
Mean shift: genre rating	**Cluster with (0, 2, 1, 4)**	The degree is part of the density in the 0 group (the highest number of results), then it will be compared with the list of the order of the cluster in the form of the results from a distance of 5831.497609771017
		Closeness is the highest part of cluster 0 to cluster 1 (high relationship between two clusters) the result of distance obtained is 1.4427276223670051
		Betweenness is part of the highest to cluster 0 (first) to cluster 2 (end), between 1 (cluster 0 the best for distance relationship with cluster 1 (between) and 2 the result of distance obtained with 1.3956092846991393
Mean shift: tags rating	**Cluster with (3, 0, 1, 2)**	The degree is part of the density in the 0 group (the highest number of results), then it will be compared with the list of the order of the cluster in the form of the results from a distance of 148.11502718011636
		Closeness is the highest part of cluster 0 to cluster 1 (high relationship between two clusters) the result of distance obtained is 0.6720449836590598
		Betweenness for part of the highest in cluster 3 (first) to cluster 1 (end), between 0 (cluster 3 is the best for distance relationship with cluster 0 (between) and 1 2 the result of distance obtained with 3.124614402228398

Table 3. Average similarity of birch method

Methods	Amount for clusters	Average for similarity
Birch: genre rating	3	0.9939695618245499
	6	0.9762854041157651
	12	0.966997782722786
Birch: tags rating	4	0.9773884050381106
	6	0.9379748183115013
	12	0.9498831456370311

Table 4. Evaluate cluster performance for the k-means and birch methods

Methods	Clustering performance for evaluation (Index)	Score
K-Means: genre rating	The Silhouette Coefficient	0.29940676129568833
	The Calinski-Harabasz	59.418329661475276
	The Davies-Bouldin	1.1381299407617178
K-Means: tags rating	The Silhouette Coefficient	0.2590800075247514
	The Calinski-Harabasz	7.477478078840098
	The Davies-Bouldin	0.8643014692398275
Birch: genre rating	The Silhouette Coefficient	0.23844858585206535
	The Calinski-Harabasz	39.03241653323649
	The Davies-Bouldin	1.2409779860630252
Birch: tags rating	The Silhouette Coefficient	0.25947335806143973
	The Calinski-Harabasz	5.734765363163111
	The Davies-Bouldin	1.1636603822506426

5   Conclusion

In this research, five clusterings is used as a grouping and comparison method for performance in making movie recommendation in systems, such as Birch Algorithm, K-Means Algorithm, K-Means Mini Batch Algorithm, Affinity Propagation, and Mean Shift. In this article, we find the best algorithm for grouping the user similarities based on genre, tags, and ratings with Movielens dataset. Optimizing K is also done for each cluster so that it will not significantly increase variance. A variance will refer to errors. In this case, in verifying the quality of the recommendation system, we use Mean Square Error (MSE) and social network analysis (SNA). We will also use average similarity, the grouping of performance evaluation measures, and computational time that have been used in comparing system performance methods.

Based on the Movielens dataset, the evaluation of the five clustering methods indicate that:

1) A system is useful as a recommendation engine that will recommend similarity users to discover movies they're likely to enjoy that are appropriate to their taste.
2) The Mean-shift algorithm is best method from all algorithm.
3) This study can propose a way to check a better algorithm of the recommendation system.

Acknowledgements. This research was supported in part by the Mitlab, National Taiwan University of Science and Technology.

References

1. Itmazi, J., Megías, M.: Using recommendation systems in course management system to recommend learning object. Int. Arab. J. Inf. Technol. **5**(3) (2008)
2. Lu, J., Wu, D.: Recommender system application development: a survey. Decis. Support Syst. **74**, 12–32 (2015)
3. Shah, N., Mahajan, S.: Document clustering: a detailed review. Int. J. Appl. Inf. Syst. (IJAIS) **4**, 30–38 (2012)
4. Wang, Z., Yu, X.: An improved collaborative movie recommendation system. J. Vis. Lang. Comput. **25**, 667–675 (2014)
5. Tayeb Himel, Md., Uddin, M.N.: Weight based movie recommendation system using K-means algorithm. IEEE (2017)
6. Wagstaff, K., Cardie, C.: Constrained K-means clustering with background knowledge. In: Proceedings of the Eighteenth International Conference on Machine Learning, pp. 577–584 (2017)
7. Subbalakshmi, C., Krishna, G.R.: A method to find optimum number of clusters based on fuzzy silhouette on dynamic data set. Procedia Comput. Sci. **46**, 346–353 (2015)
8. Fahim, A.M., Salem, A.M.: An efficient enhanced k-means clustering algorithm. J. Zhejiang Univ. Sci. A **7**, 1626–1633 (2006). https://doi.org/10.1631/jzus.2006.A1626
9. Sheikholeslami, G, Chatterjee, S.: WaveCluster: a multi-resolution clustering approach for very large spatial databases. In: Proceedings of the 24th VLDB Conference, New York, USA (1998)
10. Sculley, D.: Web-Scale K-Means Clustering. North Carolina (2010)
11. Fukunaga, K., Hostetler, L.D.: The estimation of the gradient of a density function, with applications in pattern recognition. IEEE Trans. Inf. Theory **21**, 32–40 (1975)
12. Dueck, D.: Affinity propagation: clustering data by passing messages. conformity with the requirements for the degree of Doctor of Philosophy (2009)
13. Maimon, O., Rokach, L.: Data Mining and Knowledge Discovery Handbook. Springer, Boston (2005). https://doi.org/10.1007/b107408
14. Freeman, L.C.: The Development of Social Network Analysis. BookSurge LLC, North Charleston (2004)
15. Rukmi, A.M., Iqbal, I.M.: Using k-means++ algorithm for researchers clustering. ResearchGate (2017)
16. Plattel, C. (n.d.): Distributed and Incremental Clustering using Shared Nearest Neighbours. Utrecht University (2014)
17. Maulik, U., Bandyopadhyay, S.: Performance evaluation of some clustering algorithms and validity indices. IEEE Trans. Pattern Anal. Mach. Intell. **24**, 1650–1654 (2002)

Security and BlockChain

A Group Signature Scheme for Securing Blockchain-Based Mobile Edge Computing

Shijie Zhang$^{(\boxtimes)}$ and Jong-Hyouk Lee

Protocol Engineering Laboratory, Sejong University,
Seoul, Republic of Korea
{zhangshijie,jonghyouk}@pel.sejong.ac.kr

Abstract. Blockchain-based mobile edge computing (BMEC) is a promising architecture in the fifth-generation (5G) networks. BMEC solves the problem of limited computing resources of devices in the mobile blockchain environment while ensuring the distributed deployment of computing resources and the traceable of transaction data. However, some consensus-level security threats exist in the mobile blockchain environment, i.e., double-spend attacks, long-range attacks, selfish mining. All of these threats can break the integrity of BMEC, allowing the correct block record to be overwritten with a false one. In this paper, we propose a group signature scheme on blocks of blockchain for addressing such issues. Each new block will be regarded as a valid block if it obtains a valid group aggregate signature of the group which the block creator belongs to. We describe in detail the process of authentication and key changes when nodes join and leave BMEC. We also show the role of our proposed group signature scheme in validating blocks. Lastly, the security analysis is also presented to prove that our proposed group signature scheme is effective.

Keywords: Blockchains · Group signature · Mobile edge computing

1 Introduction

Blockchain is the prevailing technology of most cryptocurrencies. Blockchain essentially creates a distributed ledger containing traceable and tamper-proof transaction records, and each update of the ledger is broadcast via a peer-to-peer (P2P) network [19]. All operations on the blockchain are in a decentralized manner, without the involvement of third-party entities, hence blockchain can change the traditional centralized business model. Blockchain nowadays has much potential application value in the supply chain, medical information record, smart grid,

This research was supported by the MSIT (Ministry of Science and ICT), Korea, under the ITRC (Information Technology Research Center) support program (IITP-2019-2015-0-00403) supervised by the IITP (Institute for Information & communications Technology Planning & Evaluation).

D.-J. Deng et al. (Eds.): WiCON 2019, LNICST 317, pp. 117–130, 2020.
https://doi.org/10.1007/978-3-030-52988-8_10

Internet of Things (IoT), etc. [13,17,18]. Meanwhile, with the rapid development of mobile devices, more and more information records and exchanges take place on the mobile end, the mobile application of blockchain is thus a hot research direction.

The emergence of the fifth-generation (5G) network has made the application of mobile devices in the IoT environment become a reality [22]. To further improve the efficiency of the use of devices with limited computing resources in the IoT environment, mobile edge computing (MEC) technology was born [12]. MEC provides cloud-computing service at the edge of the mobile network. Therefore, the computing resources originally concentrated in the central cloud service are sunk to a location closer to the users' mobile devices, providing a low-latency, high-bandwidth and location-sensitive computing service. By adopting MEC technology in the IoT environment, mobile devices with limited computing resources can perform a local analysis of data collected by IoT devices and respond to users more quickly. In addition to IoT, MEC can help enterprises and customers form a low-latency, secure and efficient business network, thus enterprises can provide customers with more efficient services, and customers can also give feedback to enterprises promptly. To sum up, MEC has a wide variety of use cases and plays an important role in the 5G era.

Blockchain and MEC technology are complementary. MEC can provide abundant computational power for devices in mobile blockchain environment [22], while blockchain can provide a decentralized database to store a variety of data, such as system logs, devices state, business transactions, etc. All these data are stored by blockchain as a series of blocks. Each block needs to be achieved consensus between nodes before it can be added after the latest block in the chain. Hence, BMEC is a combination of two promising techniques, which provides an efficient and secure IT service environment for future 5G application scenarios. Nevertheless, for the blockchain environment, there are many security threats. For instance, attackers can secretly create a longer private chain to rewrite the original record history of blockchain [2,8,19], destroying the integrity of the whole BMEC. In order to prevent such threats from happening in BMEC, we propose a new group signature scheme to verify the validity of blocks. Traditional group signature can not only reduce the tedious steps of verifying each signature, but also provide the anonymity of the signer [5]. We modify the traditional group signature scheme so that it can be suitable for BMEC and also has the function to verify blocks.

The rest of this paper is organized as follows. Section 2 introduces some basic knowledge of BMEC, security threats in blockchain, traditional group signature scheme, and bilinear pairings. In Sect. 3, we propose a modified group signature scheme used for validating blocks. In Sect. 4, the security analysis on the proposed scheme is presented. Section 5 presents some related work. We conclude this paper in Sect. 6.

2   Preliminaries

2.1   BMEC

Each mobile device can access the closest MEC server, and use the computing resource provided by the closest MEC server to perform the blockchain consensus process (block creation competition) [22]. Note that all mobile devices can act as miner nodes. Such BMEC architecture can minimize the computing resource requirements of the devices. Even if one device has limited computing power, this device can also win the block creation game. The transaction data can be authentication information of mobile devices, the security status of mobile devices, business transactions and information collected by IoT sensors, and these data are recorded into blocks after they are verified by miner nodes. Each competition winner publishes a new block containing multiple verified transaction data over the whole network. The overview of BMEC architecture is shown in Fig. 1.

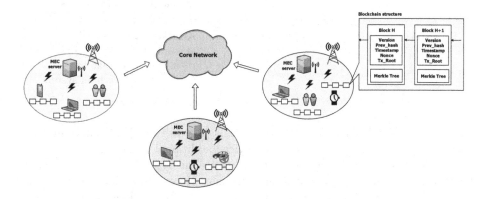

Fig. 1. Overview of BMEC architecture.

2.2   Security Threats

Since the first decentralized cryptocurrency Bitcoin came out, the consensus security issues of blockchain have always existed. Nakamoto had mentioned the problem of double-spend attack in the Bitcoin white paper [19], attackers can create a longer private chain to make the transaction that uses the same token twice valid. In recent years, more and more attacks aiming at the consensus-level of blockchain have been discovered [2,8,9,15]. We summarize some of these well-known security threats and present them in Table 1.

We can easily see from Table 1 that most consensus-level attacks happen in PoS-based blockchain systems. The reason is that attackers need to hold more than 50% share of computational power to successfully destroy the consensus

Table 1. Summary of consensus-level attacks in blockchain.

Attack name	Attack scenario	Brief description
Double spending	Most consensus protocols	Use the same coin multiple times
Selfish mining	Proof-of-Work (PoW)	Form a mining pool to privately mine blocks to get profit
Nothing at stake	Proof-of-Stake (PoS)	Mint blocks on both branches if there is a fork in the network
Bribe attack	Proof-of-Stake (PoS)	Bribe honest nodes to make them create blocks on the private fork
Stake-bleeding attack	Proof-of-Stake (PoS)	Copy transactions from the main chain and broadcast on the private fork to get extra transaction fees to increase the stake
Fake stake attack	Proof-of-Stake (PoS)	Attackers with a small amount of stake can amplify their apparent stake to deceive the blockchain system

mechanism in PoW-based blockchain systems [19]. In the BMEC environment, even if MEC servers provide mobile devices additional computational power, for one MEC server, its computing resources are far from enough to undermine the consensus of PoW-based blockchain systems. However, some recent research indicated that the threshold of computational power for breaking the blockchain consensus has dropped significantly. In [23], attackers can complete a double-spend attack with only a 32% share of computational power by conducting a concurrent Sybil attack. [1] presented that an eclipse attack can do great help to double-spend attack. Therefore, if BMEC adopts PoW as the blockchain consensus mechanism, it cannot completely guarantee the security of BMEC architecture. We thus assume that our proposed scheme can work in both PoS and PoW consensus protocols.

2.3   Group Signature

A group signature scheme allows group members to sign messages on behalf of the entire group. The current group signature technology is based on the efficient group signature scheme proposed by Camenisch and Stadler in 1997 [5]. One group signature can be verified with only a single group public key, which is more efficient. Besides, users out of the group cannot know the specific identity of the signer. Hence, group signature scheme can be applied in public resource management, critical information issuance and contract signing. The brief execution of the group signature is as follows:

Setup: The group manager computes a key pair of signature K_{sig}^{pub}, K_{sig}^{pri}, and a key pair of encryption K_{enc}^{pub}, K_{enc}^{pri}, and publishes the two public keys as a group public key. One node who wants to join the group chooses a random secret key s and computes a membership key $z = f(s)$. He signs z and sends it to the group manager. The group manager returns to him $v = K_{sig}^{pri}(z)$. The group secret key of this node consists of the triple (s, z, v).

Sign: This node encrypts a message m with his membership key z by using K_{enc}^{pub}, and computes a proof p that he knows values s, v. The signature of this node consists of the ciphertext $enc(m)$ of m and the proof p.

Verify: Checking the proof p to verify the signature of this node by using K_{sig}^{pub}. If $K_{sig}^{pub}(v) = f(s)$, this signature is proved to be correct.

Open: The group manager decrypts the ciphertext $enc(m)$ by using K_{enc}^{pri} to obtain the membership key z, which can reveal the identity of this node.

2.4 Bilinear Pairings

In this paper, we also adopt the bilinear pairings in the proposed group signature scheme. Let G_1 and G_2 denote two additive cyclic groups on the elliptic curve $F(p)$. Let G_T denote a multiplicative cyclic group. Let q be a large prime number, which is the order of G_1, G_2, and G_T. Assuming that P and Q are the generators of G_1 and G_2. The map $e : G_1 \times G_2 \rightarrow G_T$ is regarded as a bilinear map if the following properties are satisfied:

1) **Bilinearity:** $e(a \cdot X, b \cdot Y) = e(X,Y)^{a \cdot b}$ for all $a, b \in Z_q^*$ and $\forall X \in G_1$, $\forall Y \in G_2$.
2) **Non-degeneracy:** There exists a $X \in G_1$, such that $e(X, X) \neq 1_{G_T}$.
3) **Computability:** Given any two elements $\forall X \in G_1$, $\forall Y \in G_2$, $e(X, Y)$ can be efficiently computed.

3 Proposed Group Signature Scheme in BMEC

For the group signature scheme mentioned in the previous section, we need to modify it to fit the BMEC architecture, while making BMEC resistant to some of the security threats introduced in the previous section. We do not need to guarantee the anonymity of the signer, nor do we need the group manager to reveal the identity of the signer. Instead, we add the aggregate signature algorithm based on the group signature concept. The aggregate signature algorithm adopted in this paper is the BLS algorithm [3].

In our proposed BMEC, each MEC server and a set of connected mobile devices are regarded as a group, in which the MEC server acts as a group manager. In the process of blockchain consensus, we assume that MEC servers just provide the connected mobile devices some computational power instead of participating in the block creation competition, hence each mobile device acts as a consensus algorithm involved nodes (e.g., block creation nodes in case of PoW and PoS). Each mobile device has access to the data in the blockchain, and the data that needs to be processed is handed over to the MEC server in the group where each mobile device is located. All the used notations are listed in Table 2, and the main authentication process required for each mobile device and the application of the proposed group signature scheme are shown as follows:

Table 2. Notations.

Notation	Definition
$id(i, n)$	Identity of mobile device user
pk_i^{gm}	Public key of group manager in group i
sk_i^{gm}	Secret key of group manager in group i
$pk_{i,n}^{usr}$	Public key of mobile device user who has $id(i, n)$
$sk_{i,n}^{usr}$	Secret key of mobile device user who has $id(i, n)$
$f(\cdot)$	BLS aggregate function
GK_i	Group public key of group i
$sig_{i,n}^{usr}(\cdot)$	Signature of mobile device user who has $id(i, n)$
$sig_i^{usr}(\cdot)$	Aggregate signature of all members in group i
r	Random number
$v(\cdot)$	BLS signature validation function

1) Join the group

Before a new mobile device joins the group, the mobile device user needs to go through a series of authentication steps [16]. As shown in Fig. 2, a mobile device user first needs to register with a smart contract stored in the blockchain. Smart contracts are computer programs used to automatically develop contracts without any third party's participation. After registration, the smart contract issues $id(i, n)$, $pk_{i,n}^{usr}$ and $sk_{i,n}^{usr}$ to the user. i and n denotes group i and the serial number n of this mobile device, respectively. $id(i, n)$ is an identifier of mobile device n in group i, which is computed by a SHA256 function. Then, $id(i, n)$ and $pk_{i,n}^{usr}$ are stored in the blockchain. A mobile user who has $id(i, n)$ sends the first message $m_1 = (id(i, n), r, sk_{i,n}^{usr}(id(i, n), r))$ to the MEC server in group i. The MEC server queries the smart contract for the public key record of $id(i, n)$. If the record exists, the smart contract sends $pk_{i,n}^{usr}$ to the MEC server, and the MEC server uses $pk_{i,n}^{usr}$ to validate whether $sk_{i,n}^{usr}(id(i, n), r)$ is correct. If the signature is correct, the MEC server sends a message $m_2 = (id(i, n), r + 1, pk_{i,n}^{usr}(id(i, n), r + 1, pk_i^{gm}, GK_i))$ to this mobile user. The mobile user obtains pk_i^{gm} and GK_i by decryption with $sig_{i,n}^{usr}$. To prove that he has the correct $sig_{i,n}^{usr}$ and verify the identity of the MEC server, the mobile user sends the last message $m_3 = (id(i,n), r+2, pk_i^{gm}(id(i,n), r+2))$. Upon receiving m_3, the MEC server uses his secret key sk_i^{gm} to decrypt the message and validates this message. The process of the authentication between mobile user and MEC server succeeds, and then the mobile user becomes a member of this group.

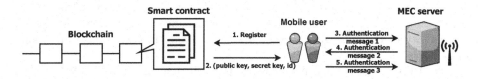

Fig. 2. Authentications before joining the group.

2) First block validation

If a new block is created by a mobile user from group i, the block needs to be verified among group members before it is broadcast over the whole network. Each group member checks the validity of transactions stored in this block. Once this block passes the validation from the side of a mobile device user with $id(i,n)$, this mobile user will use his $sk_{i,n}^{usr}$ to make a signature $sig_{i,n}^{usr}(blkhash)$ on the block hash. Only if the block receives all the signatures of members from group i, it can be broadcast to other groups to conduct a second validation. In order to greatly reduce the number of signatures, here we use the BLS aggregate signature algorithm to aggregate multiple signatures into one signature:

$$sig_i^{usr}(blkhash) = f(sig_{i,1}^{usr}(blkhash), sig_{i,2}^{usr}(blkhash), \ldots, sig_{i,n}^{usr}(blkhash)).$$

Meanwhile, the group public key GK_i of group i is also a public key aggregated from each member's public key:

$$GK_i = f(pk_{i,1}^{usr}, pk_{i,2}^{usr}, pk_{i,3}^{usr}, \ldots, pk_{i,n}^{usr}).$$

3) Update the group public key

Each time a new member joins the group after a mutual authentication or some old members exit the group, the MEC server needs to re-aggregate the current public keys from all the members to update the group public key GK_i. Since the MEC server has sufficient computing resources, the time to run the re-aggregate algorithm is negligible. After the latest block proposed from the group i is added to the longest valid chain through other groups' verifications, if there is a change in the members of the group, the MEC server stores the updated group public key information in the blockchain (through the smart contract). In this way, mobile users of other groups can share the group public key information of group i.

4) Second block validation

If one block proposed from group i passes the first block validation, it will be broadcast to other groups. Upon receiving the block proposed from group i, mobile users from other groups only check the aggregate signature on the block hash instead of checking all the transactions in the block as usual since they have already been checked, which greatly improves the efficiency of block validation. During checking the aggregate signature, mobile users first obtain the latest group public key GK_i stored in the blockchain and then use GK_i to check the validity of the aggregate signature $sig_i^{usr}(blkhash)$. The simple validation principle is shown as follows.

The BLS signature algorithm follows the principles of bilinear pairings. In the BLS aggregate signature validation, we only need to verify that whether the public key pk and the message m (two points on the BLS function curve) and the curve generation point G and the signature sig (two points on the BLS function curve) map to the same number, if these two pairs map to the same number, the signature sig is proved to be valid. The BLS signature validation function $v(\cdot)$ has two important properties [3]:

1. Assuming that P_1, P_2 are two inputs of $v(\cdot)$, for an arbitrary number x, no matter which input is multiplied by x, the result is the same:

$$v(x * P_1, P_2) = v(P_1, x * P_2).$$

2. Assuming there are multiple signatures $sig_1, sig_2, sig_3, \ldots, sig_n$, the result of aggregating signatures before input is the same as that of entering each signature before doing the final aggregation:

$$v(G, sig_1) * v(G, sig_2) * \ldots * v(G, sig_n) = v(G, f(sig_1, sig_2, \ldots, sig_n)).$$

We assume G is used to generate the public key, thus the public key of a mobile user who has $id(i, n)$ is generated from G and the secret key $sk_{i,n}^{usr}$: $pk_{i,n}^{usr} = G * sk_{i,n}^{usr}$. In the proposed scheme, the public key has been generated by the smart contract in this way. As mentioned before, each mobile user in group i makes his signature on the block hash, and the BLS aggregate algorithm will aggregate these signatures into one. According to the second property, the aggregate signature is valid and does not affect the validation result. We aim to let $v(G, sig) = v(pk, m)$, the right side of this equation can be simplified as follows:

$$
\begin{aligned}
v(G, sig_i^{usr}) &= v(G, f(sig_{i,1}^{usr}, sig_{i,2}^{usr}, \ldots, sig_{i,n}^{usr})) \\
&= v(G, f(sk_{i,1}^{usr} * blkhash, sk_{i,2}^{usr} * blkhash, \ldots, sk_{i,n}^{usr} * blkhash)) \\
&= v(G, f(sk_{i,1}^{usr}, sk_{i,2}^{usr}, \ldots, sk_{i,n}^{usr}) * blkhash) \\
&= v(f(sk_{i,1}^{usr}, sk_{i,2}^{usr}, \ldots, sk_{i,n}^{usr}) * G, blkhash) \\
&= v(f(sk_{i,1}^{usr} * G, sk_{i,2}^{usr} * G, \ldots, sk_{i,n}^{usr} * G), blkhash) \\
&= v(f(pk_{i,1}^{usr}, pk_{i,2}^{usr}, \ldots, pk_{i,n}^{usr}), blkhash) \\
&= v(GK_i, blkhash).
\end{aligned}
$$

We finally obtain the equation $v(G, sig_i^{usr}) = v(GK_i, blkhash)$, thus proving that the aggregate signature is valid. After the second block validation, the new block proposed from group i is regarded as a valid one and then added to the longest valid chain.

4 Security Analysis

We assume the security threats will happen in the blockchian systems adopting the longest-chain rule. Attackers can create a private chain to try to rewrite the blockchain history. In the BMEC without the proposed group signature scheme, if attackers create a longer private chain than the valid one, they will publish their longer fork. Since there is no way to prove that the blocks in the published private chain are fake, mobile users in the network will reach consensus on the longer one according to the longest-chain rule, then their local ledgers will be updated to the latest one (attackers' ledger). As a result, some of the most important transaction data in the original ledger such as system logs, device security status, data collected by IoT sensors have been erased, which is a devastating blow to the BMEC architecture.

4.1 General Situation

By adopting the proposed group signature scheme, each newly mined block needs to go through two rounds of validations. For the attackers, they have two choices for the behavior of publishing chains: 1) publish their private chain in the group they belong to first and 2) directly publish their private chain over the whole network. For the first choice, members of the group other than the attackers will check the validity of a set of transactions in the latest block of the private chain. If there are some double-spend transactions (double-spend attack) or transactions that have already occurred (stake-bleeding attack), the members of the group will not sign on this blocks. On the flip side, if the attackers skip the first block validation, blocks of the private chain will also not obtain signatures from other group members. Then the aggregate signatures of these blocks in this private chain will be checked by mobile users from other groups in the network.

Combining the above two cases, the attackers' privately mined blocks cannot get signatures from other group members. Even if the attackers can personally aggregate all the signatures from their alliance, the final aggregate signature cannot be verified as valid by the group public key due to the lack of signature inputs from other group members. The proof is as follows:

We assume there are q members in one group k, the attackers can insert many forged nodes into group k (e.g., leverage a Sybil attack [7,23]). Even if the attackers' forged nodes fill this group, there will inevitably be other honest mobile users joining this group. Assuming the most terrible situation: there is only one honest mobile user in this group, and the remaining users are from attackers' side. If only this honest user does not sign on the attackers' block, missing one signature input will cause the entire aggregate signature to be completely different:

$$sig_k^{usr}(blkhash) = f(sig_{k,1}^{usr}(blkhash), sig_{k,2}^{usr}(blkhash), \dots, sig_{k,q-1}^{usr}(blkhash)).$$

However, the group public key used for verifying the aggregate signature is updated in real-time by the MEC server, hence the input of the aggregate group public key contains the public key of this mobile honest user:

$$GK_k = f(pk_{k,1}^{usr}, pk_{k,2}^{usr}, pk_{k,3}^{usr}, \dots, pk_{k,q}^{usr}).$$

Since the number of inputs of $sig_k^{usr}(blkhash)$ and GK_k is different, we cannot obtain the equation $v(G, sig_k^{usr}) = v(GK_k, blkhash)$ during the second block validation. Consequently, blocks of the private chain generated by the attackers cannot pass the second block validation. Our proposed group signature scheme effectively protects the BMEC architecture from such attacks that devastate the consensus protocol of blockchain. Generally, if there are more than one honest mobile user in the group, the blocks generated by the attackers will not get the correct aggregate signature, thus the private chain cannot be supported by other mobile users in the network.

4.2   Effect of Deterring Double-Spending

Combined with the analysis in the previous subsection, in order to make the privately created blocks effective, the attackers need to ensure that mobile users within their group are all under their control. To achieve this effect, the attackers can insert Sybil nodes or botnet nodes in that group they control. Next, we analyze whether our proposed scheme works in the case the attackers launch a double-spend attack in the PoW consensus algorithm.

The attackers add a double-spending transaction TX_d into their private chain. To make TX_d valid, the attackers need to extend their private chain to exceed the length of the main chain, in that case, the original transaction in the main chain turns to be invalid, and TX_d becomes a valid one. Since blockchain is composed of a series of consecutive blocks, once one block in the private chain fails in the signature validation during catching up with the main chain, the whole private chain will become invalid. Therefore, the attackers need to ensure that no honest mobile user joins their group before the private chain overtakes the main chain. We assume the probability of one honest mobile user's joining the attacker's group per unit time is λ, thus the probability that blocks in the private chain are valid per unit time is $1 - \lambda$. We assume the proportion of the attackers' computing power to the total computing power is p_a, while the proportion of the computing power of the remaining mobile users is $p_h = 1 - p_a$. Let t_0 and z denote the average block creation time and the number of blocks created in the main chain, respectively. The time it takes for the attackers to catch up with the main chain is $\frac{t_0}{p_h} \cdot z$. Therefore, the probability that all the blocks in the private chain are valid during the attacker's pursuit of the main chain is $(1 - \lambda)^{\frac{t_0}{p_h} \cdot z}$.

Then, we adopt the formula proposed in [10] to calculate the probability of success of double-spending P_{CG}:

$$P_{CG} = 1 - \sum_{g=0}^{z-1}(p_h{}^z p_a{}^g - p_a{}^z p_h{}^g)\binom{g+z-1}{g},\tag{1}$$

where g is the number of blocks generated by the attackers during their pursuit. Hence, the probability of a successful double-spend attack under this circumstance P_{new} is:

$$P_{new} = (1-\lambda)^{\frac{t_0}{p_h}\cdot z}\cdot P_{CG}.\tag{2}$$

We use the real-data $t_0 = 10\,\text{min}$ which is adopted in the Bitcoin platform and set $\lambda = 0.05$ to calculate Eq. 2. We also compare our results with [10] using Eq. 1. The comparison results are shown in Table 3 and 4.

Table 3. P_{new} compared with P_{CG} when $p_a = 0.3$.

z	P_{new}	P_{CG}
1	0.288	0.600
2	0.100	0.432
3	0.036	0.326
4	0.013	0.252
5	0.005	0.198
6	0.002	0.156

Table 4. P_{new} compared with P_{CG} when $p_a = 0.4$.

z	P_{new}	P_{CG}
1	0.340	0.800
2	0.127	0.704
3	0.049	0.635
4	0.019	0.580
5	0.007	0.533
6	0.003	0.493

From Table 3 and 4, we can find that compared with the probability of a successful double-spend attack P_{CG} in [10], the probability of success of the double-spend attack is greatly reduced under the influence of our proposed scheme. We also find that the increase in the attackers' computing power does not contribute much to the raise of the success rate of double-spending under the proposed scheme. Besides, the safe number of block confirmations z needs to be set to more than 6 in the case without our proposed scheme, whereas in the proposed scheme, the probability of success of double-spending is less than 0.1 when $z = 3$, that is, the safe number of block confirmations can be set to 3, which can increase the throughput of transactions.

To sum up, our proposed group signature scheme effectively protects the BMEC architecture from such attacks that devastate the consensus protocol of blockchain.

5   Related Work

In 1991, Chaum et al. first proposed the group signature scheme [6]. In 1997, Camenisch et al. proposed an efficient group signature scheme that public keys and signatures have a fixed size, regardless of the number of group members [5]. Hence, this group signature scheme is suitable for large groups. Sun et al. modified group signature scheme to make it fit the blockchain environment [21]. Similarly, the research of Guo et al. presented a secure attribute-based signature scheme, which is applied in blockchain-based health records systems [11].

At present, ECDSA [14] is the most commonly used signature algorithm in most blockchain systems, but it cannot conduct signature or key aggregation, thus it can only verify signatures one by one, which is not efficient. Schnorr proposed an efficient signature algorithm [20] that can aggregate all the signatures and public keys in one transaction, but it cannot aggregate signatures from multiple transactions in one block. BLS signature algorithm [3] well addressed this issue. BLS was named after three researchers Boneh, Lynn and Shacham. The BLS algorithm is expected to be used to aggregate signatures in Ethereum Casper [4].

6   Conclusions and Future Work

In this paper, we indicated that there may be significant blockchain consensus-level security threats in the BMEC architecture. We thus proposed a modified group signature scheme for securing BMEC architecture. Comparing the current group signature scheme, we eliminated the anonymity of the group signer and the group manager's ability to reveal the signer's identity, but combined with the BLS aggregate signature algorithm, making the signature validation more efficient. Meanwhile, by using the aggregate signature to sign the block hash, the block validation process only needs to verify the validity of the aggregate signature in the block. If the signature is valid, then this block passes the validation and vice versa. Through proving the feasibility of aggregate signature and calculating the probability of a successful double-spend attack, we demonstrated that our solution makes the BMEC architecture resistant to some blockchain consensus-level attacks compared to the architecture in the absence of such a solution.

However, our proposed scheme also has some limitations. Firstly, in the proposed scheme, each MEC server acts as a group manager. Attackers can take MEC servers as the attack target so that once an MEC server is hacked, the right to update the group public key is owned by the attackers, and the attackers can easily set the group public key that can be used to pass the block validation. Besides, in the first round of block validation, once a member of the group is crashed or offline, the progress of consensus will be seriously affected, resulting in a decline in the system performance. Therefore, we need to improve the proposed scheme to address the above limitations in the future.

References

1. Bissias, G., Levine, B.N., Ozisik, A.P., Andresen, G.: An analysis of attacks on blockchain consensus. arXiv preprint arXiv:1610.07985 (2016)
2. BitFury Group: Proof of Stake versus Proof of Work White paper, September 2015. https://bitfury.com/content/downloads/pos-vs-pow-1.0.2.pdf
3. Boneh, D., Lynn, B., Shacham, H.: Short signatures from the Weil pairing. In: Boyd, C. (ed.) ASIACRYPT 2001. LNCS, vol. 2248, pp. 514–532. Springer, Heidelberg (2001). https://doi.org/10.1007/3-540-45682-1_30
4. Buterin, V., Griffith, V.: Casper the friendly finality gadget. arXiv preprint arXiv:1710.09437 (2017)
5. Camenisch, J., Stadler, M.: Efficient group signature schemes for large groups. In: Kaliski, B.S. (ed.) CRYPTO 1997. LNCS, vol. 1294, pp. 410–424. Springer, Heidelberg (1997). https://doi.org/10.1007/BFb0052252
6. Chaum, D., van Heyst, E.: Group signatures. In: Davies, D.W. (ed.) EUROCRYPT 1991. LNCS, vol. 547, pp. 257–265. Springer, Heidelberg (1991). https://doi.org/10.1007/3-540-46416-6_22
7. Douceur, J.R.: The Sybil attack. In: Druschel, P., Kaashoek, F., Rowstron, A. (eds.) IPTPS 2002. LNCS, vol. 2429, pp. 251–260. Springer, Heidelberg (2002). https://doi.org/10.1007/3-540-45748-8_24
8. Eyal, I., Sirer, E.G.: Majority is not enough: bitcoin mining is vulnerable. Commun. ACM **61**(7), 95–102 (2018)
9. Gaži, P., Kiayias, A., Russell, A.: Stake-bleeding attacks on proof-of-stake blockchains. In: 2018 Crypto Valley Conference on Blockchain Technology (CVCBT), pp. 85–92. IEEE (2018)
10. Grunspan, C., Pérez-Marco, R.: Double spend races. arXiv preprint arXiv:1702.02867 (2017)
11. Guo, R., Shi, H., Zhao, Q., Zheng, D.: Secure attribute-based signature scheme with multiple authorities for blockchain in electronic health records systems. IEEE Access **6**, 11676–11686 (2018)
12. Hu, Y.C., Patel, M., Sabella, D., Sprecher, N., Young, V.: Mobile edge computing—a key technology towards 5g. ETSI white paper, vol. 11, no. 11, pp. 1–16 (2015)
13. Huh, S., Cho, S., Kim, S.: Managing IoT devices using blockchain platform. In: 2017 19th International Conference on Advanced Communication Technology (ICACT), pp. 464–467. IEEE (2017)
14. Johnson, D., Menezes, A., Vanstone, S.: The elliptic curve digital signature algorithm (ECDSA). Int. J. Inf. Secur. **1**(1), 36–63 (2001)

15. Kanjalkar, S., Kuo, J., Li, Y., Miller, A.: Short paper: i can't believe it's not stake! resource exhaustion attacks on PoS. In: Goldberg, I., Moore, T. (eds.) FC 2019. LNCS, vol. 11598, pp. 62–69. Springer, Cham (2019). https://doi.org/10.1007/978-3-030-32101-7_4
16. Lee, J.H.: BIDaaS: blockchain based ID as a service. IEEE Access **6**, 2274–2278 (2017)
17. Liu, P.T.S.: Medical record system using blockchain, big data and tokenization. In: Lam, K.-Y., Chi, C.-H., Qing, S. (eds.) ICICS 2016. LNCS, vol. 9977, pp. 254–261. Springer, Cham (2016). https://doi.org/10.1007/978-3-319-50011-9_20
18. Mengelkamp, E., Notheisen, B., Beer, C., Dauer, D., Weinhardt, C.: A blockchain-based smart grid: towards sustainable local energy markets. Comput. Sci. Res. Dev., 207–214 (2017). https://doi.org/10.1007/s00450-017-0360-9
19. Nakamoto, S.: Bitcoin: A Peer-to-Peer Electronic Cash System (2008)
20. Schnorr, C.P.: Efficient signature generation by smart cards. J. Cryptol. **4**(3), 161–174 (1991). https://doi.org/10.1007/BF00196725
21. Sun, S.-F., Au, M.H., Liu, J.K., Yuen, T.H.: RingCT 2.0: a compact accumulator-based (linkable ring signature) protocol for blockchain cryptocurrency monero. In: Foley, S.N., Gollmann, D., Snekkenes, E. (eds.) ESORICS 2017. LNCS, vol. 10493, pp. 456–474. Springer, Cham (2017). https://doi.org/10.1007/978-3-319-66399-9_25
22. Xiong, Z., Zhang, Y., Niyato, D., Wang, P., Han, Z.: When mobile blockchain meets edge computing. IEEE Commun. Mag. **56**(8), 33–39 (2018)
23. Zhang, S., Lee, J.H.: Double-spending with a Sybil attack in the bitcoin decentralized network. IEEE Trans. Ind. Inform. **15**, 5715–5722 (2019)

A Research on Blockchain-Based Central Bank Digital Currency

Cheng-yong Liu[1] and Chih-Chun Hou[2](✉)

[1] Beijing Institute of Technology, Zhuhai, Zhuhai 519088,
Guangdong, People's Republic of China
[2] Yulin Normal University, Yulin 537000, Guangxi, People's Republic of China
ChihChun_Hou@126.com

Abstract. In recent years, the emergence of blockchain-based and privately issued digital currencies has raised a lot of concerns, including: infringement of privacy rights, the danger of such currencies being used as money laundering tools or in a way that harms consumer protection and financial stability. However, central banks have already started their research on the Central Bank Digital Currency (CBDC). To study the subject of CBDC development in China, this paper first presents a detailed introduction of the concept of private digital currency and the issues that come with it. Secondly, this paper advocates the method of establishing an easy-to-regulate CBDC system based on the two chains scheme of blockchain and making sure the complete transaction information and those used for verification are stored and accessed separately, therefore realizing a balance between protection of user privacy and facilitating regulation. At the same time, the consortium blockchain should be anchored in the public chain to ensure data credibility. Furthermore, although China has begun its CBDC development, it has yet to develop adequate laws and regulations. To this end, in addition to presenting a summary of China's CBDC system, this paper also explains the rights and obligations of the central bank, the commercial banks and the public with regards to the currency, in the hope that such contents can be of some help to the revision of relevant laws in the future.

Keywords: Blockchain · Central Bank Digital Currency · Legal framework

1 Foreword

Recently, digital currency has been a hot topic in multiple occasions and it has also raised many controversies. For another example, Facebook's plan to issue Libra in 2019 has become a global hot topic, and the program itself has raised credible concerns about privacy, money laundering, consumer protection, and financial stability. Despite the many challenges regarding digital currency, the central banks of various countries have already begun the discussion and research on issuance of legal digital currencies. For example, the State Council of China officially approved the research and development of CBDC in 2019 and corresponding works have already begun. As such, it is abundantly clear that the development of digital currency has become an irreversible trend and

© ICST Institute for Computer Sciences, Social Informatics and Telecommunications Engineering 2020
Published by Springer Nature Switzerland AG 2020. All Rights Reserved
D.-J. Deng et al. (Eds.): WiCON 2019, LNICST 317, pp. 131–139, 2020.
https://doi.org/10.1007/978-3-030-52988-8_11

that digital currencies issued by governments are more trustworthy than those issued by private entities. In order to study CBDC-related issues in China, this paper presents discussions from three aspects, namely the concept of private digital currency, CBDC development based on blockchain technology and the legal framework of China's CBDC development.

2 The Concept of Private Digital Currency

2.1 Definition and Current Development

Digital Currency can be divided into two categories, CBDC and private digital currency, the latter usually refers to a decentralized virtual currency that is issued not by any central bank but by private entities through the use of Distributed Ledger Technology (DLT) and it supports peer-to-peer transactions, examples of which include Bitcoin (BTC), ETH, Ripple and LTC etc.

In comparison to other legal currencies, the biggest innovation of digital currency is that it is based on the new blockchain technology, which boasts features such as distributed decentralization, consensus-based trust, difficult to tamper with, good traceability and security. In other words, blockchain technology makes it possible to realize digital cryptocurrencies, which requires the support of scientific and technical means that are exceptionally complex and sophisticated. By using data storage, peer-to-peer transmission, consensus mechanisms, encryption algorithms and other technologies, blockchain enables the establishment of a decentralized distributed ledger database, and the real-time, transparent, omission-free and algorithm-based calculation of the value created by each participant or node at each stage. The contribution, interaction, participation and influence of all participants in the blockchain ecosystem will be recorded in blocks, with their value being automatically determined and reflected in the form of digital cryptocurrencies shown in blockchain wallets and with also the value distribution process being automatically executed by tools such as smart contacts. With aforesaid features, blockchain technology enables the elimination of all intermediate steps such as confirmation, review and implementation, which greatly reduces the cost of building trust and brings higher economic efficiency [1].

2.2 Issues

Although the concept of Bitcoin and other private digital currencies seems very attractive, a series of risks has surfaced in their rapid development during the past decade, which can be mainly summarized as the following issues [2]:

Drastic Price Fluctuations. Since private digital currencies are issued without the backing of national credit, their values are often subject to drastic fluctuations that are detrimental to financial stability [3].

Lacking in Regulation. Due to characteristics of digital cryptocurrencies such as anonymity, decentralization and global circulation, governments can neither control their operational mechanisms nor regulate them. These characteristics make digital cryptocurrencies the best trading medium for illegal criminal activities and an ideal tool for money laundering, terrorist activities, drug transactions etc.

Technical Inadequacy. Due to the facts that digital currency is relatively new, the financial infrastructure supporting its issuance, operation and storage still needs improvements, and that blockchain and smart contracts etc. are still frontier technologies that not yet fully matured by now, it is inevitable that there are flaws and loopholes which have led to multiple incidents of digital currency theft.

The Possibility of Market Manipulation. Since a huge amount of cryptocurrency is owned by only a few entities, and the cryptocurrency exchanges don't have a sound information disclosure system like that the stock exchanges have, it's hard to root out the possibility of forgery and falsification of book records, which have given room for market manipulation.

Inadequate Consumer Protection. Due to the decentralization, anonymity and irreversibility nature of cryptocurrency transactions, when there is a problem with the transaction, even if a legitimate request for repayment is made, there is no way to force the return of corresponding amount of digital currency unless the current holder of said amount voluntarily agrees to do, so it is rather difficult for consumers to recover their losses.

3 CBDC Based on Blockchain Technology

Various central banks are actively exploring plans for CBDC, which refers to encrypted digit strings issued by central banks or monetary authorities, which represent specific amounts of real money and can be used for the consumption and trading of actual goods and services [4].

3.1 Core Elements

At present, the core elements of China's CBDC system are proposed to be configured as follows: (1) the central bank being the issuer; (2) using M0 (equivalent to electronic wallet) as the issue carrier; (3) using core technologies such as big data, distributed accounting etc.; (4) having restricted admittance; (5) having a certain degree of anonymity; (6) being available 7 days a week - 24 h a day (7) no interest [5].

3.2 The Use of Blockchain Technology

Distributed accounting and encryption technology are still used by some CBDC systems as core technologies. And the core technologies used by distributed accounting are consensus algorithms which currently mainly include: POW (Proof-of-Work), POS (Proof of Stake), DPOS (Delegated Proof of Stake), PBFT (Practical Byzantine Fault Tolerance), and DBFT (Delegated Byzantine Fault Tolerant) etc., each of which will incur costs (such as electricity consumption) at different degrees. In addition, based on practical experience, POW is applicable to public chain (permission-less chain), while PBFT is relatively more applicable to private chain and consortium blockchain (license chain), but PBFT is a preferable choice when breaking the computing power limit on a public chain. At present, many central banks have chosen PBFT rather than POW when designing their CBDC systems, the reasons for such a choice may include cost of resource consumption and non-public nature etc. [6].

Although blockchain technology has laid the foundation for trust between participants in decentralized systems, the lacking of a centralized authority means that private digital currencies are very difficult to regulate. However, regulation is a must-have for any CBDC system built on blockchain technologies. We believe that a blockchain-based CBDC system should follow the following concepts: (1) Supervision should be integrated into the operation of the system, including the supervising and back-tracing of transactions and the direct management of account behaviors; (2) Since the blockchain is essentially a distributed accounting technology, the disclosure of account transaction histories would not be conductive to privacy protection. Therefore, on the premise of user acceptance, we need to consider how to achieve a balance between protecting of the privacy of both parties to a transaction and making "safe disclosure of corresponding book records"; (3) If both conditions above are realized, it is time to maximize user participation in reaching a consensus about the system, so as to make full use of the decentralization nature of blockchain to establish the system's credibility.

To achieve the above objectives, the two chains scheme can be used to build a CBDC system that is easy to regulate: (1) The system should be built around the consortium blockchain, and its internal members should be responsible for confirmation of transactions and the encrypted storage of complete transaction data, therefore providing credentials for back-tracking of transactions while helping protect the users' privacy; central banks and other governing entities can take part in the operation and maintenance of the system as participants in the consortium blockchain. (2) Each ordinary user is allowed to access the public blockchain so that they can participate in and witness the maintenance of the system; records stored in the public chain can be used to verify account status, so that users can verify by themselves whether a transaction is valid after executing it. The consortium blockchain stores the data summary in the public chain, which can help prevent members of the consortium blockchain from colluding to tamper with the data.

4   The Legal Framework for CBDC

Although China has begun its CBDC development, there are still insufficient laws and regulations. It has yet to develop adequate laws and regulations and lacks specific regulations that can regulate CBDC related issues at all levels [7]. As such, this paper presents the following suggestions for the legislation of CBDC.

4.1   Overview of the System

Legal Nature. CBDC is a legal currency in a digital form or a new kind of legal currency that is issued by the central bank directly to the society and exists in electronic devices in the form of electromagnetic symbols. As an alternative to the traditional forms (coins and notes) of legal currency, CBDC has the same legal attributes as statutory cash or coins have. Since the currently available electronic network technologies are not advanced enough to support CBDC payments under all circumstances, it's not yet possible to completely replace traditional notes and coins with CBDC, the two form of currencies should coexist for the time being.

The Issuance System. In a CBDC system built on the two chains scheme, the central bank issues the digital currency directly to corresponding accounts of organizations or individuals and the issued CBDC can be directly transferred between such accounts. No central bank nor any third party commissioned by it will directly manage the currency accounts and they are only responsible for verifying the transactions and maintaining the normal operation of the corresponding payment and settlement system.

The Circulation Mechanism. Central banks or commercial banks and payment institutions are only responsible for maintaining the automated payment settlement system which uses blockchain technology to automatically execute currency transfer between different accounts of participating organizations or individuals. Since CBDC's credit is backed by the central bank or the country, unless the central bank or the state goes "broke", the CBDC in any customer's account will never become bankrupt property due to the insolvency of any commercial bank or payment institution.

The Account Nature. The CBDC accounts should be understood as a tool provided by the central bank to the users to deposit and make payment with this digital currency; regardless of who is responsible for direct management of the accounts, the central bank should always hold the ultimate rights to their management.

Property Relations. The parties involved are either "a user of CBDC accounts" or "a central bank or its agent" and interactions between them include currency custody and payment settlement. And based on the principle stating that "all property should be determined by law", property relations should be subject only to law and not to any agreement between the parties; in addition, account users should not be required to pay for custody and circulation of the currency all expenses arising from the relevant business handled by the central bank or its agents should be paid from the currency issuance income because such business is a part of the legal currency circulation system.

Regulatory Relations. There is little difference between the regulation of CBDC and that of traditional monetary behaviors, which mainly involves regulatory works against forgery and alteration of currency, money laundering, tax evasion and other currency-related illegal or criminal acts. However, the effectiveness of review and supervision can be improved in the case of CBDC circulation for the following reasons: Firstly, thanks to the use of blockchain technology, each transaction in the currency circulation system will have a shared complete record, which makes it impossible to carry out many illegal acts that rely on the independence of legal currency. Secondly, under the CBDC system with a double-chain structure, the regulator is also a participant in the consortium blockchain, so it can take measures to improve the efficiency of supervision of currency circulation, maintain the order of currency circulation and prevent the occurrence of illegal and criminal activities in the currency circulation system without risking breaking the basic laws of currency circulation and violating the regulations on circulation of legal currency.

4.2 Monetary Powers and Obligations of the Central Bank

Monetary Powers. Considering that CBDC is a new kind of legal currency, the central bank should hold the core monetary powers of this currency, otherwise there would be unavoidable disruption to the entire currency issuance and circulation system. Specifically, the central bank should have the power to: issue the currency, obtain issuance proceeds, conduct supervision & management and system management, authorize operations, formulate rules and regulations. To this end, China should make the following amendments to its current laws and regulations: (1) Clearly state that the central bank holds the issuing power of CBDC by amending the legal documents such as the *Law of the People's Bank of China* and the *Regulation of the People's Republic of China on the Administration of Renminbi*. (2) Amend the relevant legal documents currently in effect, including the *Law of the People's Bank of China* and the *Basic Accounting System of the People's Bank of China* etc., so as to state that issuing proceeds of CBDC as well as statutory notes and coins should all be considered as issuing proceeds of legal currency and all accounting of such proceeds should be carried out under the same accounting system. (3) Amend the *Law of the People's Bank of China*, the *Commercial Bank Law*, the *Measures for Payment and Settlement* and other regulatory documents currently in effect, so as to clearly stipulated that the central bank has the highest management authority over the CBDC circulation system, even if any commercial bank or payment institution has been entrusted by it to manage said system. (4) In order to save social resources and maintain the purity in the central bank's operations, it is required to grant the central bank the power to authorize commercial banks or payment institutions to carry out specific management of digital currency system by amending the *Law of the People's Bank of China*, the *Regulation on the Administration of Renminbi*, the *Commercial Bank Law* and other regulations. (5) Grant the central bank the power to formulate and amend the CBDC Regulations as needed, so that specific regulations can be adopted for the management of CBDC-related payment settlement and system management.

Obligations. As the central organ that governs all national or regional monetary affairs, the central bank should not only hold the necessary powers over CBDC but also bear the corresponding monetary obligations, including: system maintenance, expense payment, loss compensation and privacy protection. To this end, the following should be clearly stated in the relevant regulations: (1) The issuance and circulation of CBDC must be conducted within a specific electronic network system. In terms of specific mode of operation, the central bank can establish and operate this system all by itself or entrust commercial banks or payment agencies to run and manage specific system operations. However, no matter what specific operation mode is adopted, the central bank must assume the ultimate obligation for maintenance of this system. (2) In principle the central bank should bear all costs related to the issuance and circulation of CBDC, which mainly include system construction costs, system maintenance costs, authorization and certification fees, network resource costs etc.; The commercial banks or payment institutions may be required to bear CBDC costs in whole or in part only when the operations related to such costs are directly related to the interests of said commercial banks or payment institutions and relevant business operations and management are conductive to the recovery of expenses arising out of the CBDC circulation operations handled by said commercial banks or payment institutions. (3) CBDC owners might suffer losses due to system failures, malicious attacks, faults of the system operators, leakage of the identity info or signatures or even damage to the storage device. Where any CBDC owner claims that he/she has suffered loss to his/her CBDC property, the central bank or the system operator must assume the burden of proof with respect to self-justification and they should be liable for compensation of such loss unless they can prove that said claim is not legitimate, which should be considered as an obligation to the CBDC owners that must be assumed by the central bank as well as the system operator. (4) CBDC circulation must be contained in a network system established by a central bank or a commercial bank and it is obvious that the records of such circulation contain privacy information of the users. As such, the law must clearly stipulate the obligation of privacy protection assumed by the central bank, which shall remain one of the basic obligations of the central bank even when it has delegated operation rights to commercial banks or payment agencies.

4.3 The Monetary Rights and Obligations of Commercial Banks

Monetary Rights. The CBDC-related rights held by commercial banks or payment institutions mainly include the rights to entrusted operations, identity review, business of exchange currencies and one-way charge. As such, the current regulations should be amended for the reasons stated below: (1) In order for convergence of the currency circulation systems of the central banks and those of the commercial banks or the payment institutions, the central banks shall delegate part of the rights to CBDC issuance and circulation to commercial banks or payment institutions. (2) In order to effectively reduce and prevent illegal and criminal activities, and make sure that all transactions can be recorded in the circulation system, commercial banks or payment institutions entrusted to manage the digital currency system must be given the right to review the identities of the customers, which is also an obligation that must be fulfilled by such banks or institutions. (3) Since CBDC is a legal currency and the public can't be required to pay fees for the management and operation of a national legal currency system, the commercial banks or payment institutions should be given the right to collect fees from the central banks for conducting entrusted management and operations.

Obligations. While enjoying the above rights, commercial banks or payment institutions should also assume the corresponding obligations, including those for: entrusted maintenance, auditing and authentication, examinations for illegal behaviors and currency exchange. To this end, the current regulations should be amended for reasons stated below: (1) Generally, the central bank needs to delegate the rights to specific operation and management of the CBDC system to commercial banks or payment institutions. As such, it is required to clearly define what system maintenance obligations should be assumed by the commercial banks or payment institutions. (2) In order for the circulation of digital currency to be completed, CBDC circulation system needs to have one or more entities to check whether the payers or payees have the legitimate rights to make or receive payments with digital currency and confirm the results of the payment settlement. However, it is often impractical for central banks to assume all duties for auditing and authentication of payments, so it is necessary to clearly define the rights and obligations of commercial banks or payment institutions with respect to relevant auditing and authentication works. (3) In order to effectively prevent the occurrence of illegal and criminal acts, commercial banks or payment institutions should be required to undertake the obligations of anti-tax evasion examination, anti-money laundering examination, anti-terrorism examination and the examinations for other illegal and criminal acts.

4.4   The Monetary Rights and Obligations of the Public

Monetary Rights. In terms of monetary rights held by the public, there are certain distinctions between those with respect to ordinary legal currency and those to CBDC, which are mainly reflected in: the right to currency selection and conversion, absolute payment right, payment confirmation right and the right to claim indemnity. To this end, the current regulations should be amended for reasons stated below: (1) In order to avoid any adverse effect to the integrity of the legal currency system or the order of currency circulation, it is required to guarantee that CBDC can be unconditionally converted to the equivalent amount of statutory notes or coins; and it is forbidden to put any restriction on the free exchange between CBDC and the deposit currency on the ground of difference in the form of money or financial management needs. (2) Holders of CBDC should have absolute payment rights to such currency as long as it is authentic and meets the statutory requirements. Whether the means by which the public obtains the digital currency are legal or not, the monetary property rights to such currency shall not be affected and the absolute payment rights to such currency must be guaranteed, meaning that no payee should refuse to accept payment with it. (3) Where CBDC is used in any payment made for deposit of money, the person who owns property right to say CBDC should have the right to confirm the payment, and said payment shall have become legally valid as long as the statutory conditions for confirmation thereof are met. (4) Where any currency property in the form of CBDC stored in any account is lost due to network failure, malicious network attack, damage to network equipment, network security defects and other reasons that can't be attributed to the public, the institutions responsible for operating and maintaining relevant network should assume the liability of compensation. In order to avoid disruption to the normal currency circulation on the network system, if any indemnity claim is made by any member of the public, the institutions responsible for operating and maintaining relevant network must pay corresponding compensation in advance unless they can prove that the corresponding loss was caused by the user's own fault.

Obligations. In terms of the monetary obligations assumed by the public, in addition to the general obligations related to legal currency, the public must also assume some other obligations that are specific to online payment, including: compliance with rules, payment in good faith and reasonable care. To this end, the current regulations should be amended for reasons stated below: (1) The general public must comply with statutory rules on the online payment with digital currencies and conduct receipt and payment of money in accordance with the operating rules of the CBDC circulation system. (2) The obligation of payment in good faith means that payers must abide by the legal principle of honesty and trustworthiness, and they should make payments to the payees with legal currency that meets the corresponding requirements and never make any fraudulent attempts in the payment process. (3) The obligation of reasonable care means that property owners must exercise reasonable duty of care to the best of their abilities, including taking proper custody of their equipment that contains the digital currency as well as the electronic signatures or "private keys" that represent their identities in the currency payment network, so as to prevent others from stealing their identities and conduct monetary behaviors in a manner that violates their interests. Property owners failing to fulfill this obligation should themselves be liable for losses arising therefrom and make claims against the corresponding infringers as the digital currency payment and settlement system should not be held liable for such losses.

5   Conclusion

Despite the rapid development of private digital currencies in the last decade, many potential risks in the field have also been exposed at the same time. In such a context, central banks of various countries started to conduct theoretical research on CBDC, and many of them have already moved from the stage of concept clarification to practical examination and verification. However, even if the technologies supporting CBDC are readily available, to actually issue CBDCs the central banks still need to have relevant legal powers granted by legal documents. As such, it is of great urgency to discuss how to establish a sound legal framework for the administration of CBDC affairs. In this regard, the Chinese government is required to gradually establish a legal system that can explicitly stipulate the rights and obligations of and the relations between all parties that participate in the entire CBDC system.

Acknowledgements. This work was supported by 2019-2020 philosophy and social science research project of Zhuhai City "Study on legalization of credit management in the Guangdong-Hong Kong-Macao Greater Bay Area" (2019YB016).

References

1. Wei, W., et al.: Blockchain used by digital currency and its privacy protection mechanism. Inf. Netw. Secur. **2017**(7), 34–35 (2017)
2. Jian, C., Xue, Z.: The current development of digital currency and the experience learned from global efforts in its regulation. China Price **2018**(11), 44–47 (2018)
3. Yang, Y., Chunyu, J.: The prospect of China's CBDC development based on blockchain technology. China Market **2017**(14), 14–15 (2017)
4. Chen, W.: A research on the rights to control blockchain-based legal currency. Shanghai Finan. **2017**(1), 24–25 (2017)
5. Li, Z., et al.: Understanding of and recommended solutions to issues related to CBDC. Banker **2018**(10), 131–134 (2018)
6. Jianyi, Z., et al.: A blockchain-based digital currency model that can be regulated. Comput. Res. Dev. **55**(10), 2219–2232 (2018)
7. Shaojun, L.: Study on the legal principles and the distribution of rights and duties of legal digital currency. J. CUPL **2018**(3), 165–179 (2018)

Application of the Blockchain Technology in Smart Contracts: Legal Analysis

Chunhsien Sung[(✉)]

Department of Financial and Economic Law, Overseas Chinese University,
100, Chiao Kwang Rd., Taichung 40721, Taiwan
scotsung@gmail.com

Abstract. Smart contracts have recently been considered one of the two columns of blockchain applications. The first column is the cryptocurrency funded by the decentralized system, and the second column is the smart contracts, which are an automatic self-execution contractual program. This article provides a legal analysis of smart contracts and concludes that the application of the blockchain technology in smart contracts should be considered a guarantee to the contractual performance. Furthermore, the regulations that apply to smart contracts should focus on the codes inserted in, rather than the performance.

Keywords: Smart contract · Blockchain · Self-execution contracts

1 Introduction

In 2009, Satoshi Nakamoto set the blockchain technology for the usage of Bitcoin. Bitcoin is another important work-based application from a blockchain, which allows for the agreement of the public on the sequence of blockchain transactions. Sequence issue is regarded as an essential obstacle in decentralizing an online environment. During simultaneous transactions, an entity should confirm which transaction came first. In a centralized online environment, the central authority recognizes a tiny gap in the order amount of simultaneous transactions. However, without the central authority, the blockchain technology provides an alternative solution for such an issue. Therefore, the blockchain technology can apply multiple work-based platforms in the decentralized online environment. In other words, how can the blockchain apply for more than digital currency?

Smart contracts are regarded as one of the most important "more-than-digital-currency" applications that allow digital properties to be moved via a user's instinctively prespecified rules. Moreover, on account of the term "contract," smart contracts are characterized as "decentralized legal systems." Such systems enable entities to develop more flexible transaction methods using only a few lines of code.

This article aims to analyze smart contracts through legal doctrines. Accordingly, the blockchain technology is highly capable of replacing the position of an intermediary that concerns the legal and economic means in the society. The subject of an intermediary

D.-J. Deng et al. (Eds.): WiCON 2019, LNICST 317, pp. 140–144, 2020.
https://doi.org/10.1007/978-3-030-52988-8_12

in smart contracts refers to self-enforcing digital contracts, which allows the transfer of digital properties and currencies to others through a few lines of code and conditions settled in the software. However, the role of an intermediary is only treated as a part of a contract in the contract law, and the part is legally considered records than rights. This will provide observations and issues that are concerned by smart contracts.

2 Smart Contracts and Contract Law

The term "smart contracts" has been presented for a long time before blockchain applications. Smart contracts are the consequences of human actions [1], where contracting parties are encouraged to lower costs regardless of the advice of specialists. The term was originally described by Nick Szabo, a lawyer and technologist, in 1997. He described smart contracts as "contractual clauses embedded into hardware and software in such a way that makes breach more expensive" [2]. Szabo gave two examples to illustrate the decreasing costs of mediation, self-enforcement, and arbitration: one is vending machines and the other is devices for repossessing automobile collateral. Szabo also stated that smart contracts represent an important shift in the world toward digital systems, which is different from traditional paper-based transactions.

For computer science purposes, smart contracts refer to automated execution agreements. However, legal purposes concern more about the execution of human control. Legal purposes refer to juristic acts, which aim to establish them between two parties, including a person and a legal person. Thus, the automated execution as a result of a computer code running is considered a legal prose execution. A smart contract concerns more about the performance of a contract rather than the state of enforcement. Accordingly, the court recourse does not highly involve the process of the contract performance.

A typical example of a smart contract is the vending machine. If the machine works properly when money is inserted, then the contract for sale would be executed automatically. The process of sale depends on the code settled to the machine's interpretation. Therefore, most of the juristic acts concern "how the code is settled," not the performance of the smart contract. As a result, the existing contract law has a very limited place in situating the legal discussions of smart contracts.

3 Automated Transactions and Smart Contracts

An automated execution is the key element of smart contracts, but not every automated transaction is included. For example, automated banking payment, online standing orders, and online transactions after payment confirmation are not considered smart contracts.

First, transactions involve interventions by third parties, which may preserve the control over the respective transaction. For example, in the case of a bank payment, a bank could interfere in the transaction procedure and withdraw or add money to the account. This case is different from smart contracts, which are not administered by third parties.

Then, under a decentralization system consisted by a blockchain, no third-party computers (also known as servers) are involved in the running of a program. Transactions and records are interchanged between parties of the smart contract via the blockchain technology.

Thirdly, the blockchain technology provides an open and cryptographic nature that enables the development of trust in the decentralized system. Users are running the same codes, and the codes are kept with all users. This case is different from traditional automated contract executions, where the operation is governed by a server and is exclusively in the control of a third party.

Lastly, automated transactions in smart contracts are flexible. The developer may provide a set of ambiguous directions into the codes that enables the smart contract to be triggered and transformed. This case is different from traditional automated transactions that require ambiguous implementations for the triggers.

The aforementioned differences actually refer more about the performance than human control, and legal discussions are narrower in smart contracts. In other words, innovative technology does not equal to jurisprudence innovation, and traditional legal analyses are still the basis of rules for complex technologies [3].

4   Human Involvement

As the blockchain is capable of altering the way people manage their affairs, new software-based organizations, such as decentralized organizations and decentralized autonomous organizations, claim that the software may enable parties to get benefits without any human involvement. The blockchain technology can manage resources and interact with other humans or machines. As a result, issues regarding legal personalities, individual agencies, and their responsibilities have emerged [4]. However, the parts without human involvement, according to the blockchain technology, only refer to the performance of the contract. Such performance is still governed by the codes settled by human. Thus, the intention and activities settled in the codes are considered juristic acts and are ruled by the law of the contract.

Legal theory has principally managed a balance between individuals and states by promoting parties' autonomy and their fundamental rights. Although a smart contract and its decentralized applications have initiated several proposals of amendments for current Internet regulations, the amendments should focus on the codes inserted, rather than the performance. Therefore, once the blockchain technology is widely applied by centralized authorities, such as government agencies and large corporations, the regulation of codes inserted in smart contracts will require particular rules or principles. Otherwise, we may lose the ability to control and shape the authorities operated by decentralized systems.

5   Instantiations of Smart Contracts

Appropriately, the major benefits brought about by smart contracts is the capacities of eliminating the necessity to trust the other party by prohibiting the other part from breaching the contractual performance. The instantiations of contract terms onto machines are the key element to contract law applications. Users' instantiation inserted toward codes by either writing into the existing software or into the software connected to a machine that performs the contract. The performance of smart contracts is guaranteed, and afterward, human interference is impossible. Thus, the codes inserted will be final and deterministic to the smart contracts with blockchain applications, and moreover, the codes inserted cannot be changed; in other words, users' instantiations will be entirely enforced [5].

Consequently, the instantiations of a user or coder concerns more about the term of offer and acceptance that was inserted into the smart contract system, and the terms regarding the offer and acceptance are referred to general legal regulations not within the contract law. Inquiring the legal implications about the enforceability of the smart contract is irrational because each smart contract is direct and drafted by different instantiations and has no consistency. Recently, legal scholars have struggled to institute an organized theory regarding distinguished smart contracts from other "digital," "electronic," or "online" agreements.

Although nothing prevents smart contracts to have legal effects, smart contracts still are not considered contracts in the legal sense. In law, "contract" refers to an agreement between mutual parties or to the embodiment of an agreement. Contrarily, certain technical writings allocate "smart contracts" as a particular form of technology or entities. However, the key element, in the narrative aspect, in the "smart contract" is "self-enforcement".

Purportedly, the self-enforcement of smart contracts is established upon the blockchain technology, not upon traditional legal institutions. Thus, promissory obligations of the contract law are strengthened spontaneously without state involvement [6]. The term "self-enforcement" is ambiguous and seems to present with a combination of two distinct stages of a contract: performance and adjudication. Therefore, the confusion between rights and records involves the legality issues of smart contracts.

6 Conclusion

As the blockchain supposedly executes the "smart contract" in a balanced and unstoppable manner, the performance of the smart contract will be guaranteed. Once the party inserted the codes, neither of them can change their mind nor refuse to fulfill obligations. Therefore, the execution of the codes is equal to the performance of the obligation embodied therein. In other words, the blockchain secures and guarantees the performance of the smart contract, and the issue of enforcement should not be addressed because enforcement refers to the ability to pursue judicial assistance in the occasions of breaches.

Performance and enforcement refer to different legal notions and are mutually exclusive. Court assistance to the parties should be required when something is wrong in the contract. The guaranteed performance of the smart contract is made to prevent this situation. The essence of a smart contract is a technological tool for the automatic performance of obligations, not a tool for seeking the source of obligations [7]. Therefore, smart contracts do not eliminate the demand for judicial enforcement, and the parties still have rights to acquire it.

References

1. Frguson, A.: An Essay on The History of Civil Society, 5th edn. T. Cadell, London (1782)

2. Szabo, N.: Formalizing and securing relationships on public networks. First Monday **2** (1997). http://ojphi.org/ojs/index.php/fm/article/view/548/469
3. Easterbrook, F.: Cyberspace and the Law of the Horse. U. Chi. Legal F. 207 (1996)
4. Dixon, C., et al.: Beyond Bitcoin: The Blockchain, A16z Academic Roundtable 2014, 24 October 2014. http://a16z.com/2014/10/24/the-bitcoin-network-effect/
5. Marino, B., Juels, A.: Setting standards for altering and undoing smart contracts. In: Alferes, J.J., Bertossi, L., Governatori, G., Fodor, P., Roman, D. (eds.) RuleML 2016. LNCS, vol. 9718, pp. 151–166. Springer, Cham (2016). https://doi.org/10.1007/978-3-319-42019-6_10
6. Werbach, K., Cornell, N.: Contracts Ex Machina, 67 Duke L. J, p. 313 (2017). p. 357
7. Cieplak, J., Leefatt, S.: Smart contracts: a smart way to automate performance. Geo. L. Tech. Rev. 1, 417 (2017)

Internet of Things

Discover the Optimal IoT Packets Routing Path of Software-Defined Network via Artificial Bee Colony Algorithm

Chih-Kun Ke[1(✉)], Mei-Yu Wu[2], Wang-Hsin Hsu[1], and Chia-Yu Chen[1]

[1] Department of Information Management, National Taichung University of Science and Technology, Taichung City 40401, Taiwan R.O.C.
ckk@nutc.edu.tw
[2] Department of Business Management, National Taichung University of Science and Technology, Taichung City 40401, Taiwan R.O.C.

Abstract. The wireless sensor network is the core of the Internet of Things. However, wireless sensors have some limitations and challenges, such as limited power and computing power, data storage, and network bandwidth, especially power requirements. How to find a way to program more flexible and faster according to the state of each sensing node in the network becomes an important issue. The software-defined network separates the control functions from the hardware devices, such as switches or routers, so that these hardware devices only have the data forwarding function, and the control software dynamically controls the flow of the network and data packets according to the network state and application requirements. In order to provide flexibility and adaptability, software-defined networks require a dynamic approach to solving and optimizing routing planning problems. This study will use the artificial bee colony algorithm to monitor the state of the sensor nodes in the software-defined network through the controller and take the best decision dynamically. Artificial bee colony algorithms are used to optimize wireless sensor networks and improve sensor node energy usage and data packets routing issues. The contribution of this research is to dynamically find the optimal routing path for the sensing nodes through the artificial bee colony algorithm, and improve the overall practicability and reliability of the wireless sensor network.

Keywords: Wireless sensor network · Software-defined network · Routing path optimization · Artificial bee colony algorithm

1 Introduction

In recent years, with the rapid development of the Internet of Things (IoT), some fields have begun to introduce IoT technologies such as smart homes, smart healthcare, smart farms, and so on. Wireless sensor network (WSN) is the core of the IoT. By deploying a large variety of wireless sensors, each sensor senses the surrounding environment

D.-J. Deng et al. (Eds.): WiCON 2019, LNICST 317, pp. 147–162, 2020.
https://doi.org/10.1007/978-3-030-52988-8_13

including temperature, humidity, pressure, soil composition, etc. The data will be transmitted to specific locations, such as base stations or sinks, allowing administrators to analyze the data and make suitable decisions in various applications. However, wireless sensors have some limitations and challenges, such as limited power and computing power, data storage, and network bandwidth, especially power requirements. Whether the sensing environment communicates and shares with each other through radio signals, data processing requires a power supply. So it becomes an important issue for how to save the energy of the sensor. In addition, if the network administrator wants to manage the WSN, it usually configures the hardware devices in advance, including the routing path of the data packet. If one of the hardware devices fails or is busy, the data packet will be lost or cannot be transmitted. Therefore, it is desirable to find a way to program more flexible and faster according to the state of each sensing node in the network.

In order to overcome these limitations, the concept of a software-defined network (SDN) is proposed. The SDN separates the control functions from the hardware devices, such as switches or routers, so that these hardware devices only have the data forwarding function, and the control software dynamically controls the flow of the network and data packets according to the network state and application requirements. In order to provide flexibility and adaptability, SDN requires a dynamic approach to solving and optimizing routing planning problems. The literature has proposed swarm intelligence (SI) algorithms, such as ant colony algorithm, migratory bird algorithm, gene algorithm and so on. Collaborative approach is the main concept behind SI, which enables algorithmic programs to find solutions. The decentralized control is designed through the characteristics of the swarm to solve real-world optimization problems, and an effective solution can be obtained. The artificial bee colony algorithm (ABC) is one of the SIs. ABC algorithm is designed based on the cooperative foraging behavior among bees. Some literature pointed out that the ABC algorithm can get the best solution compared with other SI algorithms. And the ABC algorithm solves a lot of problems, such as traveling salesman problem, clustering, routing, scheduling, etc.

This study explores that SDN operates in the WSN environment and monitors the status of the sensor nodes in the WSN through the SDN controller and dynamically takes the best decision. The ABC algorithm is used to optimize the problem of how to improve the energy usage and packet routing of the sensing node in WSN. The contribution of this research is to dynamically discover the optimal routing path for the sensing nodes through the ABC algorithm and improve the overall practicability and reliability of the WSN.

The remainder of this paper is organized as follows. Related work is described in Sect. 2. Section 3 presents the system framework and process of the overall system. The experiments are presented in Sect. 4. Finally, Sect. 5 presents our conclusions.

2   Related Works

This section introduces related works, including wireless sensor network (WSN), software-defined network (SDN) and artificial bee colony (ABC) algorithm.

2.1 Wireless Sensor Network (WSN)

With the advancement of technology, the cost of sensors has decreased, and small, low-cost sensors are becoming more and more popular. A typical wireless sensor network (WSN) is a network of hundreds or thousands of sensor nodes, each sensor node sensing and controlling the environment around them in a cooperative manner, and mutually interacting with each other by radio communication [1]. These sensor nodes are small computers that include sensing, processing, and transmission functions. But for many WSNs, sensor nodes are limited by energy and communication bandwidth. Therefore, the development of innovative technologies that effectively use limited bandwidth and low energy consumption has become an important research issue. Heinzelman [2] proposed the low-energy adaptive clustering hierarchy (LEACH) method in 2000. It selects the clustering header by probability and forms a cluster using a distributed algorithm. Each non-clustering header node selects the cluster with the least amount of transmission energy to reach the clustering header and uses the clustering header node as the router to perform all data processing of the non-clustering hierarchy node in the cluster. The purpose of this clustering algorithm is to divide the network into multiple clusters. The advantages of this algorithm are to reduce routing complexity, reduce energy consumption, and extend the network life cycle. However, for the clustering header far from the base station, it is necessary to find a route that consumes less energy to transmit the collected data to the base station [3].

2.2 Software-Defined Network (SDN)

Traditional network architectures typically consist of routers and switches. As the network expands, it becomes difficult to monitor. For large networks that combine many different protocols, it is a challenge to dynamically implement management policies for changes, upgrades, or monitoring [4]. Therefore, in order to manage the network more flexibly and efficiently, software-defined networking (SDN) [5] was proposed by McKeown et al. in 2008. The structure of SDN is shown as Fig. 1. It reshapes the network structure, separating the control and data forwarding functions of traditional hardware devices, making the network hardware facilities become forwarding devices. All control is handled by the controller in the SDN. The SDN structure consists of three main components: the application, the control plane, and the infrastructure plane. The application communicates with the controller on the control plane through the northbound interface, which controls the forwarding device through a controller to implement the tasks assigned by the application. The controller is connected to the infrastructure plane through the switch's southbound interface of the SDN, and the infrastructure plane is a part that supports a protocol shared with the controller, such as OpenFlow, and processes the actual device according to the configuration issued by the controller.

Different types of sensing devices collect and generate large amounts of data, making the Internet of Things (IoT) more difficult to control, observe and protect. Some studies have used SDN as a solution to these challenges. In SDN, most energy-intensive functions are removed from the physical node to the logically centralized controller. The node becomes a device without intelligence, and the controller can determine the optimal routing strategy to reduce the energy consumption of the node. If the node is about to

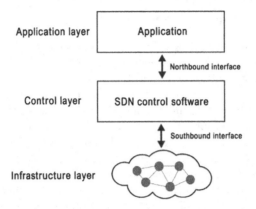

Application layer

Application

Northbound interface

Control layer

SDN control software

Southbound interface

Infrastructure layer

Fig. 1. The structure of software defined networking (SDN)

run out of energy, it will send a warning to the controller so that the routing table can be changed in time so that SDN can manage the network flexibly. Some researchers combine SDN into the WSN environment. Gante et al. [6] proposed an SDWSN in 2014, in which the controller can know the state of the entire node network and generate sensor network (SN) forwarding decisions based on the network state increasing the better cooperation between cluster header (CH) and SN. In 2015, Olivier et al. [7] proposed a cluster-based SDWSN architecture. They applied SDN to the cluster WSN to form a software-defined cluster sensor network (SDCSN). The sensor network was organized into clusters, including sensor nodes and Gateways or a cluster header, where the cluster header acts as an SDN cluster header (SDNCH), controlling and coordinating all of its sensor nodes in the cluster domain. Each SDCH can also implement its own security policy to protect its domain from external attacks and have a partial view of the network that can communicate with other SDCHs via Gateway.

2.3 Artificial Bee Colony (ABC) Algorithm

Swarm Intelligence (SI) is an algorithm developed based on the characteristics of groups in nature. Since the beginning of the 21st century, some researchers have proposed a large number of algorithms for swarm intelligence, including ant colony optimization, particle swarm optimization, artificial bee colony, fireflies' algorithms, bat algorithms, and pigeon inspiration optimization, discover the best solution from complex problems through decentralized control between groups and self-organized collective behavior. The artificial bee colony (ABC) algorithm was proposed by Karaboga et al. [8] in 2005. The design principle of ABC algorithm comes from the habit of bee feeding, simulating the behavior of bee colonies. The algorithm contains food, sources of food, employed bees, onlooker bees, and scout bees. Half of the bees in the colonies are employed bees, while the other half are bees of onlooker bees. For each food source, only one employed bee is responsible for mining the honey source currently being explored. After the exploration, they will send information about the quality of the food source to the onlooker bees. If the employed bees and the onlooker bees explore all the sources of honey and there is no better source of honey, the scout bees will randomly search the area to find new sources of food [9]. The artificial bee colony algorithm is shown in Fig. 2.

```
00  Artificial bee colony algorithm ()
01  {
02    Initialization Phase;
03      Evaluate the fitness of the population ();
04    repeat
05      Employed bee phase
06        Calculate Probabilities for Onlooker bee
07      Onlooker bee phase
08      Scout bee phase
09    Memorize the best solution;
10  }
```

Fig. 2. The artificial bee colony algorithm

The initial phase is to randomly generate a solution as a food source. Assign each employed bee to each food source and set relevant control parameters, such as a maximum number of cycles (MCN) and a maximum number of searches for each food source (Limit), then calculate for each food source's fitness value (fit) by Eq. (1).

$$fit_i = \frac{1}{1 + f_i} \tag{1}$$

Second, each employed bee finds a new source of food in the original position by Eq. (2). If the new food source has more nectar than the old one, the new food source will be replaced by the new food source. After all the employed bees have completed the mining process, they share the nectar information of the food source with the onlookers.

$$V_{ij} = Z_{ij} + \emptyset_{ij}(Z_{ij} - Z_{kj}) \tag{2}$$

Third, the probability of calculating the amount of nectar from the food source is calculated by Eq. (3). Each onlooker bee selects the food source based on the traditional roulette selection method. Then, each onlooker bee finds the source of food near its chosen food source (using a neighborhood operator) and calculates the amount of nectar from the nearby food source (fitness value).

$$P_i = \frac{fit_i}{\sum_{n=1}^{SN} fit_n} \tag{3}$$

Fourth, if the quality of the food source is not improved, the employed bee will abandon the food source as a scout bee and randomly search for new sources of food. After the scout bee finds a new source of food, the scout bee becomes an employed bee again. After each employed bee is assigned to a food source, another iteration of the

ABC algorithm is initiated. Repeat the process until the stop condition is achieved. The process is calculated by Eq. (4).

$$Z_i^j = Z_{min}^j + rand(0, 1)\left(Z_{max}^j - Z_{min}^j\right) \tag{4}$$

Karaboga and Akay [10] compared the performance of ABC algorithm with genetic algorithms (GA), differential evolution (DE), particle swarm optimization (PSO) and evolution strategy (ES) algorithms on a large number of unconstrained test functions, and concluded that the performance of ABC algorithm is better than other algorithms. Although ABC uses fewer control parameters and is effectively used to solve multimodal and multi-dimensional optimization problems, some researches have modified ABC algorithms to improve ABC deficiencies. In order to improve the performance of ABC for local search, Karaboga and Gorkemli [11] proposed the rapid artificial bee colony (qABC) algorithms which can more accurately simulate the behavior of onlooker bee and redefine the formula for onlooker bees to search for food sources. Therefore, both the employed bee and the onlooker bee search for food sources in different ways. Cui et al. [12] proposed a ranking-based adaptive artificial bee colony (RABC) algorithm, ranking the best to the worst according to the fitness value of each food source to achieve convergence and avoid stagnation to further improve ABC. Kıran and Fındık [13] proposed the dABC algorithm, which adds direction to each food source location, thereby limiting the search space to obtain a better solution.

3   System Framework

This section introduces a IoT packets routing path planning system using artificial bee colony (ABC) algorithm in the context of a software-defined wireless sensor network (SDWSN). The system framework includes the infrastructure module, ABC algorithm module, software-defined network (SDN) controller module, application module, and knowledge base. The system framework and workflow are shown in Fig. 3. The system uses an SDN structure to divide the WSN into two parts. One is the control plane and the other is the infrastructure plane. The control plane uses the SDN controller to effectively control the hardware facilities in the data layer and reduce the processing load of the forwarding nodes. The control plane improves the efficiency and reliability of the WSN and reduces energy consumption. In the infrastructure plane, a sensor network is established by a large number of sensor nodes, and the sensing elements in each sensor collect data of the surrounding environment. Then the processing elements generate data packets which transmitted through the communication components.

However, in the process of transmitting the packet to the base station, it is limited by the power problem. Therefore, the ABC module first selects the best energy node as the cluster header (CH) through the artificial bee colony algorithm and then divides the sensor network into multiple clusters. Each cluster of CHs allocates the sequence of each sensor packet transmission in the cluster through time division multiple access (TDMA) to perform data convergence. Then it plans the transmission path for all CHs through the artificial bee colony algorithm and establishes a routing table, and transmits the collected data to the SDN controllers. In the SDN controller module, it is responsible for managing information in a dynamic network environment, including a routing table constructed by ABC operations, and the status of each sensor in the infrastructure plane, such as new nodes and faulty nodes. All packets are collected for pre-processing and stored in the database. In the application module, the system can monitor and the state of the SDWSN through the webpage. The system makes the optimal data offloading decision, and avoids the problem that the data transmission congestion causes the packet to be lost.

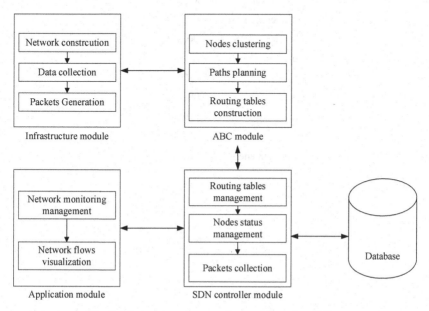

Fig. 3. The proposed system framework and workflow

4 Experiments

This section simulates the environment of the wireless sensor network. The relevant parameters are shown in Table 1. The assumptions of the simulation include that the sensors are the same; the sensor has the same initial energy; the transmission is bi-directional and symmetrical; there are no obstacles between the sensors. The simulation environment contains 100 sensors randomly distributed in a square area of 100 m × 100 m. The base station (BS) position is located at coordinates (100, 100), and the state of sensor distribution is shown in Fig. 4. Each of the sensors is connected to each other to form a large WSN, and each sensor collects data of the surrounding environment to generate a data packet and prepares to transmit the packet to the BS. The initial energy of each sensor is 2 J. When the energy of the sensor is less than 0.001 J, it can no longer be used as a faulty sensor. We preset that each sensor collects 1000 bits for transmission to the base station. When the distance between the sensor and the base station is less than the configured threshold, the free space (fs) model is used, and the energy used for transmission is ε_{fs}; otherwise, the multipath (mp) model is used, and the energy used for transmission is ε_{mp}.

Table 1. The parameters of the simulation environment of a wireless sensor network

Parameter	Value
Size of area	100×100
Number of sensors	100
Location of BS	(100, 100)
Initial energy	2 J
E_{elec}	50 J/bit
ε_{fs}	0.001 J/bit
ε_{mp}	10 J/bit
Data size	1000 bit/sensor
Minimum energy	0.001 J

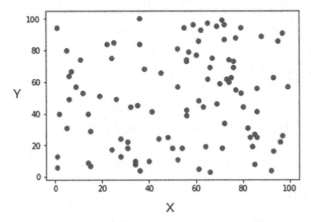

Fig. 4. The sensors distribution of the simulation environment

4.1 Sensor Clustering

There are hundreds or thousands of sensors in the wireless sensor network that communicate with the base station (BS). If the sensor is farther away from the BS, it needs to consume more energy. Therefore, we divide the sensors into clusters and select each one. The sensor with the most energy in the cluster acts as the cluster header (CH), and the CH is responsible for collecting the data of the cluster for integration, and then communicating with the BS. Before the sensors are clustered, all the sensors are numbered, and the status of each sensor is uploaded to the SDN controller for management, as shown in Table 2. The SDN controller first uses the ABC algorithm to connect the sensor network. The sensors in a SDWSN are divided into N clusters.

Table 2. The status of each sensor is uploaded to the SDN controller

Sensor_number	x	y	Energy
0	50	18	0.7
1	67	75	1.64
2	12	53	0.33
3	80	44	1.7
4	75	63	1.02
5	65	97	0.34
6	24	75	0.08
...	...	...	...

In the initialization phase of the ABC algorithm, we randomly select N sensors as CH. The remaining sensors calculate the Euclidean distance from each CH by Eq. (5). Then we select the CH with the smallest distance from itself to form an initial cluster.

$$distance = \sqrt{(x_1 - x_2)^2 + (y_1 - y_2)^2} \tag{5}$$

Suppose CH is the sensor 83, and its position is (92, 4), the distance value between sensor 0 and CH is calculated as $d = \sqrt{(50 - 92)^2 + (18 - 4)^2} = 44.27188724235731$. After the distance calculation performed with each CH, the CH closest is selected as the cluster member, thereby forming an initial cluster. Table 3 shows the result of the initial clustering.

The best CH of each cluster is calculated by the ABC algorithm to make the CH in the middle of the cluster. Each initialized cluster is the food source of the bees. Table 4 shows the parameters of the ABC algorithm. Suppose the number of employed bees and onlooker bees to be 10, and the maximum number of iteration is 100. If each solution cannot find a more solution in the preset limits 20, the food source will be obsolete. The fitness value of each food source is calculated by Eq. (6).

$$fit_i = \min \left(average \left(\sum\nolimits_{i=0}^{n} distance \right) \right) \tag{6}$$

In the employed bee phase, the employed bee mines in the food source, randomly replaces any node in the cluster as a new CH, and recalculates the fitness of the cluster. The fitness value is the average distance between the CH and the cluster members, is shown in Table 5. If the fitness value of the new CH is better than the old CH's, the original CH is replaced. If the fitness value of the old CH is better than the new CH's, the original CH is kept. If the food source is not updated, the limit value is added by 1.

Then, the probability is calculated by Eq. (3) mentioned in Sect. 2.3. According to the probability by the choice of the roulette, onlooker bees choose the cluster to go and

Table 3. The result of the initial clustering

Sensor_number of CH	Members of the cluster
83	12, 19, 38, 41, 71, 72, 99
64	2, 43, 56, 58, 66, 68, 73, 86, 92, 96
76	3, 11, 22, 36, 39, 42, 44, 49
79	10, 17, 23, 25, 27, 40, 51, 53, 55, 62, 81
7	15, 16, 18, 20, 60, 75, 89, 98
88	1, 4, 8, 24, 28, 32, 33, 35, 37, 45, 50, 67, 80, 82, 84, 87, 93, 95
48	6, 34, 46, 69, 77, 94
78	5, 13, 29, 57, 59, 63, 65, 70, 74, 91
31	9, 14, 26, 52, 61, 85
21	0, 30, 47, 54, 90, 97

Table 4. The parameters of the ABC algorithm

Parameter	Value
Max_iteration	100
Limits	20
Employed bee	10
Onlooker bee	10

Table 5. The average distance between the CH and the cluster members

Sensor_number of CH	Average distance
83	17.227143583872696
64	16.69939979492434
76	13.112180706256984
79	26.84708587963273
7	24.15624537960271
88	15.179836853843232
48	14.412849514306174
78	12.05470164676742
31	9.175234064765194
21	15.983542678595366

mine. After onlooker bees and employed bees mining, if the limit value of the food source is greater than the maximum number of mining, the scout bee will randomly replace the CH in the cluster. Then it recalculates the fitness value of the cluster and terminates the iteration. The maximum number of iterations is increased by 1 and it begins a new iteration. The final results of clustering are shown in Table 6.

4.2 ABC Path Planning

From the previous phase, the best-performing sensors are taken out from each cluster as CH. These CHs are responsible for collecting the packets of the cluster of sensors for data convergence, and then planning the route for transmitting data to the BS. In order to solve the routing optimization problem in WSN, we find the path of CH transmission data through the ABC algorithm to achieve the goal of least energy consumption. In the initialization phase, we randomly generate the paths of the sensor

CH, which serves as the food source for the bees. Table 7 shows the randomly generated path solutions.

Table 6. The final results of clustering

Sensor_number of CH	Members of the cluster
38	12, 19, 41, 71, 72, 99, 83
92	2, 43, 56, 58, 66, 68, 73, 86, 96, 83
76	3, 11, 22, 36, 39, 42, 44, 49
25	10, 17, 23, 27, 40, 51, 53, 55, 62, 81, 79
15	16, 18, 20, 60, 75, 89, 98, 7
87	1, 4, 8, 24, 28, 32, 33, 35, 37, 45, 50, 67, 80, 82, 84, 93, 95, 88
94	6, 34, 46, 69, 77, 48
70	5, 13, 29, 57, 59, 63, 65, 74, 91, 78
9	14, 26, 52, 61, 85, 31
97	0, 30, 47, 54, 90, 21

After establishing the food source, we configure the relevant parameters as shown in Table 8. Suppose the number of employed bees and onlooker bees to be 10, and the maximum number of iterations is 300. Then we calculate the fitness value of each path before performing the bee mining phase and evaluate the energy spent on each path. If the bee collects a new food source and its assessed fitness value is better than the original one, the food source is updated. If each food source cannot find a more solution in the preset limits 50, the food source will be eliminated. We consider the energy consumption of the sensor in the communication process. The total energy consumption in the transmission process is divided into two parts: the energy consumption of transmitting data and the energy of receiving data, as shown in Eq. (7).

Table 7. The randomly generated path solutions

Solution_number	Routing path
0	[38, 87, 9, 97, 76, 70, 25, 92, 94, 15, BS]
1	[92, 25, 70, 76, 15, 38, 87, 94, 97, 9, BS]
2	[76, 97, 92, 9, 94, 25, 70, 38, 15, 87, BS]
3	[25, 15, 70, 97, 87, 9, 38, 92, 94, 76, BS]
4	[15, 94, 92, 97, 70, 38, 76, 9, 25, 87, BS]
5	[87, 92, 38, 70, 15, 94, 25, 97, 76, 9, BS]
6	[94, 38, 70, 76, 9, 87, 15, 92, 25, 97, BS]
7	[70, 87, 25, 92, 9, 38, 76, 94, 97, 15, BS]
8	[9, 76, 15, 92, 25, 70, 38, 97, 94, 87, BS]
9	[97, 94, 25, 76, 9, 92, 15, 70, 38, 87, BS]

Table 8. The relevant parameters of energy consumption evaluation

Parameter	Value
Max_iteration	300
Limits	50
Employed bee	10
Onlooker bee	10

$$E_t(k, d) = E_{elec}(k) + E_{amp}(k, d) \tag{7}$$

where $E_t(k, d)$ represents the total energy consumption of k-bit data transmitted over distance d, $E_{elec}(k)$ represents the energy consumption of k-bit data, and $E_{amp}(k, d)$ represents the energy consumption of the amplifier to send k-bit data at distance d. The energy consumed in the transmission depends on the distance between the nodes. When the distance d is smaller than the threshold d_0, the free space (*fs*) model is used; otherwise, the multipath (*mp*) model is used. The energy consumed by the sensor radio to transmit 1 bit of data over distance d is given in Eq. (8) and (9). To receive k bits of data, the CH consume the E_s energy is given in Eq. (10) and (11).

$$E_t(k, d) = \begin{cases} k \times E_{elec} + k \times \varepsilon_{fs} \times d^2, d < d_0 \\ k \times E_{elec} + k \times \varepsilon_{mp} \times d^4, d \geq d_0 \end{cases} \tag{8}$$

$$d_0 = \sqrt{\varepsilon_{fs}/\varepsilon_{mp}} \tag{9}$$

$$E_s(k) = E_{elec}(k) = E_{elec} \times k \tag{10}$$

$$fit_i = \min(\sum_{i=0}^{n} E_t) \qquad (11)$$

Take solution_number 0 as an example, the path is [38, 87, 9, 97, 76, 70, 25, 92, 94, 15, BS]. At first, we calculate the amount of power consumed by this path, and collect the cluster packet by each CH. After transmitting the number of packets after convergence, the next CH, suppose that sensor number 38 has 8000 bit packets to be transmitted to the sensor number 87. It calculated by Eq. (10) and (11). $E_t = 8000 \times E_{elec} + 8000 \times \varepsilon_{mp} \times (76.4198926981712)^4 = 0.0003502387392$. In this way, the energy transferred between each node is added up to the total amount of energy that may be consumed by this path. Table 9 shows the total energy consumption of the path of each solution.

Table 9. The total energy consumption of the path of each solution

Solution_number	Total energy consumption of the path
0	0.00450164
1	0.00450021
2	0.00450116
3	0.00450145
4	0.00450119
5	0.00310163
6	0.00450076
7	0.0045009
8	0.0045013
9	0.00450095

After calculating the fitness values of all possible solutions, the employed bee phase is carried out. Each employed bee is in its current possible solution location for local mining by random exchange two nodes in the path. For example, the sequence [38, **87**, 9, 97, 76, **70**, 25, 92, 94, 15, BS] is changed to the sequence [38, **70**, 9, 97, 76, **87**, 25, 92, 94, 15, BS]

Then we evaluate whether the fitness value of the new path is higher than the original value. If it is, then update. When all the employed bees have evaluated all the paths, we calculate the probability value of each food source by the ABC algorithm Eq. (3) mention in Sect. 2.3. Let the onlooker bee based on the probability value to make the roulette selection which food source to go to. After the onlooker bee arrives the food source, we randomly exchange the order in the path and calculate whether the adapted food source has a higher fitness value than the original value. If it is higher, update it. When all the onlooker bees have been evaluated, if there is a limit value of the food source that exceeds the maximum number of iterations, the scout bee randomly generates a new solution to replace the food source, and end the iteration calculation and increase by 1 to the parameter of the maximum number of iterations. It repeats the iteration calculation until achieving the maximum number of iterations. Table 10 shows the final best paths.

Table 10. The best routing path solutions

Solution_number	Routing path
0	[38, 97, 76, 25, 87, 15, 9, BS]
1	[92, BS]
2	[76, 87, 97, 25, 15, 38, 92, 25, 9, 70, BS]
3	[25, 76, 94.97, 92, 87, 9, 70, 38, 15, BS]
4	[15, 76, 92, 70, 25, 9, 97, 94, 38,BS]
5	[87, 92, 25, 38, BS]
6	[94,92, 70,87, BS]
7	[70, 25, BS]
8	[9, 15, 38, 97, 92, 87, BS]
9	[97,15, BS]

4.3 Software Defined Network (SDN) Controller

The SDN controller is between the network administrator and the infrastructure layer. It is responsible for processing and monitoring each sensing node in the WSN, and can present the status of the current network to the administrator through the application interface. In Fig. 5, the blue dot is the distribution map of the current wireless sensor, and the red dot is the best CH node calculated by the ABC algorithm. The SDN controller software can adjust the network configuration based on the administrator's request for the application. In the SDN controller, the cluster information calculated by the ABC algorithm and the transmission path of each CH, the path information is distributed to each CH, and the data packets transmitted by each CH are collected and stored in the database.

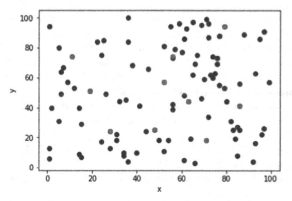

Fig. 5. The sensors and the best CHs distribution (Color figure online)

5 Conclusions

This study used the artificial bee colony (ABC) algorithm to monitor the state of the sensors in the software-defined network (SDN) through the controller and take the best decision dynamically. The ABC algorithms are used to optimize wireless sensor networks (WSN) and improve sensor energy usage and data packets routing issues. Experiments showed a simulation to illustrate the proposed system framework effectiveness to get the best routing path solutions. The contribution of this research is to dynamically find the optimal routing path for the sensors through the ABC algorithm, and improve the overall practicability and reliability of the software-defined wireless sensor network. Future works shall explore artificial intelligent and deep learning techniques to enhance the system more effectiveness.

Acknowledgement. This research was supported in part by the Ministry of Science and Technology, R.O.C. with a MOST grant 107-2221-E-025-005.

References

1. Prathap, U., Shenoy, P.D., Venugopal, K.R., Patnaik, L.M.: Wireless sensor networks applications and routing protocols: survey and research challenges. In: 2012 International Symposium on Cloud and Services Computing, Mangalore, India, pp. 49–56. IEEE (2012)
2. Heinzelman, W.R., Chandrakasan, A., Balakrishnan, H.: Energy-efficient communication protocol for wireless microsensor networks. In: Proceedings of the 33rd Annual Hawaii International Conference on System Sciences, Maui, HI, USA, pp. 1–10. IEEE (2000)
3. Chawla, S., Singh, S.: Computational intelligence techniques for wireless sensor network. Int. J. Comput. Appl. **118**(14), 23–27 (2015)
4. Kreutz, D., Ramos, F.M., Verissimo, P., Rothenberg, C.E., Azodolmolky, S., Uhlig, S.: Software-defined networking: a comprehensive survey. Proc. IEEE **103**(1), 14–76 (2015)
5. McKeown, N., et al.: OpenFlow: enabling innovation in campus networks. ACM SIGCOMM Comput. Commun. Rev. **38**(2), 69–74 (2008)

6. De Gante, A., Aslan, M., Matrawy, A.: Smart wireless sensor network management based on software-defined networking. In: 2014 27th Biennial Symposium on Communications (QBSC), Kingston, ON, Canada, pp. 71–75. IEEE (2014)

7. Olivier, F., Carlos, G., Florent, N.: SDN based architecture for clustered WSN. In: 2015 9th International Conference on Innovative Mobile and Internet Services in Ubiquitous Computing, Blumenau, Brazil, pp. 342–347. IEEE (2015

8. Karaboga, D.: An idea based on honey bee swarm for numerical optimization. Technical report-tr06, Erciyes University, Engineering Faculty, Computer Engineering Department, 200 (2005)

9. Karaboga, D., Ozturk, C.: A novel clustering approach: artificial Bee Colony (ABC) algorithm. Appl. Soft Comput. $11(1)$, 652–657 (2011)

10. Karaboga, D., Akay, B.: A comparative study of artificial bee colony algorithm. Appl. Math. Comput. $214(1)$, 108–132 (2009)

11. Karaboga, D., Gorkemli, B.: A quick artificial bee colony (qABC) algorithm and its performance on optimization problems. Appl. Soft Comput. 23, 227–238 (2014)

12. Cui, L., Li, G., Wang, X., Lin, Q., Chen, J., Lu, N., Lu, J.: A ranking-based adaptive artificial bee colony algorithm for global numerical optimization. Inf. Sci. 417, 169–185 (2017)

13. Kıran, M.S., Fındık, O.: A directed artificial bee colony algorithm. Appl. Soft Comput. 26, 454–462 (2015)

Network Protocols and Connectivity for Internet of Things

Manan Bawa[⊠] and Dagmar Caganova

Faculty of Materials Science and Technology in Trnava, Institute of Industrial Engineering and Management, Slovak University of Technology in Bratislava, 91701 Trnava, Slovakia
{manan.bawa,dagmar.caganova}@stuba.sk

Abstract. The aim of the paper is to compare different network protocols which are available for Internet of Things (IoT) systems in different industries and also to define the best practices for using these protocols in different IoT applications. IoT is a huge ecosystem of connected smart devices and objects which gathers enormous amount of data that needs to be captured, processed and communicated to and from the cloud system. The network protocols are compared based on the different IoT systems architecture and connections including smart object to object (O2O), smart object to gateway, gateway to data centers and between data centers. Furthermore, they are grouped based upon different network ranges and network topologies. Selecting the best protocol for IoT application is centered upon the proposed three-dimensional network design model which equates each of the communication protocols against the three axes of the model which are the battery life, device duty cycle and device to gateway range.

Keywords: Internet of Things (IoT) · Wireless protocols · Network design

1 Network Protocols

1.1 Introduction

Internet of Things is a network of connected devices that expands to numerous industries including automotive, manufacturing, healthcare, etc. These smart devices are able to collect, then process and send information to other devices, objects like gateways, and cloud servers [1]. IoT based solutions has specific requirements for network communication like range, power consumption, etc. There are many network protocols which are available in the market for industrial applications, as shown in the Fig. 1 below [2]. The challenge is to find the best network protocol that will work for different IoT applications. This paper will compare different network protocols and provide the best practices for the Industrial Internet of Things (IIoT) development.

1.2 IIoT Connections and Network

IoT architecture is mainly divided into three levels – smart object, gateways and systems. The systems can be application, servers and cloud network. The information flow

D.-J. Deng et al. (Eds.): WiCON 2019, LNICST 317, pp. 163–171, 2020.
https://doi.org/10.1007/978-3-030-52988-8_14

Fig. 1. Industrial Internet of Things wireless protocols [2, 3]

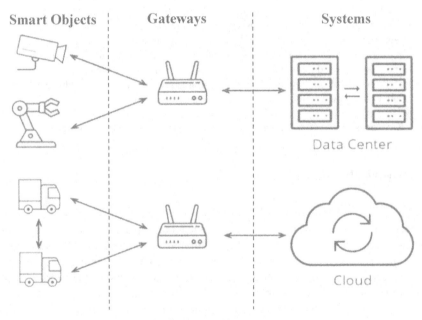

Fig. 2. IIoT architecture [1]

between the levels is categorized based upon four ways of communication: smart object to smart object (O2O), smart object to gateway, gateway to system, and between data systems.

Figure 2 above provides the system architecture for an IoT development in an industrial enterprise.

- **Smart object to smart object (O2O)** – it is a direct transmission of information between two smart objects or devices. Example – communication between sensor and industrial robot
- **Smart object to gateway** – gateways acts as a two way communication, to and from the smart object. Example – gateway will collect sensor data and send it to system which analysis and send the feedback to sensor via gateway
- **Gateway to system** – it is a direct communication between gateway and systems (one or more system). Example – smart tablet communicating back and forth with the cloud system
- **Between systems** – it is the data exchange between data centers like servers placed in-house to cloud systems

Key requirements to select an IIoT protocol depends upon the routing of the data traffic (between gateway and systems) like number of parallel connections needed, security certificate and requirements. Further, the selected IIoT network protocol should integrate with legacy applications, real-time data transmission and recovery, high availability and reliability, and ease to deploy. IIoT network can also be classified in terms of range, for example nano-network, NFC (Near-Field Communication), LAN (Local Area Network), WAN (Wide Area Network), etc. [1]. Furthermore, topology of the network protocols also provides various combinations of node connections like mesh, ring, tree, start, bus, etc.

2 Three-Dimensional Network Design Model

2.1 Introduction

The proposed method of three-dimension network design space which is the extension of the IT model (internet technology) reduces the complexity in selecting the right and the best network protocol for industrial applications. There are so many protocols available in the market and it becomes very hard to select the right one for the application. This model will help the industrial enterprises to easily choose the network protocol for their IIoT development. The model is divided into three axes as shown in the Fig. 3 below. The first dimension on the x-axis is the battery life, the second dimension on the y-axis is the duty cycle or the device data rate, and the third dimension on the z-axis is the device to gateway distance or the range [3, 4].

2.2 Comparison of Network Protocols and Hypothesis

Network protocols compared in this paper were selected based upon their popularity in the industrial environment and their wide application range in the various industries. The selected network protocols are [3]:

- **Bluetooth Low Energy (BLE):** it is very popular in diverse applications ranging from automobiles, fitness, audio, video, heart rate monitor, etc.

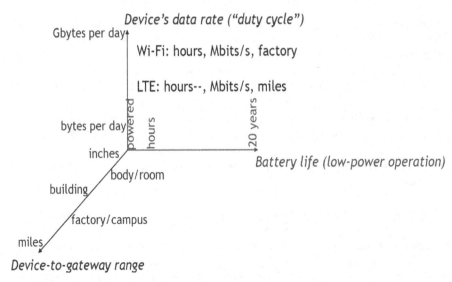

Fig. 3. IIoT network design [5]

- **ZigBee:** based on the IEEE 802.15.4 link layer and operates in 2.4 GHz ISM bank. The network layer is based upon mesh topology [6]. The applications include smart homes, smart building and home automation.
- **6LoWPAN:** acronym for IPv6 over Low Power Wireless Personal Area Networks. A mesh network topology, large area network, reliable communication and low power consumption [7].
- **Wireless HART:** it is based on IEEE 802.15.4 [8]. Designed for industrial applications processes – providing access to diagnostics, configuration and process data [6].
- **Thread:** advantage is that it is low power and low-cost over other protocols. Application includes mobile, device to device communication and smart home.

This paper predicts a hypothesis that – "wireless network protocol will be selected based upon the IIoT application and there will be no one protocol which will work for all the IIoT applications". To prove the hypothesis all the above network protocols will be placed and tested against the three-dimensional network design model.

3 Results

3.1 Three-Dimensional Model and Hypothesis Results

The Fig. 4 below shows the results of the different selected IIoT network protocols comparison. Three sets of common data sets were used and fed to different network protocols to derive the results.

To prove the hypothesis results, the survey was conducted where 117 successful responses were received to the questionnaire. The questions were asked to industry leaders, IIoT engineers, developers and R&D (research and development) specialists. The question and responses are mentioned below in the Fig. 5 and the Fig. 6:

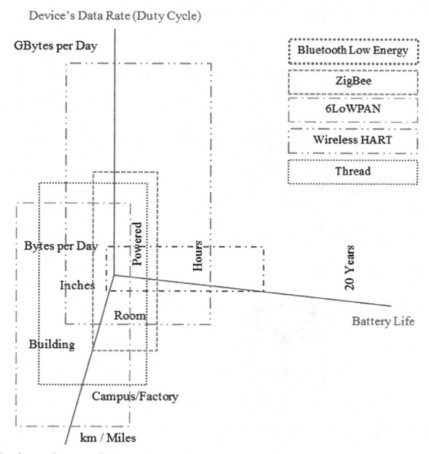

Fig. 4. Comparison results for different network protocols against three-dimensional IIoT network design model

For the hypotheses testing the "Chi-Square Goodness of Fit Test" was used since the sample fulfilled the following basic requirements:

- The sampling method is simple random sampling
- The variable under study is categorical
- The expected value of the number of sample observations in each level of the variable is at least 5.

Parameters used:
Degrees of Freedom (DF):

$$DF = (r - 1) * (c - 1) \tag{1}$$

Do you think one network protocol will fit all the IoT applications?
117 responses

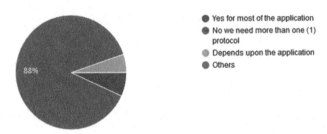

Fig. 5. Does one network protocol works for all IIoT applications

How often you change your network design after starting developing the applications?
117 responses

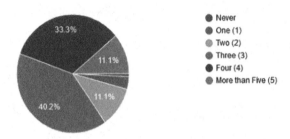

Fig. 6. Changes to the network protocols after start of the IIoT development

Where:
r: Number of levels for one categorical variable
c: The number of levels for other categorical variable

Expected Frequencies:

$$E_{(r, c)} = ((n\_r * n\_c))/n \tag{2}$$

Where:
E_(r,c): Expected frequency count for lever r of Variable A and level c of Variable B
n_r: Total number of sample observations at lever r of Variable A
n_c: Total number of sample observations at lever c of Variable B in the total sample

Test statistic:

$$x^2 = \sum (O_{(r, c)} - E_{(r, c)})^2 / E_{(r, c)} \tag{3}$$

Where:

O_(r,c): Observed frequency count at lever r of Variable A and level c of Variable B

E_(r,c): Expected frequency count at level r of Variable A and level c of Variable B

P-value:

The P-value is the probability of observing a sample statistic as extreme as the test statistic. Since the test statistic is a Chi-square, the paper authors assessed the probability associated with the test statistics using the degrees of freedom [9, 10] (Table 1).

Table 1. Observed values for question 1 and 2

Q9: Do you think one network protocol will fit all the IoT applications?	Q6: How often you change your network design after starting developing the applications?						
Q9 and Q6	Never	One (1)	Two (2)	Three (3)	Four (4)	More than Five (5)	SUM
Yes for most of the application	0	1	1	2	2	2	8
No we need more than one (1) protocol	1	3	11	43	34	11	103
Depends upon the application	0	0	1	2	3	0	6
Total	1	4	13	47	39	13	117

Degree of Freedom from Eq. (1):

$$DF = (6 - 1) * (3 - 1) = 10$$

Expected frequencies from Eq. (2) (Table 2):

Table 2. Expected values for question 1 and 2

Q9: Do you think one network protocol will fit all the IoT applications?	Q6: How often you change your network design after starting developing the applications?						
Q9 and Q6	Never	One (1)	Two (2)	Three (3)	Four (4)	More than Five (5)	SUM
Yes for most of the application	0.07	0.27	0.89	3.21	2.67	0.89	8
No we need more than one (1) protocol	0.88	3.52	11.44	41.38	34.33	11.44	103
Depends upon the application	0.05	0.21	0.67	2.41	2.00	0.67	6
Total	1	4	13	47	39	13	117

Test statistics x^2 from Eq. (3) (Table 3):

The calculated degree of freedom is 10. The calculated testing criteria/Chi-Square value is 5.8805 and p is 0.82 [10, 11].

Table 3. Test values for question 1 and 2

Q9: Do you think one network protocol will fit all the IoT applications?	Q6: How often you change your network design after starting developing the applications						
Q9 and Q6	Never	One (1)	Two (2)	Three (3)	Four (4)	More than Five (5)	SUM
Yes for most of the application	0.0684	1.9298	0.0139	0.4584	0.1667	1.3889	4.0259
No we need more than one (1) protocol	0.0163	0.0772	0.0173	0.0637	0.0032	0.0173	0.1949
Depends upon the application	0.0513	0.2051	0.1667	0.0698	0.5000	0.6667	1.6596
Total	0.1359	2.2121	0.1978	0.5919	0.6699	2.0728	5.8805

Comparing the calculated testing values against the critical value from the table, it is obvious that is calculated testing value is lesser (5.8805 < 18.307).

The used level of significance was 0.05.

Therefore, it is concluded that the hypothesis is accepted; hence proving that no one network protocol will fit all the IIoT applications and the protocol is selected based upon the IIoT application.

4 Conclusions

The three-dimensional IIoT network design model which is the extension of the internet three-axis space model was proposed to find out the best network protocol for IIoT application. The three-dimension included – data rate, battery life, and device to gateway range.

The test results were verified by placing the different network protocols like ZigBee, Bluetooth LE, Wireless HART, 6LowPAN, Thread, etc. against the three-dimensional IIoT network model. Furthermore, the hypothesis was tested by performing questionnaire and surveys and successfully verifying the results and findings to prove that more than one protocol is needed for developing a single IIoT application. The main observations or the best practices that were concluded during the experimentation and the testing of the network protocols are mentioned below:

- The network design for IIoT application is based on the terms of which technology or combinations of technology are the best suited for that particular IIoT application by placing the requirements.
- Take the three-dimensional models and place the preferred technology and see if it fits the requirements of the intended IIoT application.

Acknowledgments. This research was supported and funded by 030STU-4/2018 KEGA project titled "E-platform as basis for improving collaboration among universities and industrial enterprises in the area of education" and with support of 2/0077/19 VEGA project titled "Work competencies in the context of Industry 4.0".

References

1. Sakovich, N.: Internet of Things (IoT) Protocols and Connectivity Options: An Overview. https://www.sam-solutions.com/blog/internet-of-things-iot-protocols-and-connectivity-options-an-overview/
2. Sarma, S.: The Internet of Things: Roadmap to a Connected World, MIT Professional Education, Digital Programs, Massachusetts Institute of Technology (2016)
3. Caganova, D., Bawa, M., Sobrino, D.R.D., Saniuk, A.: Internet of Things and Smart City, University of Zielona Góra, Poland (2017). ISBN 978-83-65200-07-5
4. Korowajczuk, L.: LTE, WiMAX and WLAN Network Design, Optimization and Performance Analysis. Wiley (2011). ISBN-10: 047074149X, ISBN-13: 978-0470741498
5. Balakrishnan, H.: The Internet of Things: Roadmap to a Connected World, MIT Professional Education, Digital Programs, Massachusetts Institute of Technology (2016)
6. Gerber, A.: Connecting all the things in the Internet of Things, Paper Published in the Developer Works Magazine, Issued by IBM (2018). https://developer.ibm.com/articles/iot-lp101-connectivity-network-protocols/
7. Lethaby, N.: Wireless connectivity for the Internet of Things: one size does not fit all, paper published by Texas Instruments, SWRY010A (2018)
8. Zhang, Y., Yang, L.T., Yan, H.N.L.: The Internet of Things: From RFID to the Next-Generation Pervasive Networked Systems. CRC Press (2008). ASIN: B0089A5C42
9. Columbia University (2016). http://ccnmtl.columbia.edu/projects/qmss/the_chisquare_test/about_the_chisquare_test.html
10. Szilva, I.: Increasing efficiency of assembly process through innovative KM tool. Dissertation thesis, Trnava: Slovenská Technická Univerzita v Bratislave MTF (2017)
11. Stanford (2016). http://web.stanford.edu/class/psych252/cheatsheets/chisquare.html

BatTalk: Monitoring Asian Parti-Colored Bats Through the IoT Technology

Yun-Wei Lin[1]([✉]), Cheng-Han Chou[2], Yi-Bing Lin[3], and Wen-Shu Lai[4]

[1] College of Artificial Intelligence and Green Energy, National Chiao Tung University, Tainan, Taiwan
jyneda@nctu.edu.tw

[2] Department of Forestry and Natural Resources, National Chiayi University, Hsinchu, Taiwan
shockchouau@gmail.com

[3] Department of Computer Science, National Chiao Tung University, Hsinchu, Taiwan
liny@nctu.edu.tw

[4] Institute of Applied Arts, National Chiao Tung University, Hsinchu, Taiwan
wendylai@g2.nctu.edu.tw

Abstract. In the past, we studied the activities of Asian parti-colored (APC) bats through visual observation, which is very labor intensive. This paper develops an IoT platform called BatTalk to continuously monitor the APC bats population, understand its compositional changes, life history, and environmental factors. With BatTalk, the above visual observations can be achieved with reduced man power and minimal interference to the bat activities. The most important task is to use BatTalk to automate the process to understand APC bats' regular annual cycle of life history and estimate the percentage of the baby bats born and raised there would return to their original habitat in the coming year. Also, we proposed an inexpensive manner to identify the bat habitats and bat movement paths by identifying the bat's ultrasonic signal strength and GPS position, and then show the information in a map.

Keywords: Internet of Things · IoTtalk · Asian parti-colored bats

1 Introduction

Lewis Carroll's Alice's Adventures in Wonderland has a "Twinkle Twinkle Little Star" parody saying: "Twinkle, twinkle little bat, How I wonder what you're at! Up above the world you fly, Like a tea-tray in the sky". Clearly, bats are lovely animals that deserve better attention and study. This paper describes an Internet of Things (IoT) technology for studying Asian Parti-colored Bats (*Vespertilio sinensis*) that mainly distribute in Northeast Asia. This species was first found in 1880. In 1952, David H. Johnson confirmed that Taiwan is the most southern habitat for Asian parti-colored (APC) bats [1]. Since then, no APC bats had been found for more than half a century, and academia almost identified them as "regional extinctions". In 2006 an APC bat was captured by a Harp trap at Guanwu in Shei-Pa National Park, which excitedly inspired the bat researchers

D.-J. Deng et al. (Eds.): WiCON 2019, LNICST 317, pp. 172–183, 2020.
https://doi.org/10.1007/978-3-030-52988-8_15

of Taiwan [2]. Although APC bat is evaluated as a least-concern species by the International Union for Conservation of Nature (IUCN) in 2018, it is listed as vulnerable or data deficient in Japan [3]. Taiwan ranks APC bat as an endangered species in the country and is of the same class as Formosan Black Bear (*Ursus thibetanus formosanus*) and Leopard Cats (*Prionailurus bengalensis chinensis*). Therefore, observation of APC bat behavior is an important bat research topic in Taiwan.

Cluster of 600–700 APC bats was first found in the Imperial Japanese Navy's Sixth Fuel Factory in Hsinchu (Fig. 1 (1)), a World War II industrial relic. From April to September of a year, a herd of bats perched on the seams in the abandon big chimney (Fig. 1 (2)). Although this cluster of APC bats has only inhabited Hsinchu City for about 5 months, the chimney and surrounding environment are very important for their survival and reproduction of baby bats, which also provides a rare opportunity for the researcher to understand and conserve this particular and rare species from the existential crisis. However, the traditional approach for bat observation requires significant involvement of manual operation. Through the IoT technology, the man power in bat observation can be reduced. This paper develops an IoT platform called BatTalk to support continuous monitoring of the APC bat population, understanding its compositional changes, life history, and environmental factors. The paper is organized as follows. Section 2 provides the background about the APC bats. Section 3 proposes BatTalk and describes the sensors and the actuators for bat observation. Section 4 conducts performance evaluation to investigate how communications delays affect the accuracy of positioning bat locations in BatTalk.

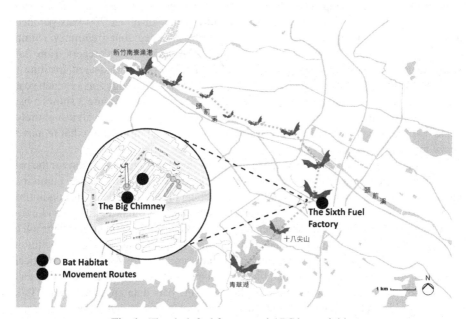

Fig. 1. The sixth fuel factory and APC bat activities

2   An Overview to Asian Parti-Colored Bat in the Big Chimney

Figure 2 shows an APC bat. Its head is about 7 cm long, the tail length is about 5 cm, the forearm is about 5 cm long, the wingspan is about 35 cm long, and the weight is 15 to 25 g. APC bats have dark brown hair on the back, mixed white hair, frosty white at the end, and gray belly. The face is black with prominent mouth kiss, recessed side, dull circle at the end of the ear shell, and edgy ear-ball. APC bats are medium-sized insect-eating bats that have a preference for insects with half-winged and fins.

Fig. 2. Asian parti-colored bat (*Vespertilio sinensis*)

In July 2010, the Hsinchu municipal government planned to develop a cultural park at the former Imperial Japanese Navy's Sixth Fuel Factory and the surrounding village. During the survey, the city officials found a group of about 700 bats perched in the slits of the drainage channel while exploring the abandoned chimney within the fuel factory area, which was later confirmed as APC bats. Researchers from Bat Association of Taiwan (台灣蝙蝠學會) and Endemic Species Research Institute (行政院農業委員會特有生物研究保育中心) have conducted edgy surveys each year including annual population estimation, larvae growth, and so on. Figure 3 shows a bat group in the chimney. The study confirmed that APC bats population is almost entirely made up of pregnant female bats through very tedious visual observation that required heavy manual operation.

To reduce manual operation overhead, the paper develops BatTalk to monitor the bat ecosystem in the chimney of the former fuel factory, including temperature, humidity, ultrasonic and video cameras. The ability to understand in real time the living conditions of APC bats in the big chimney from April to September through the image and non-image signals, BatTalk detects environmental changes caused by climate anomalies in a timely manner, so that the bat habitat can be remedied as quickly as possible. In addition to ecological conservation and education, we have created the APC Bat Ecological Education Space (Fig. 1 (3)) that combines the benefits of ecological conservation and sightseeing. This space will not only display the APC bats data produced by BatTalk in real time, but also allow observing the activity of bats through video streaming. Through participating in the educational activities of science, art and technology held at the education space, the audiences can further understand APC bats. Both BatTalk and the APC Bat Ecological Education Space serve the functions of ecological conservation,

Fig. 3. A bat group in the chimney

research and education. For example, the space interacts with the audience with the bat habitats (Fig. 1 (4)) and the bat movement paths (Fig. 1 (5)).

By effectively avoiding human stoic interaction with APC bats, BatTalk allows people to know bats in a way they see with their own eyes, to observe bats' activities inside the big chimney through the streaming video images shown on the screen. The adoption of BatTalk monitoring is also expected to create a sustainable and automatic operation of ecological model and further applications.

3   The BatTalk Architecture

BatTalk is a platform derived from an IoT device management system called IoTtalk [4]. In BatTalk, a sensor or a control switch is called an input device feature (IDF), and an actuator such as the heater is called an output device feature (ODF). An IDF sends sensor/control data to the BatTalk server (Fig. 4 (1)). An ODF receives the instruction data from the BatTalk server. The input (output) device features that share the same communications hardware are grouped as an input (output) device. In the big chimney scenario, we install an input device called micro weather station, which consists of the sensors (Fig. 4 (2)–(6)) for barometric pressure (BARP), temperature (TEMP), relative humidity (RH), luminance (LUM), CO2 and ultra-violet (UV). The physical appearance of the micro weather station is illustrated in Fig. 5. These sensors are connected to the input pins of a control board (Fig. 4 (7)) that can be based on Arduino, ESP8266 ESP-12F, and so on [5]. The physical appearance of the control board is illustrated in Fig. 4(b) and (c).

To create a comfortable living environment for the APC bats, we may install actuators including the heater, the fan and the dehumidifier (Fig. 4 (8)–(10)) in the big chimney. These actuators are grouped as an output device "actuators", which are connected to the output pins of the control board. The control board communicates with the BatTalk server through Ethernet (ADSL) or Wi-Fi connections.

We have installed multiple cameras in the chimney (Fig. 4 (11)), which allow the viewers (i.e., the bat researchers and the general audiences) to observe the bats (Fig. 4 (12)) without interfering their activities. The cameras are connected to a streaming server

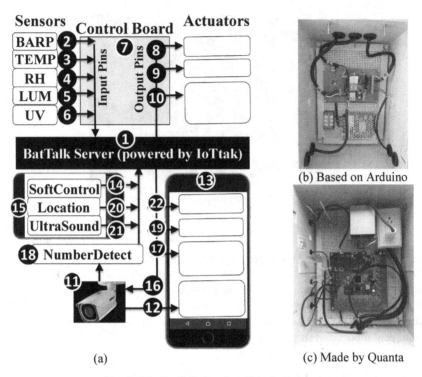

(a)

(b) Based on Arduino

(c) Made by Quanta

Fig. 4. The BatTalk functional block diagram

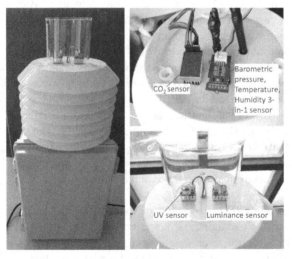

Fig. 5. Micro weather station

through Ethernet. By accessing the streaming server the viewer can use the browser of any smartphone (Fig. 4 (13)) to watch the bat activities in real time. Specifically, the viewer can press the soft control switches (Fig. 4 (14)) of a smartphone (Fig. 4 (15)) to control the cameras (Fig. 4 (16)) as well as other actuators. All sensor data (Fig. 4 (2)–(6)) are sent to the BatTalk server, and the server will show them in the dashboard (Fig. 4 (17)). Note that Fig. 4 (13) is a smartphone that represents an output device and Fig. 4 (15) is another smartphone representing an input device. In reality, both Fig. 4 (13) and (15) can be the web-based BatTalk browser in the same smartphone as illustrated in Fig. 6, which communicates with the BatTalk server through 4G or NB-IoT [6].

Fig. 6. The BatTalk browser

The BatTalk web-based window is partitioned into four areas: the video (Fig. 6 (1)) for Fig. 4 (12)), the camera control (Fig. 6 (2) for Fig. 4 (14)), the actuator control (Fig. 6 (3) for Fig. 4 (14)) and the dashboard (Fig. 6 (4) for Fig. 4 (17)). The videos produced from the cameras can be analyzed to, for example, count the number of bats in the chimney using AI techniques. Then through the "NumberDetect" IDF (Fig. 4 (18)), the number of bats is sent to the BatTalk server. If the change of the bat number is larger than a threshold, the server will send an alert to inform the viewer (Fig. 4 (19)).

The video together with the non-image sensors are used to automatically observe various bat activities. In the past, we conducted 2-days visual observation every month to detect when the first bat leaved the chimney, when the first 50% of the bats leaved the chimney, and when all bats leaved, and see how temperature, humidity, barometric pressure and illumination affect bat behavior. BatTalk automates that the above task. For example, through the TEMP and NumberDetect IDFs, Fig. 7 shows that when temperature decreases from 28 °C to 25 °C, the bat group tends to be more crowed and the bat number is reduced. Most bats fly outside the chimney individually before the sky turns completely dark. Such activity and the exact timing can also be automatically observed by the NumberDetect IDF.

The ultrasonic sensor (Fig. 4 (20)) is used to detect and record bats' foraging audio in Hsinchu urban areas. By identifying the ultrasonic signal strength and its GPS position (Fig. 4 (21)), we can identify the bat habitats (Fig. 1 (4)) and bat movement paths (Fig. 1 (5)), and then show the information in a map (Fig. 4 (22)) [7]. In [8], the ultrasonic sensor and the GPS device can be separated and independently send signals to the BatTalk server. The server then pairs both signals to identify the locations of the ultrasonic signal sources. Since the delays of sending ultrasonic signal and the GPS signal may be

25°C   28°C

Fig. 7. Potential effect of temperature

different, the "ultrasonic-GPS" pairing may not be accurate. To resolve this issue, we have developed the MorSensor Chip solution [9], where the ultrasonic sensor (Fig. 8 (1)) can be plugged in a smartphone. The ultrasonic data will be automatically shown in the screen of the smartphone (Fig. 8 (2)). Furthermore, the smartphone will continuously send the ultrasonic signal together with the GPS signal to the BatTalk server. In this way, the "ultrasonic-GPS" pairing is guaranteed to be accurate.

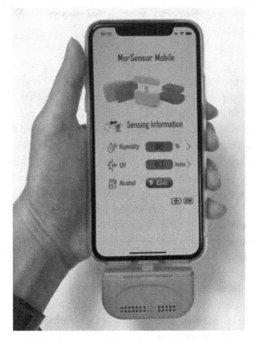

Fig. 8. MoSensor chip solution for bat detection

4   Location Accuracy of Bat Tracking

Although MorSensor chip solution perfectly synchronizes the ultrasonic and the GPS signals, we may still use inexpensive stand-alone ultrasonic sensor together with a nearby locator (e.g., a smartphone with GPS) to provide GPS information through the IoTtalk location tracking technique developed in [8]. In this approach, several bat observers (either pedestrians or cars) are equipped with inexpensive ultrasonic sensors. When the ultrasonic sensors move around, the ultrasonic signals and the GPS signals of the locators are periodically and independently sent from the smartphones of the observers to the BatTalk server. In the current implementation, the signals are sent from the smartphones to the server through the 4G communication technology.

Since the 4G delays are not fixed delays, the ultrasonic signal and the GPS signal measured at the same time (at the sensors) may arrive at the BatTalk server at different times such that the BatTalk server will pair the ultrasonic signal with the wrong GPS coordinates. Suppose that the ultrasonic and the GPS signals are sent out by the smartphone at time τ. The ultrasonic signal arrives at the BatTalk server at time $\tau + t_0$, and the GPS signal arrives at the sever at time $\tau + t_1$ where t_0 and t_1 are 4G communication delays. In [10] we have obtained the histograms for $t_0(t_1)$ through 1000 measurements for each of the ADSL (Ethernet used for communication between the control board (Fig. 4 (7)) and the BatTalk server (Fig. 4 (4)) and the 4G transmission scenarios, which are illustrated in Fig. 9. The ADSL delays are the message delays for the fixed sensors and the actuators installed in the big chimney. The 4G delays are $t_0(t_1)$ for the mobile ultrasonic and GPS signals.

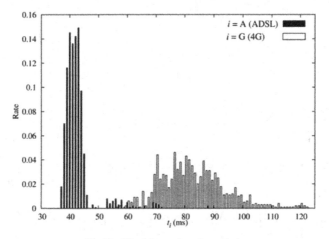

Fig. 9. The histograms for $t_0(t_1)$

From the measured data illustrated in Fig. 9, we computed the expected value $E[t_0] = 42.638$ ms and the variance $V[t_0] = 0.018\ E[t_0]^2$ for ADSL transmission, and $E[t_0] = 85.958$ ms and $V[t_0] = 0.057\ E[t_0]^2$ for 4G transmission. It is clearly that the delays for 4G are about twice of that for ADSL. Also, the variance for 4G is higher than ADLS, which means that wireless communications is not as stable as wired communications. Therefore $t_2 = |t_1 - t_0|$ may be large. If the observer (particularly in car) moves for a long distance during t_2, then the ultrasonic signal may be paired with a GPS location very different from its actual location. For example, if the car moves at 30 km/h, then it moves 8.3 m in $t_2 = 1$ s. If t_2 is less than 1 s, then the moving distance is within the

GPS measurement error. Therefore, in the remainder of this section, we assume that the threshold time $t_3 = 1$ s, and we see if $t_2 < t_3$ so that ultrasonic signal positioning will not cause inaccuracy. Specifically, we derive the probability $\Pr[t_3 < t_2]$ and see if it is sufficiently large.

From the 4G delay histogram illustrated in Fig. 9, $t_0(t_1)$ can be approximated by an Erlang density function $f_1()$ with the shape parameter n and the scale parameter λ.

$$f_1(t) = \frac{\lambda^n t^{n-1} e^{-\lambda t}}{(n-1)!} \tag{1}$$

where

$$n = 17 \text{ and } \lambda = 0.198 \tag{2}$$

The approximation is validated by the Kolmogorov-Smirnov test for goodness of fit [10]. From the above analysis, it is reasonable to let t_0 and t_1 be two random variables with the same Erlang density function. Then From Eq. (1), the density function $f_2(t_2)$ is expressed as

$$f_2(t_2) = 2\int_{t_0=0}^{\infty} f_1(t_0)f_1(t_0+t_2)dt_0$$

$$= 2\int_{t_0=0}^{\infty} \left[\frac{\lambda^n t_0^{n-1} e^{-\lambda t_0}}{(n-1)!}\right]\left[\frac{\lambda^n (t_0+t_2)^{n-1} e^{-\lambda(t_0+t_2)}}{(n-1)!}\right]dt_0$$

$$= 2\left[\frac{\lambda^{2n} e^{-\lambda t_2}}{(n-1)!\,(n-1)!}\right]\int_{t_0=0}^{\infty} t_0^{n-1}(t_0+t_2)^{n-1} e^{-2\lambda t_0}dt_0$$

$$= \left[\frac{2\lambda^{2n} e^{-\lambda t_2}}{(n-1)!\,(n-1)!}\right]\int_{t_0=0}^{\infty} \sum_{i=0}^{n-1}\binom{n-1}{i}\left(t_0^i t_2^{n-i-1}\right)t_0^{n-1} e^{-2\lambda t_0}dt_0$$

$$= \left[\frac{2\lambda^{2n} e^{-\lambda t_2}}{(n-1)!\,(n-1)!}\right]\sum_{i=0}^{n-1}\binom{n-1}{i}t_2^{n-i-1}\left[\int_{t_0=0}^{\infty} t_0^{n+i-1} e^{-2\lambda t_0}dt_0\right]$$

$$= \left[\frac{2\lambda^{2n} e^{-\lambda t_2}}{(n-1)!(n-1)!}\right]\sum_{i=0}^{n-1}\binom{n-1}{i}t_2^{n-i-1}\left[\frac{(n+i-1)!}{(2\lambda)^{n+i}}\int_{t_0=0}^{\infty}\left[\frac{(2\lambda)^{n+i}t_0^{n+i-1}}{(n+i-1)!}\right]e^{-2\lambda t_0}dt_0\right]$$

$$= \left[\frac{2\lambda^{2n} e^{-\lambda t_2}}{(n-1)!\,(n-1)!}\right]\sum_{i=0}^{n-1}\binom{n-1}{i}t_2^{n-i-1}\left[\frac{(n+i-1)!}{(2\lambda)^{n+i}}\right]$$

$$= \left[\frac{2\lambda^{2n} e^{-\lambda t_2}}{(n-1)!\,(n-1)!}\right]\sum_{i=0}^{n-1}\left[\frac{(n-1)!}{i!(n-i-1)!}\right]t_2^{n-i-1}\left[\frac{(n+i-1)!}{(2\lambda)^{n+i}}\right]$$

$$= \sum_{i=0}^{n-1}\binom{n+i-1}{i}\left(\frac{1}{2^{n+i-1}}\right)\left[\frac{\lambda^{n-i}t_2^{n-i-1}}{(n-i-1)!}\right]e^{-\lambda t_2} \tag{3}$$

Let t_3 be the period that the observer moves for the threshold distance, which is a random variable with the density function $f_3(t_3)$. Then the bat tracking may not be accurate if $t_3 < t_2$. From Eq. (3), the probability $\Pr[t_3 < t_2]$ is expressed as

$$\Pr[t_3 < t_2] = \int_{t_3}^{\infty} \int_{t_2=t_3}^{\infty} f_3(t_3) f_2(t_2) dt_2 \, dt_3$$

$$= \int_{t_3=0}^{\infty} f_3(t_3) \int_{t_2=t_3}^{\infty} \sum_{i=0}^{n-1} \binom{n+i-1}{i} \left(\frac{1}{2^{n+i-1}}\right) \left[\frac{\lambda^{n-i} t_2^{n-i-1}}{(n-i-1)!}\right] e^{-\lambda t_2} dt_2 \, dt_3$$

$$= \sum_{i=0}^{n-1} \binom{n+i-1}{i} \left(\frac{1}{2^{n+i-1}}\right) \int_{t_3=0}^{\infty} f_3(t_3) \left\{\int_{t_2=t_3}^{\infty} \left[\frac{\lambda^{n-i} t_2^{n-i-1}}{(n-i-1)!}\right] e^{-\lambda t_2} dt_2\right\} dt_3$$

$$= \sum_{i=0}^{n-1} \binom{n+i-1}{i} \left(\frac{1}{2^{n+i-1}}\right) \int_{t_3=0}^{\infty} f_3(t_3) \left\{\sum_{j=0}^{n-i-1} \left[\frac{\lambda^j t_3^j}{j!}\right] e^{-\lambda t_3}\right\} dt_3$$

$$= \sum_{i=0}^{n-1} \binom{n+i-1}{i} \left(\frac{1}{2^{n+i-1}}\right) \left\{\sum_{j=0}^{n-i-1} \int_{t_3=0}^{\infty} f_3(t_3) \left[\frac{\lambda^j t_3^j}{j!}\right] e^{-\lambda t_3} dt_3\right\}$$

$$= \sum_{i=0}^{n-1} \binom{n+i-1}{i} \left(\frac{1}{2^{n+i-1}}\right) \left[\sum_{j=0}^{n-i-1} \left(\frac{\lambda^j}{j!}\right) \int_{t_3}^{\infty} t_3^j f_3(t_3) e^{-\lambda t_3} dt_3\right] \qquad (4)$$

Let $f_3^*(s)$ be the Laplace transform for $f_3(t_3)$. From the frequency-domain general derivative of Laplace transform, we have

$$\int_{t=0}^{\infty} t^j f(t) e^{-st} dt = (-1)^j \left[\frac{f^{*(j)}(s)}{ds^j}\right]$$

and Eq. (4) is written as

$$\Pr[t_3 < t_2] = \sum_{i=0}^{n-1} \binom{n+i-1}{i} \left(\frac{1}{2^{n+i-1}}\right) \left\{\sum_{j=0}^{n-i-1} \left(\frac{\lambda^j}{j!}\right) \left\{(-1)^j \left[\frac{f_3^{*(j)}(s)}{ds^j}\right]\Bigg|_{s=\lambda}\right]\right\}\right\}$$

$$= \sum_{i=0}^{n-1} \binom{n+i-1}{i} \left(\frac{1}{2^{n+i-1}}\right) \left\{\sum_{j=0}^{n-i-1} \left[\frac{(-\lambda)^j}{j!}\right] \left[\frac{f_3^{*(j)}(s)}{ds^j}\right]\Bigg|_{s=\lambda}\right\} \qquad (5)$$

Assume that t_3 is exponentially distributed with the mean $1/\beta = 1$ s, then the Laplace transform $f_3^*(s)$ is expressed as

$$f_3^*(s) = \frac{\beta}{s+\beta}$$

and Eq. (5) is re-written as

$$\Pr[t_3 < t_2] = \sum_{i=0}^{n-1} \binom{n+i-1}{i} \left(\frac{\beta}{2^{n+i-1}}\right) \sum_{j=0}^{n-i-1} \left[\frac{\lambda^j}{(\lambda+\beta)^{j+1}}\right]$$

$$= \sum_{i=0}^{n-1} \binom{n+i-1}{i} \left[\frac{\beta}{2^{n+i-1}(\lambda+\beta)} \right] \sum_{j=0}^{n-i-1} \left(\frac{\lambda}{\lambda+\beta} \right)^j$$

$$= \sum_{i=0}^{n-1} \binom{n+i-1}{i} \left[\frac{\beta}{2^{n+i-1}(\lambda+\beta)} \right] \left[\frac{1 - \left(\frac{\lambda}{\lambda+\beta} \right)^{n-i}}{1 - \frac{\lambda}{\lambda+\beta}} \right]$$

$$= \sum_{i=0}^{n-1} \binom{n+i-1}{i} \left(\frac{1}{2^{n+i-1}} \right) \left[1 - \left(\frac{\lambda}{\lambda+\beta} \right)^{n-i} \right]$$

$$= \sum_{i=0}^{n-1} \binom{n+i-1}{i} \left(\frac{1}{2^{n+i-1}} \right) - \sum_{i=0}^{n-1} \binom{n+i-1}{i} \left(\frac{1}{2^{n+i-1}} \right) \left(\frac{\lambda}{\lambda+\beta} \right)^{n-i} \quad (6)$$

Since

$$\sum_{i=0}^{n-1} \binom{n+i-1}{i} \left(\frac{1}{2^{n+i-1}} \right) = 1$$

Equation (6) is simplified as

$$\Pr[t_3 < t_2] = 1 - 2 \left[\frac{\lambda}{2(\lambda+\beta)} \right]^n \sum_{i=0}^{n-1} \binom{n+i-1}{i} \left(\frac{\lambda+\beta}{2\lambda} \right)^i \quad (7)$$

If $n = 1$, Eq. (7) is re-written as

$$\Pr[t_3 < t_2] = \frac{\beta}{\lambda+\beta} \quad (8)$$

We have validated both Eqs. (7) and (8) by simulation, and the discrepancies are within 1%. Therefore, the analytic analysis is consistent with the simulation. The simulation model follows the same approach used in [4–6], and the details are omitted.

5 Conclusion

In the past, we studied the activities of Asian parti-colored (APC) bats through visual observation, which is very labor intensive. This paper described how the IoT platform BatTalk allows automatic APC bat observation without interfering their activities.

The most important task is to use BatTalk to automate the process to understand APC bats' regular annual cycle of life history: every year in late March or early April, sporadic individual APC bats fly to Hsinchu City habitat. The number of gathering gradually increased, and stabilized in May. Most individual female bats are pregnant in late May. Reproductive seedling continued into late June, and July has the largest population of the year (1330 in 2016 was the highest estimate to date). After August, when temperature began to drop significantly, the bats moved out. They flew out of

Hsinchu City completely in October. With BatTalk, the above visual observations can be achieved with reduced man power and minimal interference to the bat activities.

In the future, we would like to attach small location sensors to the bats so that BatTalk can exactly track the bat movement. Our observation in the chimney indicates that a female bat can produce two cubs per birth, but young bats in the growth stage will suffer a variety of survival tests, and may not grow up. Therefore, only a few new born bats successfully flew away in the winter. Through BatTalk, the marking study can be automated to estimate the percentage of the baby bats born and raised there would return to their original habitat in the coming year. These bats hibernate in the caves of the mountains in winter, and fly back to the warm Hsinchu city to breed and raise their children in the spring.

Through multiple-year monitoring, we suspect that female bats have experienced a variety of survival hardships, including man-made interference, rapid changes in the landscape, potential predators, and changes in the climate (temperature and humidity) conditions inside and outside the main habitat, resulting in a sharp decline in the number of ethnic groups from the tens of thousands in the 1950s to more than a thousand in recent years. Through BatTalk, it was the first time to install the micro weather station in the big chimney, and the bat observer can accurately detect the climate change in the chimney.

We sincerely hope that APC bats will continue to return to the reproductive habitat of Hsinchu City, eat a happy meal of insects every night, and successfully complete the reproductive and offspring-rearing events, increase the number of ethnic groups and survive in Taiwan. At the same time, we should also think about, though BatTalk what can we do more for them?

References

1. TaiBIF. Vespertilio sinensis Peters (1880). 霜毛蝠《臺灣生物多樣性資訊網-TaiBIF》. http://taibif.tw/zh/namecode/380578
2. Cheng, H.-C.: (2018). 煙囪裡的夜行客 — 霜毛蝠. Sci. Am. (2018). http://sa.ylib.com/MagArticle.aspx?Unit=columns&id=4172&fbclid=IwAR1G6Shy4BOBOQXp-P8ytbMVJcXVXDhTMku662o-edMXOJnO5G_Bve1ClL4
3. Stubbe, M., et al.: Vespertilio sinensis. The IUCN Red List of Threatened Species, IUCN 2008 (2008)
4. Lin, Y.-B., Lin, Y.-W., Huang, C.-M., Chih, C.-Y., Lin, P.: IoTtalk: a management platform for reconfigurable sensor devices. IEEE Internet Things J. 4(5), 1152–1562 (2017)
5. Lin, Y.-W., Lin, Y.-B., Yang, M.-T., Lin, J.-H.: ArduTalk: An Arduino network application development platform based on IoTtalk. IEEE Syst. J. 13(1), 468–476 (2019)
6. Lin, Y.-B., Tseng, H.-C., Lin, Y.-W., Chen, L.-J.: NB-IoTtalk: a service platform for fast development of NB-IoT applications. IEEE Internet Things J. 6(1), 928–939 (2019)
7. Lin, Y.-B., Shieh, M.-Z., Lin, Y.-W., Chen, H.-Y.: MapTalk: mosaicking physical objects into the cyber world. Cyber-Phys. Syst. 4(3), 156–174 (2018)
8. Lin, Y.-B., Lin, Y.-W., Hsiao, C.-Y., Wang, S.-Y.: Location-based IoT applications on campus: the IoTtalk approach. Pervasive Mob. Comput. 40, 660–673 (2017)
9. Lin, Y.-B., Huang, C.-Mi., Chen, L.-K., Sung, G.-N., Yang, C.-C.: MorSocket: an expandable IoT-based smart socket system. IEEE Access 6, 53123–53132 (2018)
10. Chen, W.-L., et al.: AgriTalk: IoT for precision soil farming of turmeric cultivation. IEEE Internet Things J. 6(3), 5209–5223 (2019)

Using Multi-channel Transmission Technology to Construct an IoT Mechanism for Homecare Service

Lun-Ping Hung[1]([✉]), Shih-Chieh Li[1], Kuan-Yang Chen[2], and Chien-Liang Chen[3]

[1] Department of Information Management, National Taipei University of Nursing and Health Sciences, Taipei, Taiwan, R.O.C.
lunping@ntunhs.edu.tw

[2] Department of Leisure Industry and Health Promotion, National Taipei University of Nursing and Health Sciences, Taipei, Taiwan, R.O.C.

[3] Department of Innovative Living Design, Overseas Chinese University, Taichung, Taiwan, R.O.C.

Abstract. Owing to the issue of silver tsunami, the number of widow and widower arises day by day. Patient's families couldn't accompany elders due to the job. Thus, the elders' self-care ability becomes an ordeal in daily lives. Even if the advanced medical tech allows elders to have a perfect medical service or to enhance his/her self-care ability, the medical institution is still facing the heavy-burden predicament because of the short of medical manpower and the restriction of medical resource while most caring services are concentrated in hospital or institution, and fail to decentralize them to various home environments. Whereas the target of "Aging in place" sets in the Long-term Care 2.0, we extend the professional care to individual resident through Long-term Care A, B, and C, and to relieve the pressure of Chinese-type treatment and the hardship of long journey. Nevertheless, the popularizing performance is confined due to lack of self-care environment and professional integrating care platform for elders.

We intend to use the module of medical internet to conduct clinical field simulation and deployment, through multiple transit technique and fog-computing environment to produce an appropriate aging-care module. It is livable for patients' health, and can save the unnecessarily medical resource and the manpower cost expenditure. Such a module can be extended to broaden the range of medical service, introduction of smart high-tech, create a livable environment for elders' healthcare and life.

Keywords: Home care · Internet of Things · Low power wide area network · Edge computing · Long-term care

1 Introduction

According to the population projections released by the National Development Council in R.O.C. (Taiwan) in August 2016 [1], the percentage of the population aged 65 and

D.-J. Deng et al. (Eds.): WiCON 2019, LNICST 317, pp. 184–190, 2020.
https://doi.org/10.1007/978-3-030-52988-8_16

over will reach 20.6% of total population in 2026, which means there will be one in every five people at 65 years of age or older, and a huge social cost to caring for the elderly by the young adult. In view of the impacts to the family and society, the government of the ROC promotes community and home-based care policies, and expands the scope of medical services gradually [2]. The main goal is to address the problem of excessive concentration of medical resources and to serve more people who need medical care.

The specific aim of this study is to achieve information technology-supported life. It will be introduced into home medical services, and as described above, with IoT as the main axis, edge and fog computing technologies will be developed via the LPWAN characteristics of NBIoT, through the intelligent communications switching network, data processing and care supporting behaviors will be managed according to the priority of urgency. Three major aspects, i.e., emergency rescue, protection via data tracking, and general daily care, in the home care environment for the elderly will be established to improve the home care quality, as well as to implement the government's long-term care policy.

2   Literature Review

2.1   Home Care

The global elderly population continues to grow at an unprecedented rate [3]. The elders over the age of 60 are estimated to have a population number of 2 billion in the world by 2050. The demand for health care and the cost of long-term care for the elders are relatively high. For the government, finding alternative care strategies to meet the specific needs of the elders and their families is also a challenge. However, home care services can help the elders get the care they need in their homes, encourage the elders to live as independently as possible at home [4], and reduce the pressure of the elders' family members.

2.2   Smart Home

In recent years, the rapid development of IoT technology has made most of the practical applications attempt to introduce such a communication environment. The users can control a variety of home appliances such as air conditioners, electric lights, dehumidi-fiers, etc., from outside their house through the IoT technology. Asif Iqbal et al. proposed an interoperable IoT platform for a smart home system using web-of-objects and cloud infrastructure [5]. Raspberry PI based gateway was provided for interoperability among various home appliances, different communication technologies and protocols, as well transmits the data to the cloud server for analysis [5].

2.3   Edge Computing and Fog Computing

With the rapid growth of IoT services, the data generated by sensors also grow rapidly and complicated. With the help of edge and fog computing for dispersed operation, the proximity of edge modes allows the responding to urgent needs, and only the filtered data will be sent to the cloud for complex analysis or permanent storage, so as to reduce data transmission, power consumption, network bandwidth and to minimize the delay [6, 7]. With the advantage of edge and fog computing, a technical architecture with promptly reply for faster and more convenient notification can be created to meet the requirement of latency-sensitive healthcare applications.

In summary, the development of the health care industry is facing the problem of insufficient medical human resources, therefore, the main goal is to develop a home technology and assistive technology, aimed at close integration with the back-end platform. Through remote data access and monitor by the medical-grade platform, telemedicine can minimize the transport inconvenience and medical expenses of the patients, lower the burden on medical units, and eventually improve the overall home care effectiveness and quality.

3   Research Method and Analysis

In this study, an integrated medical-grade home care service system with the characteristics of life-saving, protection, and general healthcare was proposed based on the IoT architectures of perception, network and application layers. As illustrated in Fig. 1, the system include emergency home life-saving module, data tracking home protection module, life-assisted home health module, multi-channel gateway (edge computing) entity development and medical-grade health cloud platform (fog and cloud computing).

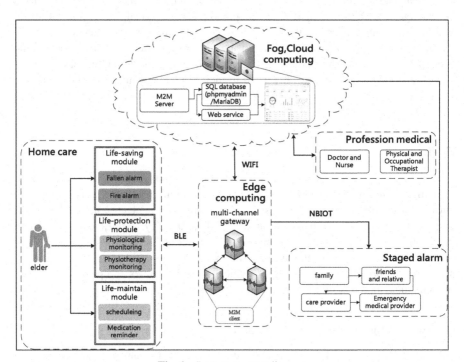

Fig. 1. System context diagram

3.1 Multi-channel Gateway Entity Development

Here we developed a smart multi-channel gateway, which is collected physiological data of various low-power peripheral devices through BLE and connected to the Internet mainly by SIM7020 communication chip and Wifi-based wireless transmission channel. NBIoT is mainly used as the wireless communication channel for the most emergency (level 3) alarm mechanism, and Wifi is used for the secondary emergency and non-emergency events (level 2, level 1), respectively. The fixed licensed band property of NBIoT enables direct communication with the cell cite, and speed-up of the event notification efficiently, as well as the prevention of Wifi disconnection.

Here we use NBIoT transmission technology as the communication channel for staged alarms, mainly relies on the intelligent switch of communication mode according to different level of emergency, i.e., life-saving (most urgent), protection (secondary urgent), and general care (non-urgent), to ensure no omission of message to be conveyed. Figure 2 illustrates the process of staged alarm notification. Based on different home care modules, the level is judges and appropriate alarm mode is selected. Among them, the bold line box represents the most urgent events (level 3) for the immediate notification to the emergency center at fire or fall accidents; the doubled line box represents the secondary urgent events (level 2) for physiological data detection as well as data monitoring according to the needs of medical staff; and the dashed line represents the non-urgent events (level 1) for schedule and medication reminding. The staged alarm system accelerates the notification, enables the automatic alarm of accidents when the elderly is at home alone, and to ensure the safety of the seniors living alone. Steps of internal programing of the alarm process will be described in the following sections.

3.2 Staged Alarm Notification Mechanism

The staged alarm notification is to notify the specific person according to the extent of the emergency. To decentralize and disperse the data processing by cloud computing efficiently, we introduce the combination of edge and fog computing. Based on the proximity characteristics of these two computing, data can be processed in the first time for quick response to urgent events and to eliminate the delay resulted from data transmission to the cloud. Therefore, a staged event notification mechanism is proposed, as shown in algorithm 1, to accelerate the notification via automatic trigger of the wearable IoT devices when there is an accident at home. In the Algorithm 1, entering the signals of the modules of life-saving, protection, and general health care deployed for elderly home care, then the alarm notification module will release different levels of notifications based on the alarm settings inside the module. In case of the emergency situation (level 3) announced by the alarm notification module, it will be notified to the medical emergency units; in case of the secondary emergency situation (level 2), it will be notified to the case managers or their family members; in case of the non-emergency situation (level 1), the alarm notification system will release the notifications repeatedly. Finally, confirm the event exclusion status and the event exclusion status will be interpreted to perform a higher level of notification module, which are to ensure whether the completion status of the alarm notifications has been completely transmitted to the distant terminals of the family members and professional medical staffs.

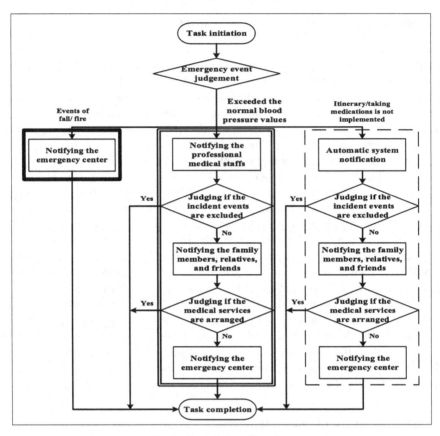

Fig. 2. Staged alarm flowchart

In summary of the above mentioned three aspects and integrated multi-channel transmission technology in assisting the elders' home health care module, the main purpose of this study is to extend the scope of current medical services. We aim to promote the development of information technology for a comprehensive home care by applying the existing professional services based on the long-term care, and to complete the integration of front-end and back-end architectures to achieve the goal of improving reablement efficiency for the elders.

Algorithm 1 Event Alarm Mechanism

```
Input: HCD
Output: The most suitable alarm process
Level ← GetAlarmMode(HCD);
NotificationConfirm =false;
While true do
  If Level==Garde_1 Then
    send message to peripheral ;
  Else If Level==Garde _2 Then
    send message to care provider/family;
  Else If Level== Garde _3 Then
    send messageto emergency;
  End
  If Rule Out Then
    NotificationConfirm =ture;
    Break;
  Else
    Level ← Level +1;
    Notification again(loop)
  End
End
```

---

4 Example and Discussion

Figure 3 is a visualized chart showing the measurement data of the back-end health cloud platform. The left column shows the elders' personal data and the total numbers in terms of their physiological measurements out of normal ranges. The right column shows the average data of the elders' daily measurement data. According to the definitions of hypertension threshold defined by the WHO, an abnormal value exceeding the normal range is defined if the systolic blood pressure exceeds 140/mmHg or the diastolic blood pressure exceeds 90/mmHg. The SBP and DBP in the Fig. 3 have exceeded the threshold, so the grade2 alerting procedure for Algorithm 1 will be triggered, it will be notified at the same time. It may help professional medical practitioners to quickly analyze and judge the influence on the elders with special risk factors or the appropriateness of individual prescriptions. However, this study has not been added the functions of artificial intelligence and machine learning function. In the future, the technology of big data analysis can be combined with this platform. Through the prediction and judgment of artificial intelligence on the data, we can remind the elders to have a follow-up health check in order to prevent the disease from getting worse. This system has the quasi-medical level of intelligent judgment, which may save the medical and labor costs, and thus disperse the load of centralized medical care.

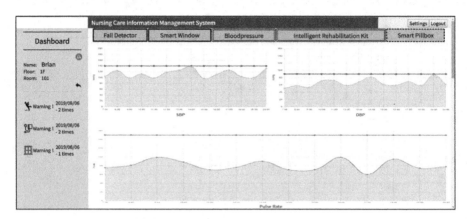

Fig. 3. Dashboard of physiological data

5 Conclusion

The staged alarm notification module proposed in this study can effectively help the elders to improve their home security through the module's intelligent notification or alarm function when they are alone in the house. Our system can store the long-term records of the elders' health status and information, thereby economizing the medical resources and labor costs. With the introduction of IoT technology, when the elders' data are abnormal, the logistics medical personnel can be quickly notified, and the physical therapists and nursing staffs can be effectively assisted to track the health status of the elders, analyze the physiological parameters and treatment conditions, so as to improve the quality of home care, as well as the home care service model can be expanded gradually.

References

1. National Development Council (R.O.C): Population Projections (105–150 year) (2016). https://www.ndc.gov.tw/Content_List.aspx?n=84223C65B6F94D72
2. Ministry of Health and Welfare (R.O.C): Long-Term Care Projection 2.0 (106–115 year). https://1966.gov.tw/LTC/cp-4001-42414-201.html
3. Organization, W.H.: US National Institute of Aging. Global health and aging. National Institutes of Health, Bethesda (2011)
4. Tomita, N., Yoshimura, K., Ikegami, N.: Impact of home and community-based services on hospitalisation and institutionalisation among individuals eligible for long-term care insurance in Japan. BMC Health Services Research, vol. 10, p. 345 (2010)
5. Iqbal, A., et al.: Interoperable internet-of-things platform for smart home system using web-of-objects and cloud. Sustain. Cities Soc. **38**, 636–646 (2018)
6. Aazam, M., Huh, E.: Fog computing: the cloud-IoTVIoE middleware paradigm. IEEE Potentials **35**(3), 40–44 (2016)
7. Kumari, A., et al.: Fog computing for healthcare 4.0 environment: opportunities and challenges. Comput. Electr. Eng. **72**, 1–13 (2018)

The Application of Internet to Evaluation of Land Expropriation

Huan-Siang Luo[1]([✉]) and Yee-Chaur Lee[2]

[1] Department of Civil Engineering, College of Architecture and Design, Chung Hua University, 707, Sec.2, WuFu Rd., Hsinchu 30012, Taiwan
j2006ms660822@yahoo.com.tw
[2] Department of Landscape Architecture, College of Architecture and Design, Chung Hua University, 707, Sec.2, WuFu Rd., Hsinchu 30012, Taiwan
joeychuc@yahoo.com.tw

Abstract. The evaluation mechanism of land expropriation policy has contributed a lot for land acquisition in Taiwan. The purpose of this study is to investigate the result of Internet application to evaluation of land expropriation by means of evaluating land expropriation policy, interviewing professional experts, employing Analytical hierarchy process (AHP), ranking of different factor weight, and prioritizing various factors and dimensions in order to provide relevant information and reference for further development.

Keywords: Land expropriation · Internet · Hierarchy analysis

1 Introduction

The purpose of this study is to investigate the result of Internet application to evaluate land expropriation policies and regulations by means of evaluating land expropriation policy, interviewing professional experts, employing analysis of hierarchy and prioritizing various factors and dimensions in order to provide relevant information and reference for further development. Analytical hierarchy process (AHP) is used to determine the weight of the different identified Internet factors. The Internet application Index, including four dimensions, is developed using weight of various factors and condition rating of various factors.

2 Literature Reviews

According to land expropriation policies and regulations in Taiwan, land can only be acquired on the condition of proper use, guarantee of protection on individual properties, and ensurance to enhance public interest and welfare. It is of great interest for both individuals and government to understand how and why land expropriation policies are made and employed. The new technology has been able to expedite and transparentize

D.-J. Deng et al. (Eds.): WiCON 2019, LNICST 317, pp. 191–198, 2020.
https://doi.org/10.1007/978-3-030-52988-8_17

things so that personal rights and government duties can be guaranteed. The aim of this study is to investigate the application of Internet in evaluation of land expropriation in Taiwan. The findings of this study would shed new lights on the evaluation method and on the legislations of land expropriation in general.

3 Methodology

Internet is famous for its imminence and convenience. Analytical hierarchy process (AHP) is used to determine the weight of the different identified Internet factors. The Internet application Index, including four dimensions, is developed using weight of various factors and condition rating of various factors.

Analytical hierarchy process (AHP), suitably appropriate for uncertain or multi-criteria decision-making process, is to help decision makers to analyze complicated problems by means of categorizing factors into a hierarchical structure. The decomposition and calculation of the hierarchical structure will explain the consequence of factors and decrease the risks of wrong strategic decisions.

The relative weights of the proposed factors are determined using analytical hierarchy process (AHP). AHP can find the contribution of each individual factor in each section. Moreover, if there is a hierarchy of items, as is the case in this study, factors will be ranked accordingly. Mathematically, AHP uses pair-wise comparisons to systematically scale the items. It calculates the eigenvalues of the Relative Weight Matrix (RWM), and determines the relative weights by determining the eigenvector (Agarwal 2006).

3.1 Steps of the Hierarchy Analysis

1. The definition of the proposed problem, the creation of the population, and the establishment of the two elements are as the followings:

In order to put all possible considerations in the problem-solving process, it is the best policy to expand the environment in which the problem took place. At the same time, it is suggested to form a discussion group or a forum to discuss the content and the limit of the proposed problem. It is important to form a group of 5 to 15 experts to demarcate the scope of the proposed problem to consider the complication that the problem is involved. Based on these potential risks and obstacles, a hierarchical order of problems and possible solutions are proposed and arranged. Each subordinate phase, however independent, is only governed by its superior phase.

2. The design of the questionnaire, collection of the data, and establishment of the paired matrix

The possible matrix works like this. Suppose there are n factors being compared with each other, there are $n(n - 1)$ 2 pairs being compared. For instance, suppose the ratio of factor i to factor j is a_{ij}, $1/a_{ij}$ then is the reciprocal of its ratio, indicating its contrast.

In a similar vein, as it is shown in the Formula (1) in the following, the matrix A is the reciprocal of the inverted triangle.

$$A = [a_{ij}] = \begin{bmatrix} 1 & a_{12} & \cdots & a_{1n} \\ 1/a_{12} & 1 & \cdots & a_{2n} \\ \cdots & \cdots & & \cdots \\ 1/a_{1n} & 1/a_{2n} & \cdots & 1 \end{bmatrix} = \begin{bmatrix} w_1/w_1 & w_1/w_2 & \cdots & w_1/w_n \\ w_2/w_1 & w_2/w_2 & \cdots & w_2/w_n \\ \cdots & \cdots & & \cdots \\ w_n/w_1 & w_n/w_2 & \cdots & w_n/w_n \end{bmatrix} \tag{1}$$

w_{ij}: the weight of factor i; $i = 1, 2, \ldots, n$
a_{ij}: The ratio of relative importance between the two factors, i and j

$$i = 1, 2, \ldots, n; j = 1, 2, \ldots, n$$

3. Calculation of the characteristic value and the characteristic vector

After the paired comparison matrix is obtained, then we calculated the optimized vector and the characteristic vector by means of characteristic formula, which is generated from the numerical analysis. The purpose of this calculation is to gain the weight of each factor. As the calculation is described in Formula (2) in the following, we gained Geometric mean by the multiplication of all factors before we did the normalization.

$$W_i = \frac{\left(\prod_{j=1}^{n} a_{ij} \right)^{\frac{1}{n}}}{\sum_{i=1}^{n} \left(\prod_{j=1}^{n} a_{ij} \right)^{\frac{1}{n}}}, \; i, j, = 1, 2 \ldots \ldots, n \tag{2}$$

After Formula (2), W_i was obtained and was multiplied by the paired comparison matrix A. As a result, W_i' was a new characteristic vector In Formula (3), to get the value of λ_{max}, every characteristic vector W_i' was divided by its corresponding characteristic vector W_i, and then we calculated their arithmetical mean.

$$\lambda_{max} = \frac{1}{n} \left(\frac{W_1'}{W_1} + \frac{W_2'}{W_2} + \cdots \frac{W_n'}{W_n} \right) \tag{3}$$

To become a consistent indicator, consistent verification was conducted next, aiming to examine the validity of the paired comparison matrix undertaken by each decision maker. It is suggested that consistency can be guaranteed on the condition that C.I. < 0.1, allowing the acceptable error value to be C.I. < 0.2. The consistence index was generated in Formula (4).

The consistent indicator (Consistence Index, C.I.)

$$C.I. = \frac{\lambda_{max} - n}{n - 1} \tag{4}$$

In Formula (4), λ_{max} stands for the maximal characteristic value of the matrix. "n" is the number of factors being evaluated. In Formula (5), it is called the Consistency Ratio, C.R., meaning the ratio of C.I. to R.I. under the same matrix with the same level.

$$C.R. = \frac{C.I.}{R.I.} \tag{5}$$

If fact, the Consistency Ratio was satisfactory if C.R. < 0.1. Here is how it was compared. First of all, the basis of the evaluation was usually the factors from the previous level. The factors from the same level, taken as a pair, were compared, adopting the evaluation scale of 1 to 9 for the comparison of matrix A (Table 1).

Table 1. The explanation of evaluation criteria for AHP

Evaluation scale	Definition	Explanation
1	"Equal Importance", Equal Imp.	Equal importance of the contribution
3	"Slight Importance", Weak Imp.	Slight preference of one or the other
5	"Noticeable Importance", Essential Imp.	Intense likes of one or the other
7	"Total Importance", Very Strong Imp.	Strong tendency of one or the other
9	"Complete importance", Absolute Imp.	Sufficient evidence to support absolute favor of the selection
2, 4, 6, 8	"Value between adjacent scales", Intermediate Values	Necessary to compromise

Source: Deng & Tseng

Based on our calculation, the positive reciprocal matrix will generate different random index (R.I.) under different levels. However, under the same levels of the matrix, we got the value of the C.R., which specified the ratio of C.I. to R.I. As can be seen in Table 2, the values of the R.I. at different scales were demonstrated.

Table 2. The random index of R.I. for each level

N	1	2	3	4	5	6	7	8	9	10	11	12	13	14	15
R.I.	0.00	0.00	0.58	0.90	1.12	1.24	1.32	1.41	1.45	1.49	1.51	1.48	1.56	1.57	1.58

4   Results and Discussion

The purposes of this study are to calculate weight for various factors and to set up a criteria for land expropriation. The analysis for evaluation of land expropriation includes three dimensions. To begin with, the first stratum includes weight, the target level, and the optimal level. The second stratum includes four dimensions: social factor, economical factor, cultural and ecological factor and sustainability factor. The third stratum includes population factor, ages of population factor, current condition factor in society, group health factor, living styles factor of minority group, taxation factor, food safety factor, agriculture, forestry, fishery and animal husbandry factor, factor of number of changing jobs, levying expenses factor, financial expenses factor, factor of complete use of land, city scenery factor, living style factor, ecological environments factor, residents factor, society factor, Sustainability development factor, and territorial planning factor. The structure of evaluation of various factors can be seen in Fig. 1.

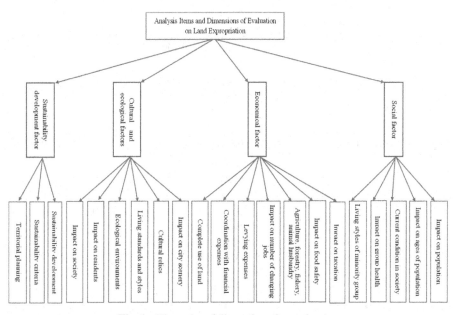

Fig. 1. Hierarchy of dimensions for evaluation

The subjects of this study include professionals from public sectors, development industries, and academic institutions and universities. Five professionals from each specific field were invited to fill in the proposed questionnaire and to conduct interviews focusing on the experience and the application of Internet on land expropriation. The arithmetic means and calculation of weight in addition to the comparisons of matrix between factors were conducted to generate C.I. and C.R. Table 3 demonstrated the structure of evaluation and the calculation of factor weight including the factor weight and factor ranking.

Table 3. Analysis of Relative importance (weight) of factors

Dimension	Dimension weight	Dimension ordering	Factors	Factor weight	Factor ordering	General weight	General ordering
D1 Social factor	0.247	2	C1 Impact on population	0.195	5	0.036	17
			C2 Impact on ages of population	0.199	3	0.047	10
			C3 Impact on current condition in society	0.203	2	0.057	6
			C4 Impact on group health	0.206	1	0.068	2
			C5 Impact on living styles of minority group	0.197	4	0.042	14
D2 Economical factor	0.271	1	C6 Impact on taxation	0.135	6	0.034	19
			C7 Impact on food safety	0.138	5	0.037	16
			C8 Impact on agriculture, forestry, fishery and animal husbandry	0.131	7	0.032	21
			C9 Impact on number of changing jobs	0.149	3	0.049	9
			C10 Levying expenses	0.154	1	0.069	1
			C11 Coordination with financial expenses	0.151	2	0.058	5
			C12 Impact on complete use of land	0.142	4	0.043	13

(*continued*)

Table 3. (*continued*)

Dimension	Dimension weight	Dimension ordering	Factors	Factor weight	Factor ordering	General weight	General ordering
D3 Cultural and ecological factors	0.242	3	C13 Impact on city scenery	0.167	3	0.045	11
			C14 Impact on cultural relics	0.169	2	0.056	7
			C15 Impact on living standards and styles	0.158	5	0.035	18
			C16 Impact on ecological environments	0.185	1	0.064	3
			C17 Impact on residents	0.165	4	0.041	15
			C18 Impact on society	0.156	6	0.033	20
D4 Sustainability development factor	0.240	4	C19 Sustainability development	0.332	2	0.051	8
			C20 Sustainability criteria	0.341	1	0.059	4
			C21 Territorial planning	0.327	3	0.044	12

5   Conclusion

The findings of this study has demonstrated that the weight for Levying expenses, Impact on group health, Impact on ecological environments and Sustainability criteria are ranked the highest, which is consistent with general public's expectation and cognition of land expropriation. Despite that, more observations and evaluation on land expropriation regulations need to be conducted if legislations of relevant land expropriation policies are to be made.

References

Agarwal, P.K.: Road condition, prioritization and optimal resource allocation for highway maintenance at network level. Ph. D. thesis, Department of Civil Engineering. IIT Kanpur, Kanpur (2006)

Patil, P.K.: Development of a methodology for ranking road safety hazardous locations using analytical hierarchy process. M.Tech thesis unpublished, Department of Civil Engineering. Maulana Azad National Institute of Technology, Bhopal (2013)

Wireless Internet

An Edge Computing Architecture for Object Detection

Endah Kristiani[1,2], Po-Cheng Ko[3], Chao-Tung Yang[3(✉)],
and Chin-Yin Huang[1]

[1] Department of Industrial Engineering and Enterprise Information,
Tunghai University, Taichung City, Taiwan R.O.C.
[2] Department of Informatics, Krida Wacana Christian University, Jakarta, Indonesia
[3] Department of Computer Science, Tunghai University,
Taichung City, Taiwan R.O.C.
ctyang@thu.edu.tw

Abstract. Edge computing services are contingent on several constraints. There is a requirement needed to provide a proper function, such as low latency, low energy consumption, and high performance. Object detection analysis involves high power resources, it is because of the need to process the images or videos. In this paper, the architecture of edge computing for object recognition is proposed, and the performance of the edge node is examined. The resources performance comparison on Raspberry Pi and Neural Compute Stick are inspected. This study combined the Neural Compute Stick (NCS) to enhance the ability of image processing on Raspberry Pi. Through the aid of NCS, the Raspberry Pi's frames per second (FPS) is increased by four times when the object detection program is executed, and the energy consumption of the Raspberry Pi is also recorded.

Keywords: Edge computing · Object detection · Raspberry Pi · Neural Compute Stick

1 Introduction

In recent years, edge computing has become an increasingly valued solution. Edge computing makes computation at the edge of the network, where data is stored at the edge of the network to improve data processing efficiency [2]. Edge computing is conceived as a promising promoter of the ability to exploit edge computing and solve problems in cloud computing [9]. With the rapid development of the Internet of Things and 5G networks in smart urban environments, it is expected that a large amount of data will be generated, increasing the latency

Some of the illustrations in this paper have already been published in:
On Construction of Sensors, Edge, and Cloud (iSEC) Framework for Smart System Integration and Applications, in IEEE IoT Journal on 22 June 2020,
https://doi.org/10.1109/JIOT.2020.3004244.
https://ieeexplore.ieee.org/document/9122603.

D.-J. Deng et al. (Eds.): WiCON 2019, LNICST 317, pp. 201–209, 2020.
https://doi.org/10.1007/978-3-030-52988-8_18

of traditional cloud computing. To reduce latency, consider using an edge computing architecture to offload some workloads from mobile devices to nearby edge servers with sufficient computing resources [7].

Object detection is a part of computer vision and image processing. It is deal with detecting objects based on the classification, such as cars, humans, or buildings. Computer vision uses an image processing task, for example, object segmentation, face detection, tracking object, or tracking movement. Object detection analysis involves high power resources, it is because of the need to process the images or videos. There is a requirement needed to provide a proper function, such as low latency, low energy consumption, and high performance.

In this paper, the architecture of edge computing for object recognition is proposed, and the performance of the edge node is examined. The specific purposes are listed as follows.

1. Implement edge computing architecture for object detection by using
2. Raspberry Pi and Intel Neural Compute Stick. Evaluate the performance and energy consumption of the edge node.

2   Method

In this section, the method used and related works are discussed as the background review of this work.

2.1   Edge Computing

Edge computing is a concept of near-computation (distributed computing architecture). It calculates the computation closer to the location of the resource. It does not transfer data back to the cloud and reduces the cost of data to and from the cloud. The difference with the cloud is that the operation is moved to the edge node for processing. Edge computing usually performs operations near the local and cloud interfaces, that is, the location of data in and out of the local area network, which is convenient for the simultaneous connection with the cloud and the local processing.

Although edge computing's performance is lower than cloud computing, it has the advantage of the number of nodes being large and densely, providing lower latency services and higher mobility support. Edge computing provides various types of monitoring services, including medical data, soil, temperature, and humidity, which can be used to a simple calculation by edge computing and store the processed data in the cloud. In brief, edge computing provides services on the edge of the network closer to the end device. Currently used in IoT, AR/VR, autopilot vehicles, drones, and robots. In the high transmission speed and low latency environment of modern networks, edge computing is an essential layout for 5G networks.

In summary, edge computing has the characteristics of low network latency, support for massive data access, and flexible infrastructure. At the same time, the benefits of shortening the spatial distance not only shorten the transmission delay but also reduce the delay of various routing and processing and network device processing in complex networks. Also, the overall latency can be significantly reduced due to the greatly reduced chance of network link contention. Edge computing adds decentralized capabilities to traditional cloud centers. Deploying some of the business logic on the edge side and completing related data processing can significantly alleviate the pressure to send data back to the central cloud. Edge computing also provides the ability to flexibly virtualize based on edge-position computing, networking, storage, and so on, and truly achieve "cloud-side collaboration". Edge computing can also provide targeted computing resource to data sources on the end device side. These computing resources can process some of the data on the edge side, while others can be processed and then sent back to the cloud. Edge computing provides a new elastic allocation solution of computing resources.

2.2   Neural Compute Stick

Movidius Neural Compute Sticks (NCS) can assist artificial intelligence application developers in analyzing, debugging, verifying neural networks, and accelerating deep learning. The SDK includes Tool and API. The part of Tool has three components: Profiler, Checker, and Compiler. The Profiler analyzes the network model and reports the operational efficiency of each layer of the network to assist developers in optimizing the network structure. The Checker tests the results and performance of the network before the developer starts deploying the network. The Compiler converts the network model (Caffe model or TensorFlow model) into a graph file that NCS can recognize. Moreover, part of API is hardware call interface for deep learning developers. The network model obtained through training can be compiled into a model format that can be used by the neural compute stick using the compiler tool. By calling the API, it is convenient to communicate between the host (the computer connected to the NCS) and the NCS. The NCS uses the trained model to calculate the results of the image analysis and transmits it to the host to complete the work.

Movidius's Myrid chip is not only used for neural network training and deep learning. Due to its relatively low power consumption and excellent visual processing performance, Movidius's first-generation visual processing chip was used in Google's Project Tango mobile phone and used to process data from various sensor feedbacks and draw pictures. We can see that Movidius's Myrid chip has gradually penetrated all walks of life. This work also uses the NCS API to perform computer vision experiments on the Raspberry Pi, while recording the power consumption and performance of the execution program. The future is the era of artificial intelligence and the Internet of Things. Supporting these two areas is the deep learning and communication network. At that time, mobile devices pay attention to power consumption. Movidius' low-power Myrid chip, which will make future mobile devices more intelligent.

2.3   Related Works

Morabito et al. [3] introduced a lightweight edge gateway for the Internet of Things (LEGIoT) architecture. It relies on the modular nature of microservices and the flexibility of lightweight virtualization technology to ensure a scalable and flexible solution. Song et al. [5] proposes a new information infrastructure called the Energy Internet of Things (IoET) to make DSM practical based on the latest wireless communication technology: LPWAN. The main advantage of LPWAN over General Packet Radio Service (GPRS) and Regional IoT is its wide-area coverage, which has the lowest power and maintenance costs. The monitoring network proposed by Addabbo et al. [1] consists of very low power sensor nodes with LoRa connections capable of measuring the displacement of structural cracks in buildings with 10 micron resolution. Ponce et al. [4] proposes an IoT system for predicting climatic conditions in closed areas using supervised learning methods, artificial hydrocarbon network models, using artificial intelligence, over ten days of data. The experimental results conclude that the artificial hydrocarbon network model helps predict remote temperatures.

Yin et al. [9] proposed an advanced decision model to solve the computational unloading problem in edge computing. It uses the inherent hierarchical topology of the Internet to perform online scheduling in a decentralized manner to eliminate the expected modeling. The concept proposed by Yang et al. [8] is realized by parallel MPI and OpenMP parallel programming in C language. Since the parallel loop self-scheduling consists of static and dynamic allocation, the static part adopts the weighting algorithm, and the dynamic part adopts the famous cyclic self-scheduling. This study use MPI for parallel data preprocessing. Tiwary et al. [6] introduced a non-cooperative broad game model in which players can maximize their rewards to minimize response time. The game model achieves a balance by using a reverse induction technique. This work also handles device availability by clustering previous availability data. Finally, the performance of the proposed model is evaluated based on response time, user efficiency, and memory utilization.

3   Experimental Procedure

This study integrated Raspberry Pi 3 B+ with camera module as show in Fig. 1 and NCS as show in Fig. 2 for object detection.

The specification of Raspberry Pi 3 model B+ as edge part is shown in Table 1.

Start from install the NCS SDK Tools on Ubuntu Desktop, and compile the model written in Caffe or Tensorflow into the graph file that can be executed at the edge node through the SDK Tool. On the other hand, you only need to install the NCS SDK API on the Raspberry Pi, and put the graph file generated by Tools on the Raspberry Pi. The Raspberry Pi has the deep learning ability to do object detection as shown in Fig. 3.

4   Results and Discussion

In this section, the results of edge node implementation and evaluation are described in detail.

 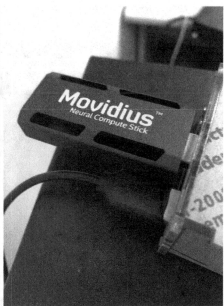

Fig. 1. Raspberry Pi with camera module

Fig. 2. Neural Compute Stick

Table 1. Raspberry Pi specification

Item	Description
Model	Raspberry Pi 3 B+
Operate system	Raspian strtch
CPU	Broadcom BCM2837B0, Cortex-A53 (ARMv8) 64-bit SoC @ 1.4 GHz
RAM	1 GB LPDDR2 SDRAM
Storage	MicroSD
Network	Gigabit Ethernet over USB 2.0 (maximum throughput 300 Mbps)
WiFi	2.4 GHz and 5 GHz IEEE 802.11.b/g/n/ac wireless LAN
Bluetooth	Bluetooth 4.2, BLE
Power	5V/2.5A DC power input

4.1   Object Detection on the Edge Node

This work use the Neural Compute Stick (NCS) to enhance the computing power of the Raspberry Pi in processing computer vision with NCS SDK to load the graph file and just call SDK API by edge node, speed up the recognition efficiency

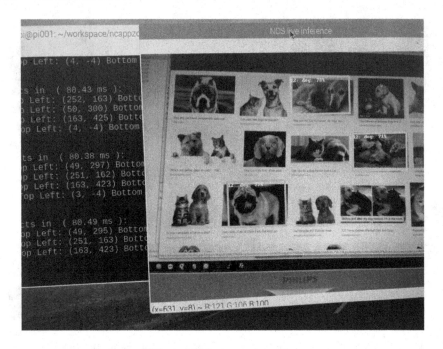

Fig. 3. NCS object detection

of the Raspberry Pi, and obtain nearly 4 times upgrades without NCS in Frames Per Second (FPS).

The FPS without NCS roughly is 0.8 as shown if Fig. 4. On the another side, the FPS with NCS roughly is 3.6 as shown in Fig. 5. This study also use the Power Distribution Unit (PDU) to record the power consumption w/ and w/o NCS. On average, it consumed 18.5 watt during the execution of the object recognition program without NCS. On the contrary, it consumed 15.47 watt with NCS. NCS saved roughly 16.37% consumption. The power consumption depict on Fig. 6.

4.2   Resource Performance

This study also record the CPU, RAM and temperature utilization during the program was executed. In terms of CPU usage, a reduction of 82.96% was achieved as shown in Fig. 7. In terms of RAM, it is 66.67% reduction as shown in Fig. 8, and the average temperature is also reduced roughly 8.8 degrees Celsius as shown in Fig. 9.

Fig. 4. Object detection without NCS

Fig. 5. Object detection with NCS

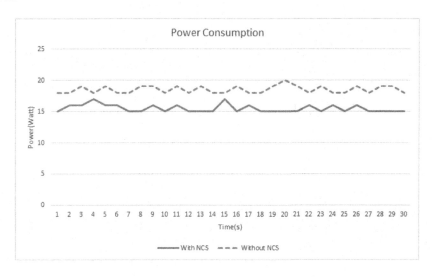

Fig. 6. Power consumption during object detection

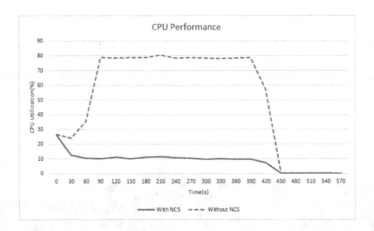

Fig. 7. CPU utility during object detection

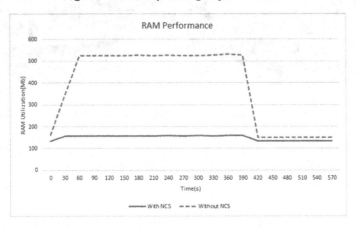

Fig. 8. Memory utility during object detection

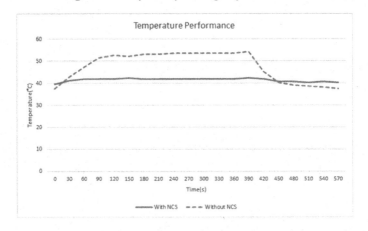

Fig. 9. Temperature during object detection

5   Conclusion

This work implement and evaluate the edge node on object detection case. The edge node utilize Raspberry Pi and Neural Compute Stick. The usage of Neural Compute Stick to implement object detection on the Raspberry Pi achieved a good performance and energy consumption based on the experiments. The FPS achieved four times improvement by comparing Raspberry Pi with NCS and not using NCS.

Acknowledgment. This research was supported in part by Ministry of Science and Technology, Taiwan R.O.C., under grants no. 107-2218-E-029-004.

References

1. Addabbo, T., Fort, A., Mugnaini, M., Panzardi, E., Pozzebon, A., Vignoli, V.: A city-scale IoT architecture for monumental structures monitoring. Measurement **131**, 349–357 (2019). https://doi.org/10.1016/j.measurement.2018.08.058. http://www.sciencedirect.com/science/article/pii/S0263224118307978
2. Li, C., Bai, J., Tang, J.: Joint optimization of data placement and scheduling for improving user experience in edge computing. J. Parallel Distrib. Comput. **125**, 93–105 (2019). https://doi.org/10.1016/j.jpdc.2018.11.006. http://www.sciencedirect.com/science/article/pii/S0743731518302661d
3. Morabito, R., Petrolo, R., Loscrì, V., Mitton, N.: Reprint of: Legiot: a lightweight edge gateway for the internet of things. Fut. Gener. Comput. Syst. **92**, 1157–1171 (2019). https://doi.org/10.1016/j.future.2018.10.020. http://www.sciencedirect.com/science/article/pii/S0167739X18325123
4. Ponce, H., Gutiérrez, S.: An indoor predicting climate conditions approach using internet-of-things and artificial hydrocarbon networks. Measurement **135**, 170–179 (2019). https://doi.org/10.1016/j.measurement.2018.11.043. http://www.sciencedirect.com/science/article/pii/S0263224118310972
5. Song, Y., Lin, J., Tang, M., Dong, S.: An internet of energy things based on wireless LPWAN. Engineering **3**(4), 460–466 (2017). https://doi.org/10.1016/J.ENG.2017. 04.011. http://www.sciencedirect.com/science/article/pii/S2095809917306057
6. Tiwary, M., Puthal, D., Sahoo, K.S., Sahoo, B., Yang, L.T.: Response time optimization for cloudlets in mobile edge computing. J. Parallel Distrib. Comput. **119**, 81–91 (2018). https://doi.org/10.1016/j.jpdc.2018.04.004. http://www.sciencedirect.com/science/article/pii/S0743731518302430
7. Wang, S., Zhao, Y., Xu, J., Yuan, J., Hsu, C.H.: Edge server placement in mobile edge computing. J. Parallel Distrib. Comput. **127**, 160–168 (2019). https://doi.org/10.1016/j.jpdc.2018.06.008. http://www.sciencedirect.com/science/article/pii/S0743731518304398
8. Yang, C.T., Huang, C.W., Chen, S.T.: Improvement of workload balancing using parallel loop self-scheduling on intel xeon phi. J. Supercomput. **73**(11), 4981–5005 (2017). https://doi.org/10.1007/s11227-017-2068-9. https://www.scopus.com/inward/record.uri?eid=2-s2.0-85019215725&doi=10.1007
9. Yin, Z., Chen, H., Hu, F.: An advanced decision model enabling two-way initiative offloading in edge computing. Future Generation Computer Systems **90**, 39–48 (2019). https://doi.org/10.1016/j.future.2018.07.031. http://www.sciencedirect.com/science/article/pii/S0167739X17329527

The Implementation of an Edge Computing Architecture with LoRaWAN for Air Quality Monitoring Applications

Endah Kristiani[1,2], Chao-Tung Yang[3(✉)], Chin-Yin Huang[1],
and Po-Cheng Ko[3]

[1] Department of Industrial Engineering and Enterprise Information,
Tunghai University, Taichung City, Taiwan R.O.C.
[2] Department of Informatics, Krida Wacana Christian University, Jakarta, Indonesia
[3] Department of Computer Science, Tunghai University,
Taichung City, Taiwan R.O.C.
ctyang@thu.edu.tw

Abstract. Cloud computing enables a user to access and analysis the data at any time, anywhere, and any devices with internet access. However, the need for faster and more reliable cannot adequately be handled by cloud computing. By combining cloud computing and edge computing along with low power wide area networks (LoRaWAN), it can provide excellent services. In this paper, a campus air quality using edge computing monitoring system and integrated Arduino and LoRaWAN air quality sensor was proposed. The air quality monitoring data collected by the LoRaWAN sensor is visualized using a web page to monitor and analyze the real-time air pollution data. The air quality data obtained from the open government data and LoRaWAN sensors.

Keywords: Internet of Things · Edge computing · Deep learning · LoRaWAN

1 Introduction

Cloud computing is an essential trend in the development of today's technology. Artificial intelligence and the rapid development of big data technology have enabled many models or patterns based on data science to be stored in the cloud server. In this case, the cloud service rented by the user is still placed in a data center. However, the analysis result cannot respond to the user immediately, and also, the massive amount of data causes the cloud to be unloaded. Cisco has proposed Edge Computing, also known as Fog Computing. It refers to the processing and operation of data, moving the data source closer to the data source on the logical network to shorten the network. In this way, they can diminish delay in transmission for faster data analysis or faster data acquisition. iThome pointed out that cloud service leader Amazon announced its emphasis

© ICST Institute for Computer Sciences, Social Informatics and Telecommunications Engineering 2020
Published by Springer Nature Switzerland AG 2020. All Rights Reserved
D.-J. Deng et al. (Eds.): WiCON 2019, LNICST 317, pp. 210–219, 2020.
https://doi.org/10.1007/978-3-030-52988-8_19

on edge computing at the re-invent global user conference held in Las Vegas last year. Another cloud service vendor Microsoft also proposed at the Build 2017 Developer Conference. Commercial software SAP also bought an Italian enterprise IoT platform provider Plat in 2016, to plan for edge computing development. Even the majority of cloud manufacturers that have strongly supported the cloud in the past have simultaneously changed dramatically and began to pay attention to edge computing. Because these cloud vendors suddenly discovered their limitations, they found that only cloud products are not enough. Therefore, they must launch non-cloud products and deploy cloud technology devices closer to users.

In this paper, two stages of an air quality monitoring system were established to facilitate the condition of regional air environmental changes and early warning system. First, the Arduino and LoRa air quality sensors were integrated, and the LoRa sensors were tested and calibrated, after that the sensor nodes were deployed on campus. In the system part, Raspberry Pi 3 is set up as the hardware device of the Edge side. Kubernetes and Docker are deployed to provide container services, and a MySQL database is built for data storage. The Cloud-based deployment of OpenStack clusters provides the subsequent infrastructure through virtualization. Second, in the main implementation of the system integration part, OpenStack and Ceph distributed storage system was integrated to provide storage solutions for OpenStack virtual machine resources, and in the Edge side data for backup processing [3–5].

In the term of the network management of IoT devices, the system collects relevant air pollution data through LoRa sensors. On the Cloud side, TensorFlow is used to implement a neural network training to produce a predictive model [2]. Moreover, we optimize the accuracy by integrating the open data of the Taiwan Environmental Protection Agency into the eigenvalues. The objectives of this paper are listed as follows.

1. Design the architecture of cloud edge computing.
2. Visualize the AQI on the map.

2   Method

In this section, the method used and the related works are discussed as the background review of this work.

2.1   Internet of Things (IoT)

IoT first appeared in 1998 and was proposed by Kevin Ashton, director of the MIT Auto-ID Center, a global network infrastructure. With the ability to capture and communicate, linking physical objects and virtual data for various types of control, detection, identification, and service. The emerging of IoT can be seen as a smart infrastructure revolution. The development of the IoT will connect every machine, every company, every resident and every car into a communication network. In the future, the energy network and the logistics network consists of a smart network, and all networks are embedded in a single operating system. In 2007, 10 million sensors linked a variety of human inventions to the IoT, but by 2013, the number had risen to more than 3.5 billion, and even more surprisingly, estimates by 2030, there will be a hundred mega sensors connected to the IoT networks.

2.2 Cloud Computing

Cloud computing is the only information technology model that provides access to shared configurable system resource pools and more advanced services at any time. These services are typically available quickly over the Internet with minimal administrative effort. Cloud computing relies on resource sharing to achieve scale consistency and economy, similar to a utility. Third-party clouds enable companies or developers to focus on their core business rather than costing server infrastructure and maintenance resources. Cloud computing enables companies to avoid or minimize the cost of upfront IT infrastructure, enabling cloud computing to run applications faster, improve manageability, reduce maintenance, and bring through IT teams to adjust resources more quickly to meet volatility And unpredictable business needs. Cloud providers typically use a "pay as you go" model, and if an administrator is not familiar with the cloud's pricing model, it can result in unexpected operating expenses [1, 10].

2.3 Edge Computing

The rapid development of Big Data has enabled many of the Models or Patterns based on Data Science to be stored in Cloud Computing's computer room. Although the results of data analysis can be obtained through Cloud Computing, Cloud Computing's primary data centers are still in a fixed geographical location. For example, in Taiwan, data analysis is sent to the United States, and unavoidable network delays still exist. Several of Cloud Computing's providers have come up with the concept of edge computing. Edge Computing, also known as Fog Computing, refers to the processing and operation of data, moving closer to the data source on the logical network to shorten the delay of network transmission and obtain data, analyze, and get results faster [6–9].

2.4 Low Power Wide Area Networks (LoRaWAN)

Recently, information technology grows fast. After the Internet, the IoT has caused widespread concern. With the rapid rise of the IoT and the increasing number of applications, the wireless communication transmission protocols of WiFi, Zigbee, Bluetooth, and so on, have made many options in the construction of the Internet of Things. The LoRa radio modulation technology was first invented by the company Cycleo in 2010 and is currently supported and open by the LoRa®Alliance. LoRa is the abbreviation of Long Range, a kind of low power wide area networks (LPWAN) communication technology. Semtech released ultra long-distance low-power data transmission technology in 2013. In the past, before LPWAN created, it seemed that trade-offs between long distances and low power consumption were impossible. The emergence of LoRa wireless technology has changed the trade-off between transmission distance and power consumption, which not only enables long-distance transmission but also has the advantages of low power consumption and low cost.

2.5 Related Works

Tsai et al. [11] at APNOMS 2017 proposed a distributed analysis of the fog computing platform. The platform integrates data center to end device resources. This study uses these devices to run IoT and multimedia applications that use different sensor data, including cameras and microphones. In this article, they focus on implementing a platform that supports complex analysis, such as deep learning, to avoid sending large amounts of raw data to a robust data center for analysis.

Lo et al. [12] published a paper on deep learning applied to edge computing. The authors understand the unstable communication channels at the edge and the limited computing resources for mobile battery-powered devices such as unattended surveillance cameras and robots.

3 Experimental Procedure

First, the cloud infrastructure platform will be implemented, and the sensors will be set up to collect data. The platform applied to the air pollution monitoring system. We have considered the use and data from the sensors. With a variety of aspects, such as transport mode, back-end architecture design, and virtual network power, this platform can implement a variety of different IoT applications. This study establishes an edge computing architecture for the IoT to cope with various IoT applications. The primary system of our study divide into three parts: device, cloud and edge computing as shown in Fig. 1, and the device is the sensor and alarm. It can accommodate a variety of different IoT devices and transport protocols. The cloud part is the host of the virtual machine and Kubernetes, and also handles applications that do not require fast response, such as data backup, complex operations, and data visualization. Finally, the part of the edge ramp is mainly responsible for running services and applications, such as data reception and exception notification. Data reception is pre-processed via edge ramps, which can significantly reduce a load of cloud transmission and storage, while the abnormal notification is instantaneous. All application services run on the Docker container to implement the microservices architecture. Moreover, the data is also stored on the edge ramps. If the cloud stores unexpected conditions, it can also be run through the data stabilization service on the edge ramp.

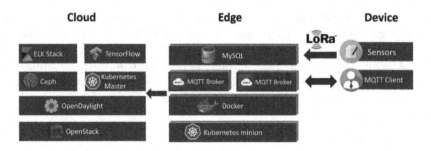

Fig. 1. The architecture of cloud edge computing

3.1   System Implementation

On the device side, that is, the terminal device, such as the sensor, Raspberry Pi 3, Arduino, and so on. This platform is also applicable to various transmission protocols. The overall architecture of this study is shown in Fig. 2. The Arduino equipped with LoRa Shield module and Pms5003t sensor as the overall sensing module. The sensing data collected by LoRa Nodes is transmitted to LoRa Gateway through LoRa. LoRa provides low-power WAN and star topology, and the is also connected to the micro-edge ramp made by Raspberry Pi 3, and finally transmitted to the data center, which is the cloud.

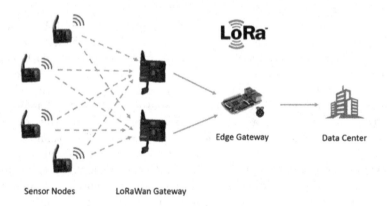

Fig. 2. The flowchart of the device side

On the Edge side, it is mainly designed as a service provider. The overall environment is set up on the Raspberry Pi 3. We can build the required software as needed. The main services are received from the LoRa terminal. Data transfer in the cloud, data storage in the MySQL relational database, and abnormal push system of the MQTT Broker. Figure 3 shows the system data flow on the device side and the edge side. With this Unified Data Modeling (UML) system, we can show the application flow and data flow at each stage.

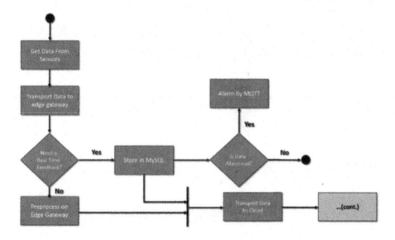

Fig. 3. The flowchart the edge side

On the Cloud side, mainly built OpenStack cluster infrastructure services, providing the servers needed for the IoT through virtualization technology. OpenStack also provides network virtualization through the neutron suite, and the project integrates OpenDaylight. As an SDN Controller used by OpenStack, ODL uses OpenFlow and OVSDB to manage Open vSwitch for OpenStack compute nodes. Moreover, on the storage of Ceph Storage, Ceph provides decentralized storage and supports both block storage and file storage. It can also store image files and some computing resources, with Ceph, users in the entire OpenStack environment, only Need to face a single storage system. Also, the Cloud side mainly handles complex operations. Finally, visualize the results of the operations through web pages. Figure 4 shows the operational flow after entering the cloud. We can view this UML to understand the data processing mechanism in the cloud.

4   Results and Discussion

In this section, the results of system implementation and evaluation are described in detail.

4.1   Data Collection

This study implements an air pollution monitoring system that will actually be used on campus. There are many aspects to consider in terms of sensors.

1. Buildings: campus has many buildings, building shelter will cause interference data transmission
2. Distance signals: the campus covers an area of 1,333,096 m^2 wide, in such a large application environment, resulting in transmission distance limit

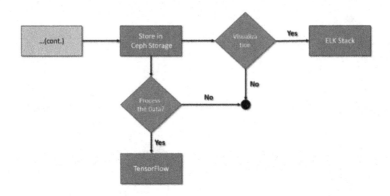

Fig. 4. The flowchart the cloud side

3. Power consumption: The general transmission mechanism plus the sensor needs to consume a certain amount of power, but the location where we want to set up does not necessarily have a power supply system. If we use battery power, we need to replace it with a new one.

Under such conditions, we have chosen LoRa. LoRa has long-distance and low-power wireless network technology. Through this technology, we can build a low-power wide-area network. The low-power features make IoT applications excellent. Endurance and the advantage of long-distance allows a single gateway or base station to cover the entire city or hundreds of square kilometers, which will enable the system to be more scalable in the future. Hardware assembly, LoRa Shield and Arduino Uno development boards are integrated and connected to a four-in-one sensor. Test the transmission distance and stability of LoRa, and calibrate the sensor, and finally modularize the hardware, which is conducive to rapid deployment in the future. To prevent moisture, we use a 3D printing mechanism to make a waterproof casing. Figure 5 and 6 show the LoRa node and Gateway hardware device.

All Nodes will transfer data to the cloud via Gateway. Through the combination with Arduino, LoRa integrates the temperature and humidity and PM2.5 sensing modules on the LoRa Node and periodically transfers them to the Thingspeak IoT cloud database for further data access and visual analysis as shown in Fig. 7.

4.2   Data Visualization Platform

Web system built through an interactive visual suite. Figure 8 shows the air pollution index information. The system collects air pollution from station data.

Fig. 5. LoRa node   **Fig. 6.** LoRa Gateway

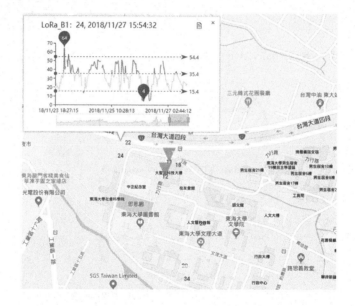

Fig. 7. Visualization of LoRa sensing nodes in the campus map

Moreover, the detail information of the air quality is described in the Radial gauge charts in the Fig. 9.

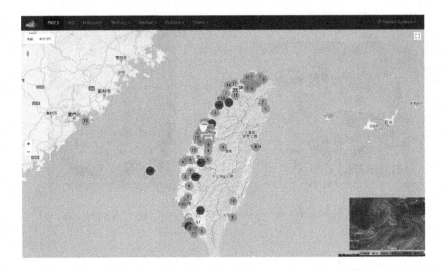

Fig. 8. Visualization of Taiwan air pollution index status

Fig. 9. Visualization of PM2.5 status in the Radial gauge charts

5   Conclusion

In this study, we present a complete big data ecosystem environment, which consists of data collected from air quality for data analysis and monitoring. In terms of infrastructure, performance optimization has been improved. The framework of edge computing and cloud platform can enhance the efficiency of decision-making. Also, the deployment of a complete wireless transmission system and visual presentation.

In the future, this system can implement deep learning for the prediction of air quality status. In addition to the webpage, it can also provide air pollution information in Taiwan, and it can also notify the air pollution alarm through MQTT.

Acknowledgment. This research was supported in part by Ministry of Science and Technology, Taiwan R.O.C., under grants no. 107-2221-E-029-008-, 107-2218-E-029-004-, 108-2221-E-029-010, and 108-2119-M-029-001-A.

References

1. Autenrieth, A., Elbers, J.-P., Kaczmarek, P., Kostecki, P.: Cloud orchestration with SDN/OpenFlow in carrier transport networks. In: 2013 15th International Conference on Transparent Optical Networks (ICTON), pp. 1–4. IEEE (2013)
2. Abadi, M., et al.: Tensorflow: Large-scale machine learnin G on heterogenous distributed systems. Preliminary White Paper, 09 November 2015
3. Malik, A., Ahmed, J., Qadir, J., Ilyas, M.U.: A measurement study of open source SDN layers in OpenStack under network perturbation. Comput. Commun. **102**, 139–149 (2017)
4. Solano, A., Dormido, R., Duro, N., Sánchez, J.M.: A self-provisioning mechanism in OpenStack for IoT devices. Sensors (Switzerland) **16**(8), 1306 (2016)
5. Yang, C.-T., Chen, C.-J., Chen, T.-Y.: Implementation of ceph storage with big data for performance comparison. In: Kim, K., Joukov, N. (eds.) ICISA 2017. LNEE, vol. 424, pp. 625–633. Springer, Singapore (2017). https://doi.org/10.1007/978-981-10-4154-9_72
6. Satria, D., Park, D., Jo, M.: Recovery for overloaded mobileedge computingRecovery for overloaded mobileedge computing. Future Gener. Comput. Syst. **70**, 138–147 (2017)
7. Shankar, D., Lu, X., Panda, D.K.D.K.: Boldio: a hybrid and resilient burst-buffer over lustre for accelerating big data i/o, pp. 404–409 (2016)
8. Ahmed, E., Rehmani, M.H.: Mobile edge computing: opportunities, solutions, and challenges (2017)
9. Cicirelli, F., Guerrieri, A., Spezzano, G.C., Vinci, A.: An edge-based platform for dynamic smart city applications. Future Gener. Comput. Syst. **76**, 106–118 (2017)
10. Toffetti, G., Brunner, S., Blöchlinger, M., Spillner, J., Bohnert, T.M.: Self-managing cloud-native applications: design, implementation, and experience. Future Gener. Comput. Syst. **72**, 165–179 (2017)
11. Tsai, P.-H., Hong, H.-J., Cheng, A.-C., Hsu, C.-H.: Distributed analytics in fog computing platforms using tensorflow and Kubernetes. In: 2017 19th Asia-Pacific Network Operations and Management Symposium (APNOMS), pp. 145–150. IEEE (2017)
12. Lo, C., et al.: A dynamic deep neural network design for efficient workload allocation in edge computing. In: 2017 IEEE 35th International Conference on Computer Design (ICCD). IEEE (2017)

Combination of OFDM and CDMA Techniques for a High Bandwidth Optimization and a Great Improvement of Signal Quality in OFDM Systems

Agnès Ngom[1]([⊠]) and Ahmed Dooguy Kora[2]

[1] Ecole Supérieure Polytechnique, Université Cheikh Anta Diop, Dakar, Senegal
mameagnes@yahoo.fr
[2] Ecole Supérieure Multinationale des Télécommunications, Dakar, Senegal
ahmed.kora@esmt.sn

Abstract. The use of OFDM modulation has become a priority in recent years as it is an ideal platform for wireless data transmissions. Its implementation can be seen in most of the newer broadband and high bit rate wireless systems, including Wi-Fi, cellular telecommunications and more. This is due to the many benefits this technology provides. These include immunity to selective fading, inter-symbol interference resistance, intercarrier interference resistance, more efficient spectrum utilization and simpler channel equalization.

But with the increasing demand from users, the scarcity of the radio spectrum and the use of OFDM for a large number of recent wireless applications, the optimization of bandwidth and signal quality must be a major concern.

Thus, in this paper, we propose in a multipath Additive White Gaussian Noise environment, a more efficient wireless transmission system that combines OFDM and CDMA techniques. It is a 4-QAM OFDM-CDMA synchronous multiuser system that uses OVSF codes to differentiate users. It can be applied on the downlink of a wireless cellular system based on a simple OFDM access and even be a system for 5th generation mobiles where OFDM is considered in combination with a multiple access technique.

It turns out that, compared to a 4-QAM OFDM single-user system, a 4-QAM OFDM-CDMA synchronous multi-user system offers better performances that increase with SF the length of the OVSF codes used to differenciate users.

Thus with SF = 32 and in the case of a six paths Additive White Gaussian Noise channel, a user of a 4-QAM OFDM-CDMA system can share the same OFDM subcarriers with twenty (20) other users of the same system and have a lower BER than a user of a 4-QAM OFDM single-user system having the same power profiles.

It is therefore possible with values of SF greater than or equal to 32, to optimize bandwidth and signal quality in systems based on an OFDM access.

Keywords: ADSL · CDMA · FFT · IFFT · LTE · OFDM · OFDMA · OVSF · QAM · SF

1 Introduction

OFDM is a multicarrier modulation technique that consists of distributing a high bit rate bit stream over N low bit rates orthogonal sub-channels (or sub-carriers). This gives it several advantages in the frequency selective channels because, unlike the single carrier modulations, OFDM exhibits high resistance to selective fading and interference while offering a high degree of spectral efficiency.

Also, it lends itself to digital signal processing techniques while allowing to increase the bit rates of a transmission system and to simplify the equalization technique in reception.

For all these reasons, OFDM has been used during the last decade for a wide range of applications [1–6].

We can particularly mention ADSL for a wired context, WiFi, LTE (4G) and Digital Terrestrial Television for wireless systems. In addition, it is still considered for 5th generation mobiles (5G) in combination with a multiple access technique. However, among the multiple access techniques, the CDMA may be mentioned since it has the privilege of using the same bandwidth for all users, with each identified by a code. The codes have the effect of spreading the spectrum of the transmitted signal, which also provides a number of advantages including:

- Good resistance to narrow-band disrupters
- Low interference of conventional narrowband emissions
- Insensitivity to the multipath effects (fading hollows)
- Low probability of interception
- Multiplexing and selective addressing

Faced with the use of OFDM for a large number of recent wireless applications, the scarcity of the spectrum and the increasing demand of users, the objective of this article is to combine the OFDM and CDMA techniques to propose a new mobile radio system that minimizes the use of the radio spectrum and greatly improves the quality of the transmitted signal.

Thus in this paper, we propose in a multipath Additive White Gaussian noise channel, a 4-QAM OFDM-CDMA synchronous multiuser system using OVSF codes.

The rest of the paper is organized as follows. In Sect. 2, we will first study the performance of a M-QAM OFDM single-user system. Then in Sect. 3, we will present the proposed system before studying its performance in Sect. 4. Section 5 concludes the paper.

2 Performance of a M-QAM OFDM Single User System

In this section, we consider an OFDM transmission in a multipath Additive White Gaussian Noise channel. Our goal is to see the impact of the constellation size and of the number of paths on the single user system BER.

2.1   Presentation of a M-QAM OFDM System

Consider a system emitting in a multipath Additive White Gaussian Noise channel an OFDM signal $x(t)$ formed by **P** OFDM symbols. To avoid the presence of OFDM symbols interferences and OFDM carriers interferences, we add a cyclic prefix between two successive OFDM symbols.

$x(t)$ is given by:

$$x(t) = \sum_{i=1}^{P} x_i(t) = \sum_{i=1}^{P} (\sum_{k=1}^{N_c} c_i(k) e^{j2\pi f_k(t - iT_s)}) \tag{1}$$

with **P** representing the total number of OFDM symbols, $\boldsymbol{x_i}(t)$ the ith OFDM signal or the ith OFDM symbol transmitted, $\boldsymbol{N_c}$ the total number of subcarriers, $\boldsymbol{c_i}(k)$ the kth M-QAM complex symbol of the ith OFDM symbol, $\boldsymbol{f_k}$ the kth subcarrier frequency and $\boldsymbol{T_s}$ the OFDM symbol duration.

By sampling $x_i(t)$ at the times $t = t_n = iT_s + nT$ where T represents the $c_i(k)$ symbol duration and knowing that:

$$f_k = \frac{k}{T_s} = \frac{k}{N_c T} \tag{2}$$

we obtain the discrete OFDM signal expression x_n corresponding to $x(t)$ and given by:

$$x_n = \sum_{i=1}^{P} x_i(n) = \sum_{i=1}^{P} (\sum_{k=1}^{N_c} c_i(k) e^{\frac{j2\pi kn}{N_c}}) = \sum_{i=1}^{P} IFFT[c_i(k)] \tag{3}$$

Thus according to the discrete Fourier transform properties, we have:

$$c_i(k) = \frac{1}{N_c} FFT[x_i(n)] \tag{4}$$

We rely on x_n expression to make a digital OFDM transmission system (Fig. 1) involving a cyclic prefix to avoid OFDM symbols interferences and OFDM carriers interferences.

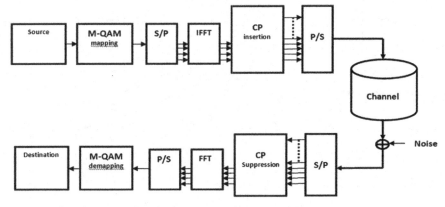

Fig. 1. M-QAM OFDM system

2.2 Constellation Size Impact on the Single User System BER

In this sub-section, we study for a three paths Additive White Gaussian Noise channel, the constellation size impact on the BER of a M-QAM OFDM single user system.

The SNR in dB is given by the relation:

$$\mathbf{SNR} = \mathbf{Eb/No} + 10.\log(\mathbf{k}) + 10.\log(\mathbf{number\ of\ data\ sub\text{-}carriers/N\_fft}) \quad (5)$$

with **SNR** the signal to noise ratio, **Eb** the energy per bit, **No** the noise power spectral density, **k** the number of bits per symbol QAM and **N_fft** the FFT size.

The considered simulation parameters are summarized at Table 1 with **M** the constellation size, **N** the number of bits transmitted, **N_fft** the FFT size, **Ncyc** the cyclic prefix size and **Nt** the number of channel paths.

Table 1. Simulation parameters

M	N	N_fft	Ncyc	Nt	1rst path power profile (dB)	2nd path power profile (dB)	3rd path power profile (dB)
4, 16, 32, 64, 128, 256	430080	128	N_fft/4	3	0	−8	−17

Figure 2 shows the obtained results for **number of data sub-carriers = N_fft**

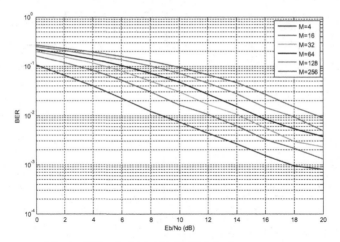

Fig. 2. BER of a M-QAM OFDM single user system

The simulation results of Fig. 2 show that for Eb/N0 varying from 0 dB to 20 dB, the best performance is obtained for the smallest constellation size which is **M = 4.**

2.3 Number of Paths Impact on the Single User System BER

In this sub-section, we study the number of paths impact on the BER of a 4-QAM OFDM single user system. The considered simulation parameters are: **M** = 4, **N_fft** = 128, **N** = 430080 bits, **Ncyc** = 8. The paths power profiles are given at Table 2.

Table 2. Simulation parameters

Power profile (dB)	1st path	2nd path	3rd path	4th path	5th path	6th path	7th path	8th path	9th path	10th path
1 path channel	0									
3 paths channel	0	−2	−4							
6 paths channel	0	−2	−4	−6	−8	−10				
10 paths channel	0	−2	−4	−6	−8	−10	−12	−14	−17	−20

The obtained results are at Fig. 3.

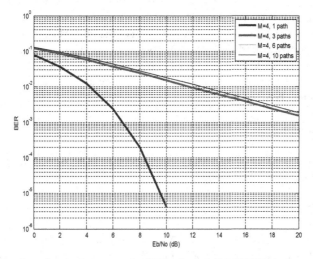

Fig. 3. Number of paths impact on the BER of a 4-QAM OFDM single user system

Figure 3 shows best performance for a single path channel and the same performance for a 6 and a 10 paths channel.

3 Presentation of the Proposed System

In this section, we propose in a multipath Additive White Gaussian Noise channel, a M-QAM OFDM-CDMA synchronous multiuser system. In this system, the different users are identified by orthogonal spreading codes (OVSF codes).

The principle of this system is illustrated in Fig. 4.

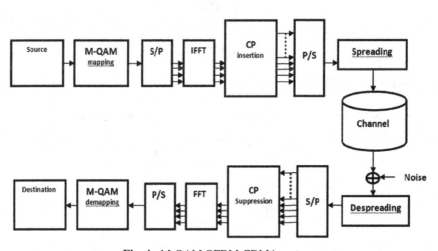

Fig. 4. M-QAM OFDM-CDMA system

This system differs from a simple OFDM transmission system with the presence of the two blocks **"Spreading"** (before transmission of the OFDM symbols of each user in the channel) and **"Despreading"** (after the spread OFDM signals of the different users cross the channel so as to find the signal corresponding to each user). It is of a great spectral advantage because the same OFDM carriers are used for all users and each user is identified by an OVSF code.

- **M-QAM mapping**

If we consider a system transmitting simultaneously to **K** users, a M-QAM mapping of the bits of each user is first made.

- **"S/P" and "IFFT" blocks**

With the help of the **S/P** block, M-QAM symbols of each user are then grouped by block of size N_{fft} to enter the **"IFFT"** module in order to generate the N_{fft} OFDM symbol samples.

If for each user **u** is sent **P** OFDM symbols, then the **n**th OFDM symbol sample of the **i**th OFDM symbol of a user **u** is given by:

$$x_i^u(n) = \sum_{k=1}^{N_{fft}} c_i^u(k) e^{\frac{j2\pi kn}{N_{fft}}} = IFFT\left[c_i^u(k)\right] \tag{6}$$

with $1 \le i \le P$, $1 \le u \le K$, $1 \le n \le N_{fft}$, $c_i^u(k)$ the **k**th M-QAM symbol of the **i**th OFDM symbol of the user **u** and $1 \le k \le N_{fft}$.

Let's consider $N_{fft} = N_c$, then the **i**th vector of the N_c OFDM symbol samples of the user **u** is:

$$x_i^u = \begin{bmatrix} x_i^u(1) \\ x_i^u(2) \\ \vdots \\ x_i^u(N_c) \end{bmatrix} \tag{7}$$

- **Cyclic prefix insertion**

After insertion of the cyclic prefix of size N_{cyc}, we get the vector v_i^u given by:

$$v_i^u = \begin{bmatrix} x_i^u(N_c - N_{cyc} + 1) \\ \vdots \\ x_i^u(N_c) \\ x_i^u(1) \\ x_i^u(2) \\ \vdots \\ x_i^u(N_c) \end{bmatrix} \tag{8}$$

- «P/S» and «Spreading» blocks

It follows the **P/S** phase where the elements of v_i^u are sent in series in the «Spreading» block so that they can be spread one by one by the spreading code $C^u = \left[C^u(1)C^u(2)\ldots\ldots\ldots\ldots C^u(SF) \right]$ assigned to the user **u**. **SF** is the spreading factor.

Thus at the output of the «**Spreading**» block, we have for the user **u** the matrix E_i^u given by:

$$
E_i^u = v_i^u . C^u =
\begin{bmatrix}
x_i^u\left(N_c - N_{cyc} + 1\right) \\
\vdots \\
x_i^u(N_c) \\
x_i^u(1) \\
x_i^u(2) \\
\vdots \\
x_i^u(N_c)
\end{bmatrix}
. [C^u(1)C^u(2)\ldots\ldots C^u(SF)
$$

$$
=
\begin{bmatrix}
x_i^u\left(N_c - N_{cyc} + 1\right).C^u(1) & \cdots & x_i^u\left(N_c - N_{cyc} + 1\right).C^u(SF) \\
\vdots & \ddots & \vdots \\
x_i^u(N_c).C^u(1) & \cdots & x_i^u(N_c).C^u(SF)
\end{bmatrix}
\tag{9}
$$

- **Channel crossing**

Let's consider $E_{i,j}^u$ the **jth** column of E_i^u. After crossing the channel, the vector corresponding to it is $R_{i,j}^u . R_{i,j}^u$ is given by the convolution product of $E_{i,j}^u$ with the impulse response h_i^u.

$$
R_{i,j}^u = E_{i,j}^u * h_i^u =
\begin{bmatrix}
R_{i,j}^u(1) \\
R_{i,j}^u(2) \\
\cdot \\
\cdot \\
R_{i,j}^u(N)
\end{bmatrix}
\tag{10}
$$

And after the **SF** vectors $E_{i,j}^u$ of the matrix E_i^u cross the channel, we have the matrix R_i^u given by:

$$
R_i^u =
\begin{bmatrix}
R_{i,1}^u(1) & R_{i,2}^u(1)\ldots\ldots\ldots\ldots\ldots\ldots\ldots R_{i,SF}^u(1) \\
R_{i,1}^u(2) & R_{i,2}^u(2)\ldots\ldots\ldots\ldots\ldots\ldots\ldots R_{i,SF}^u(2) \\
& \cdot \\
& \cdot \\
R_{i,1}^u(N) & R_{i,2}^u(N)\ldots\ldots\ldots\ldots\ldots\ldots\ldots R_{i,SF}^u(N)
\end{bmatrix}
\tag{11}
$$

with:

$$N = N_c + N_{cyc} \tag{12}$$

• Adding White Gaussian Noise

At the output of the channel, the **K** users'signals are summed together with White Gaussian Noise B given by:

$$B = \begin{bmatrix} B_{i,1}(1) & B_{i,2}(1) \dots\dots\dots\dots\dots\dots\dots B_{i,SF}(1) \\ B_{i,1}(2) & B_{i,2}(2) \dots\dots\dots\dots\dots\dots\dots B_{i,SF}(2) \\ & \cdot \\ & \cdot \\ B_{i,1}(N) & B_{i,2}(N) \dots\dots\dots\dots\dots\dots\dots B_{i,SF}(N) \end{bmatrix} \tag{13}$$

This gives the matrix Y_i

$$Y_i = \sum_{u=1}^{K} (R_i^u) + B = \begin{bmatrix} \sum_{u=1}^{K} R_{i,1}^u(1) + B_{i,1}(1) \dots\dots\dots \sum_{u=1}^{K} R_{i,SF}^u(1) + B_{i,SF}(1) \\ \sum_{u=1}^{K} R_{i,1}^u(2) + B_{i,1}(2) \dots\dots\dots \sum_{u=1}^{K} R_{i,SF}^u(2) + B_{i,SF}(2) \\ \cdot \\ \cdot \\ \sum_{u=1}^{K} R_{i,1}^u(N) + B_{i,1}(N) \dots\dots \sum_{u=1}^{K} R_{i,SF}^u(N) + B_{i,SF}(N) \end{bmatrix} \tag{14}$$

$$Y_i = \begin{bmatrix} Y_{i,1}(1) & Y_{i,2}(1) \dots\dots\dots\dots\dots\dots\dots Y_{i,SF}(1) \\ Y_{i,1}(2) & Y_{i,2}(2) \dots\dots\dots\dots\dots\dots\dots Y_{i,SF}(2) \\ & \cdot \\ & \cdot \\ Y_{i,1}(N) & Y_{i,2}(N) \dots\dots\dots\dots\dots\dots\dots Y_{i,SF}(N) \end{bmatrix} \tag{15}$$

• «Despreading» and «S/P» blocks

The signal Z_i^u of a user **u** is obtained by multiplying successively each line of Y_i by the transpose of the code C^u. that we note C_u^T

$$C_u^T = \begin{bmatrix} C^u(1) \\ C^u(2) \\ \cdot \\ \cdot \\ C^u(SF) \end{bmatrix} \tag{16}$$

$$Z_i^u = Y_i . C_u^T = \begin{bmatrix} Z_i^u(1) \\ Z_i^u(2) \\ \cdot \\ \cdot \\ Z_i^u(N) \end{bmatrix} \tag{17}$$

with:

$$Z_i^u(n) = \sum_{j=1}^{SF} Y_{i,j}(n)\, C_u^T(j) \tag{18}$$

$$Z_i^u(n) = \sum_{j=1}^{SF} \left[\left(\sum_{u=1}^{K} R_{i,j}^u(n) + B_{i,j}(n) \right) C_u^T(j) \right] \tag{19}$$

$$Z_i^u(n) = \sum_{j=1}^{SF} \left[\left(\sum_{u=1}^{K} R_{i,j}^u(n) \right) C_u^T(j) + B_{i,j}(n) C_u^T(j) \right] \tag{20}$$

$$Z_i^u(n) = \sum_{j=1}^{SF} \left[\left(\sum_{u=1}^{K} \left\{ E_{i,j}^u(n) * h_i^u(n) \right\} \right) C_u^T(j) + B_{i,j}(n) C_u^T(j) \right] \tag{21}$$

$$Z_i^u(n) = \sum_{j=1}^{SF} \left[\left(\sum_{u=1}^{K} \left\{ [v_i^u(n).C^u(j)] * h_i^u(n) \right\} \right) C_u^T(j) + B_{i,j}(n) C_u^T(j) \right] \tag{22}$$

$$Z_i^u(n) = \sum_{j=1}^{SF} \left[\left[\left\{ \left[v_i^1(n).C^1(j) \right] * h_i^1(n) + \cdots + \left[v_i^u(n).C^u(j) \right] * h_i^u(n) \right. \right. \right.$$
$$\left. \left. \left. + \cdots + \left[v_i^K(n).C^K(j) \right] * h_i^K(n) \right\} C_u^T(j) + B_{i,j}(n) C_u^T(j) \right] \right] \tag{23}$$

$$Z_i^u(n) = \sum_{j=1}^{SF} \left[\left[v_i^1(n).C^1(j) C_u^T(j) \right] * h_i^1(n) + \cdots . \left[v_i^u(n).C^u(j) C_u^T(j) \right] \right.$$
$$\left. * h_i^u(n) + \cdots + \left[v_i^K(n).C^K(j) C_u^T(j) \right] * h_i^K(n) + B_{i,j}(n) C_u^T(j) \right] \tag{24}$$

$$Z_i^u(n) = \sum_{j=1}^{SF} \left[\left[C^1(j) C_u^T(j) \right] v_i^1(n) * h_i^1(n) + \ldots + \left[C^u(j) C_u^T(j) \right] v_i^u(n) \right.$$
$$\left. * h_i^u(n) + \ldots + \left[C^K(j) C_u^T(j) \right] v_i^K(n) * h_i^K(n) + B_{i,j}(n) C_u^T(j) \right] \tag{25}$$

But $C_u^T(j) = C^u(j)$ and (25) becomes

$$Z_i^u(n) = \sum_{j=1}^{SF} \left[\left[C^1(j) C^u(j) \right] v_i^1(n) * h_i^1(n) + \ldots + \left[C^u(j) C^u(j) \right] v_i^u(n) \right.$$
$$\left. * h_i^u(n) + \ldots + \left[C^K(j) C^u(j) \right] v_i^K(n) * h_i^K(n) + B_{i,j}(n) C^u(j) \right] \tag{26}$$

Because of orthogonality of the codes we have:

$$Z_i^u(n) = SF.v_i^u(n) * h_i^u(n) + \sum_{j=1}^{SF} B_{i,j}(n) C^u(j) \tag{27}$$

And finally,

$$Z_i^u(n) = SF.v_i^u(n) * h_i^u(n) + B_i^u(n) \tag{28}$$

- **Cyclic prefix suppression**

After the suppression of the cyclic prefix, we obtain the vector W_i^u given by:

$$W_i^u = \begin{bmatrix} Z_i^u(N_{cyc} + 1) \\ Z_i^u(N_{cyc} + 2) \\ . \\ . \\ . \\ Z_i^u(N) \end{bmatrix} \tag{29}$$

- **«FFT» and «P/S» blocks**

The FFT of the vector W_i^u generates N_c symbols. After channel equalization, these symbols are successively sent through the **«P/S»** block towards the **«M-QAM demapping»** block.

- **M-QAM demapping**

Finally, at the «**M QAM demapping**» block, QAM demodulation of the symbols is performed in a hard decision taking

4   M-QAM OFDM-CDMA System Performance

4.1   Constellation Size Impact on the BER of a Two Users System

In this sub-section, we assume that the system transmits simultaneously the signals of two users: *user1* and *user2*. Our objective is to study user1 signal BER evolution according to the constellation size **M**.

The SNR in dB is given by:

$$\mathbf{SNR = Eb/No + 10.log(k) + 10.log(number\ of\ data\ carriers/N\_fft)}. \quad (30)$$

Eb is the energy per bit, **No** the noise power spectral density and **k** the number of bits per QAM symbol.

The considered simulation parameters are in Table 3 with **M** the constellation size, **N** the number of bits transmitted, **N_fft** the FFT size, **Ncyc** the cyclic prefix size, **Nt** the number of paths in the channel and **SF** the spreading factor.

Figure 5 shows the obtained results for a number of data carriers equal to **N_fft**.

Table 3. Simulation parameters

M	User	N (bits)	N_fft	Ncyc	Nt	1st path power profile (db)	2nd path power profile (db)	3rd path power profile (db)	SF
4, 16, 32, 64, 128, 256	User 1	860160	128	8	3	0	−8	−17	8
	User 2	860160	128	8	3	0	−5	−15	8

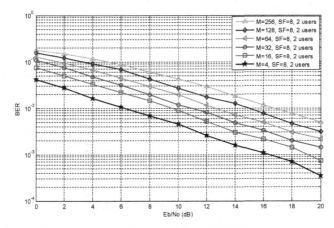

Fig. 5. User 1 signal BER in a M-QAM OFDM-CDMA system

The results in Fig. 5 show that for a fixed value of Eb/N0, the user1 signal BER increases with the constellation size **M.** Also for a fixed **M,** the user1 signal BER decreases when Eb/N0 increases. Consequently, the best performance is obtained with **M = 4.**

4.2 SF Impact on the BER of a 4-QAM OFDM-CDMA Two Users System

Here we consider a 4-QAM OFDM-CDMA two users system with the simulation parameters of Table 3 for **N, N_fft, Ncyc, Nt** and the **path power profiles.** By varying **SF** we get the results in Fig. 6 giving the user 1 signal BER.

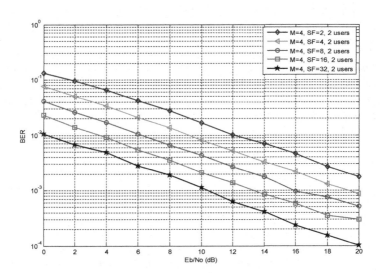

Fig. 6. SF impact on the user1 signal BER

Figure 6 shows that in a 4-QAM OFDM-CDMA synchronous two users system, user1 signal performance increases with the code length **SF**.

4.3 Number of Paths Impact on the BER of a 4-QAM OFDM-CDMA Two Users System

Here we study for a 4-QAM OFDM-CDMA synchronous two users system, the number of paths impact on the user1 signal BER. The considered simulation parameters are: **M** = 4, **N_fft** = 128, **N** = 430080 bits, **Ncyc** = 8 and **SF = 32**. The paths power profiles are given at Table 4 and the simulation results at Fig. 7.

Table 4. The paths power profiles of the 2 users

Power profile (dB)		1st path	2nd path	3rd path	4th path	5th path	6th path	7th path	8th path	9th path	10th path
User 1	1 path channel	0									
	3 paths channel	0	−2	−4							
	6 paths channel	0	−2	−4	−6	−8	−10				
	10 paths channel	0	−2	−4	−5	−8	−10	−12	14	−17	−20
User 2	1 path channel	0									
	3 paths channel	0	−3	−5							
	6 paths channel	0	−3	−5	−7	−9	−11				
	10 paths channel	0	−3	−5	−7	−9	−11	−13	−15	−18	−20

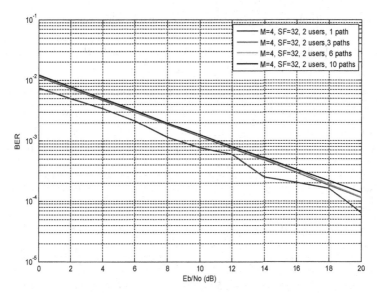

Fig. 7. Number of paths impact on the user1 signal BER

The results show that the best performance is obtained for a single path channel. For a 6 and a 10 paths channel, we see the same performance up to 16 dB. Beyond 16 dB, the best performance is obtained for a 6 paths channel.

4.4 Comparison of a 4-QAM OFDM Single User System and of a 4-QAM OFDM-CDMA Multiuser System

Consider a synchronous multiuser system based on OFDM access. It remains obvious that this system will give better performance in the event that it only transmits the signal of a single user.

In this sub-section, we want to determine the OFDM transmission system optimizing bandwidth and providing better signal quality. For this, we will compare the signals BER of two users having the same paths power profiles. One (**user1**) is in a 4-QAM OFDM single user system and the other (**always user1**) is in a 4-QAM OFDM-CDMA synchronous multiuser system. The comparison is made in a six paths Additive White Gaussian Noise channel and the considered simulation parameters are $N = 860160$ bits, $N\_fft = 128$, $Ncyc = 8$ and $Nt = 6$. The users power profiles are given at Table 5 and the results at Fig. 8.

Table 5. The users power profiles in a 6 paths channel

Power profile (dB)	1st path	2nd path	3rd path	4th path	5th path	6th path
User 1	0	−4	−8	−14	−17	−20
User 2	0	−6,5	−12,5	−14,5	−18	−20
User 3	0	−5	−13	−15	−18,5	−20
User 4	0	−8	−12	−14	−16	−17,5
User 5	0	−4,5	−11	−13	−15	−16,5
User 6	0	−3,5	−6	−10	−13,75	−15
User 7	0	−5	−8	−12	−14	−17
User 8	0	−2,75	−8	−10	−13	−15
User 9	0	−9	−13	−16	−18	−19,5
User 10	0	−6,75	−12,75	−14,75	−18,5	−19,5
User 11	0	−9,5	−13,5	−15,5	−19	−20
User 12	0	−8,5	−14	−16	−18	−19,5
User 13	0	−6,75	−11,5	−15,75	−17	−18,5
User 14	0	−7	−12	−16	−18	−20
User 15	0	−4	−8	−11	−15	−18
User 16	0	−2	−10	−14	−16	−19
User 17	0	−3	−12	−16	−18	−20
User 18	0	−5,75	−10	−15	−17	−19
User 19	0	−6	−12	−14	−16	−18
User 20	0	−2	−8	−13	−15	−17,5

The simulation results at Fig. 8 show for the values of Eb/N0 going from 0 dB to 11,5 dB, that the user1 signal BER is better in the 4-QAM OFDM-CDMA synchronous 20 users system. Beyond 11,5 dB, the user1 signal BER is the same in the two systems.

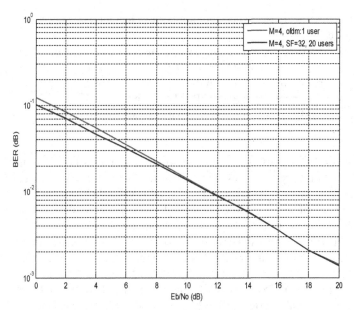

Fig. 8. User1 signal BER in a 4-QAM OFDM single-user system and in a 4-QAM OFDM-CDMA twenty users system

5 Conclusion

This work has been undertaken in a multipath Additive White Gaussian Noise (AWGN) channel to compare two types of systems: **M-QAM OFDM** systems and **M-QAM OFDM-CDMA** systems.

First, we studied the BER evolution of a M-QAM OFDM single-user system as a function of the constellation size M. This study showed that the lowest BER is reached with M = 4. Subsequently, we relied on a 4-QAM OFDM single-user system to study the impact of the number of channel paths on the system BER. This resulted in a BER which becomes smaller and smaller when the number of channel paths decreases (therefore better performance for a one path channel).

In a second step, we went on to study the performances in terms of BER of a M-QAM OFDM-CDMA synchronous multiuser system.

- The first study was to consider a M-QAM OFDM-CDMA two-user system to see the impact of the value of M on the user1 signal BER. This resulted in a lower BER for M = 4.
- In the second study, we considered a 4-QAM OFDM-CDMA two-user system with FFT = 128 to assess the impact of the spreading factor SF on the user1 signal BER. As a result, we came up with a weaker BER due to the increase of SF.
- In the third study, we considered with FFT = 128 and SF = 32, a 4-QAM OFDM-CDMA two-user system to see the impact of the number of channel paths on the user1 signal BER. As a result (in a 10, 6, 3 and 1 path channel), we observed a user1

signal BER that decreases when the number of channel paths decreases. So, better performance for a one path channel.

- Finally, we compared for a six paths channel, user1 signal BER in a 4-QAM OFDM single-user system and in a 4-QAM OFDM-CDMA synchronous multiuser system. For the same paths power profiles in the two systems application, FFT = 128 and SF = 32, we see that the user1 signal BER is better in the synchronous multiuser system where the OFDM symbols are spread; that is to say in the 4-QAM OFDM-CDMA system.

If in terms of BER a 4-QAM OFDM single-user system is normally more efficient than a 4-QAM OFDM synchronous multiuser system, we note from the simulations made in this paper that when SF is great, a 4-QAM OFDM-CDMA synchronous multi-user system is far better than a 4-QAM OFDM single user system. In the case for example of a 6 paths channel and for SF = 32, we do not obtain a sole better quality of user1 signal in the 4-QAM OFDM-CDMA twenty-user system, but also a less use of radio resources because the same OFDM carriers are allocated to the twenty users each identified by an OVSF code.

In the OFDMA multiple access technique which is based on OFDM, each user has his block of N sub-carriers. Therefore, it is necessary to have as many different blocks of N subcarriers as users to perform the OFDMA multiple access. But when SF is great, we have just seen that a 4-QAM OFDM-CDMA synchronous multi-user system offers better signal quality and greatly optimizes bandwidth. A **4-QAM OFDM-CDMA transmission system** can nowadays be used on wireless OFDM systems such as the OFDMA-based LTE downlink or even be a 5th generation mobile system.

References

1. Dahlman, E., Parkvall, S., Sköld, J.: 4G: LTE/LTE-Advanced for Mobile Broadband, pp. 27–43. Academic Press, Cambridge (2011)
2. Galih, S., Karlina, R., Nugroho, F., Irawan, A., Adiono, T., Kurniawan, A.: High mobility data pilot based channel estimation for downlink OFDMA system based on IEEE 802.16e standard. In: International Conference on Electrical Engineering and Informatics, Selangor, Malaysia, pp. 478–483 (2009)
3. ETSI TS 101 475 V1.2.2, ETSI Broadband Radio Access Networks (BRAN), HIPERLAN Type 2: Physical Layer, August 1999
4. DVB, A122: Framing structure, channel coding and modulation for a second generation digital terrestrial television broadcasting system (DVB-T2), June 2008
5. IEEE, Part 16: Air interface for fixed and mobile broadband wireless access systems - amendment 2: physical and medium access control layers for combined fixed and mobile operation in licensed bands (2005)
6. Sesia, S., Toufik, I., Baker, M.: LTE-The UMTS Long Term Evolution-From Theory to Practice. Wiley Press, Chichester (2009)

Traffic Load Perception Based OFDMA MAC Protocol for the Next Generation WLAN

Jianfei Cheng, Bo Li, Mao Yang$^{(\boxtimes)}$, and Zhongjiang Yan

School of Electronics and Information, Northwestern Polytechnical University,
Xi'an, China
434321310@mail.nwpu.edu.cn, {libo,yangmao,zhjyan.npu}@nwpu.edu.cn

Abstract. With the rapid development of wireless local area network (WLAN) and the proliferation of intelligent terminals, the current WLAN protocol is no longer able to meet the needs of users. Therefore, the next generation WLAN: IEEE 802.11ax has emerged to meet the growing demand for user traffic. Orthogonal Frequency Division Multiple Access (OFDMA), which enables simultaneous transmission of data by different User Equipment (UEs), is considered to be one of the key technologies of IEEE 802.11ax. In order to achieve high throughput rates and low access latency to ensure quality of service (QoS), IEEE 802.11ax supports two uplink access modes: scheduling access and random access. However, how to adaptively and efficiently switch these two access mechanisms in the process of real-time operation of the system, and effectively reduce the drawbacks caused by these two mechanisms is a thorny problem. This paper proposes an evaluation mechanism of network traffic load based on OFDMA-MAC protocol, and its performance is verified by simulation. The simulation results show that the traffic load assessment mechanism effectively improves the network throughput and quality of service (QoS), and also adapts to the dynamic changes in network traffic.

Keywords: OFDMA · UORA · 802.11ax · Traffic load perception

1 Introduction

Due to the rapid development of wireless local area networks, existing WLAN protocols is no longer able to meet the needs of users [1]. Now, key technologies and standardized IEEE 802.11ax are under study and will be promoted globally. For the next generation of WLAN, there are inevitably two needs: large network capacity and higher quality of service requirements. 1) Large network capacity. Increasingly diverse services require wireless networks to provide greater network capacity. For example, the potential users of the entire stadium may be 50,000–100,000 [2]. The WLAN in the stadium should provide users with video streaming and video calling services, which greatly challenges the capacity of the network [3]. 2) Higher quality of service requirements. In a high-density scenario, each

© ICST Institute for Computer Sciences, Social Informatics and Telecommunications Engineering 2020
Published by Springer Nature Switzerland AG 2020. All Rights Reserved
D.-J. Deng et al. (Eds.): WiCON 2019, LNICST 317, pp. 237–248, 2020.
https://doi.org/10.1007/978-3-030-52988-8_21

AP needs to associate tens or even hundreds of STAs [4]. Due to different user service requirements, wireless networks are required to ensure QoS requirements for different services. Therefore, next-generation WLANs need to find ways to meet large network capacity and high QoS requirements [5].

Next-generation communication networks have several emerging communication technologies, including uplink MU-MIMO [6] non-orthogonal multiple access [7], massive MIMO [8] and FD techniques [9], and orthogonal frequency division. Multiple Access (OFDMA) [10].

OFDMA allows users to share band resources and is one of the key technologies of 802.11ax. Orthogonal frequency division features can support more STAs, and a single transmission can carry more information. Therefore, OFDMA technology can significantly meet the needs of larger network capacity and higher quality of service. And 802.11ax also joined the management of the uplink. Prior to 802.11ax technology, uplink management was a random contention bandwidth; the new protocol in 802.11ax technology added some functions that can coordinate between terminals and uplink resource management scheduling. However, the scheduling-based access results in high access latency, since the STA always feeds back the buffer status to the AP, and then the AP finds the appropriate resource unit (RU) for the STA. Therefore, in order to guarantee QoS and achieve low access latency, 802.11ax supports two access modes: scheduling access and random access.

But how to effectively allocate resources to scheduling access and random access becomes a problem. Intuitively, this simple allocation method will result in inefficiencies if fixed allocation of radio resources to same access method. This is because the needs of STAs change over time. These two access methods should be dynamically changed, but if the selective access method is selected, it will lead to waste of resources or high collision.

Most scholars have proposed effective algorithms to support scheduling access and UOR A, Lou et al. [11] propose that the AP is able to achieve UL OFDMA transmission through the centralized scheduling approach. Mishima et al. [12] propose that AP sends RTS frame to multiple nodes, the nodes reply CTS frames sequentially, and then AP respectively schedules OFDMA UL transmission. Lanante et al. [13] compute the saturated throughput in the UL under the assumption that UL OFDMA-based RA (UORA) is the only mechanism for transmitting UL packets.

Few people pay attention to how to dynamically switch between scheduled access and random access, so that these two ways can better play their strengths.

This paper proposes a network traffic load perception mechanism to meet this need. The TLP-MAC supports dynamic switching of scheduled access and random access. We introduced the principles of the TLP-MAC and explained in detail the advantages of using the TLP-MAC. Then we model the TLP-MAC and analyze its performance from the simulation. The simulation results prove that the TLP-MAC can effectively alleviate the disadvantages caused by the two access modes, and the performance is better than the strictly separated access method.

We can summarize the contributions of this article as follows:

1) The protocol based on network load perception is proposed to enable the network to dynamically switch access modes.
2) Effectively improve the utilization efficiency of wireless resources, and effectively improve the overall throughput of the network under the premise of ensuring QoS.
3) TLP-MAC is not only applicable to 802.11ax, It has good scalability and portability.

This paper is mainly divided into five parts:

In the second part, the model of scheduling and random access is introduced. Then, in the third section, a MAC protocol based on network traffic load Perception mechanism is designed. The fourth section gives the performance verification based on the simulation platform, and the fifth section is the summary of this paper.

2 System Model

The IEEE 802.11ax D4.1 draft was completed in April 2019. It proposes a standard for next-generation WLANs. Therefore, we chose 802.11ax as a typical example for designing network traffic load perception mechanisms.

OFDMA is an evolution of OFDM technology that combines OFDM and FDMA technologies [14]. The OFDMA mechanism divides the bandwidth into sets of orthogonal subcarriers that do not overlap each other [15]. Different sets of subcarriers are allocated to different users to implement multiple access technology.

OFDMA has been used extensively in both 802.11ax and cellular networks [16]. We introduce the proposed network traffic load perception mechanism based on OFDMA technology.

In 802.11ax, there are a total of two methods of channel access, scheduling-based access and contention-based access. In the scheduling-based channel access, the AP sends a trigger frame containing the scheduling result information, and the AID12 in the user info field is set to the AID of the user in the cell. After receiving the trigger frame, the STA is in the allocated resource block. Transmission for data transmission, the specific process is shown in Fig. 1.

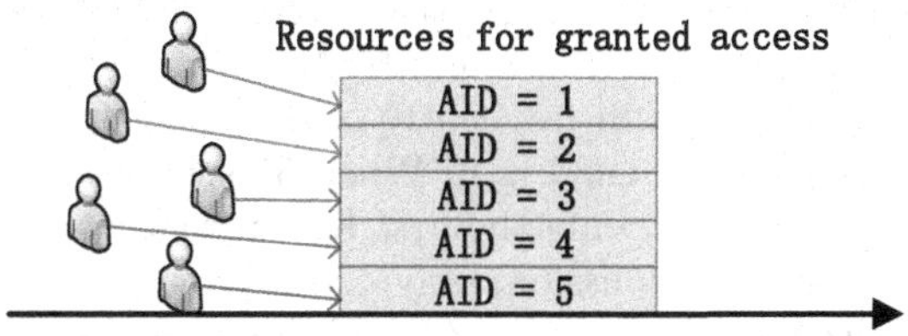

Fig. 1. Resource allocation for scheduling access.

802.11ax recently introduced uplink OFDMA random access (UORA), and the AID12 in the user info field is set to 0 in the trigger frame sent by the AP to indicate that these RUs are used for random contention. The STA randomly selects the RU for data transmission in these RUs for random competition. The specific process is shown in Fig. 2.

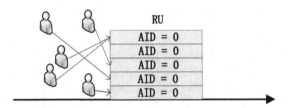

Fig. 2. Resource allocation for random access.

In our proposed network traffic load assessment mechanism, we adopt a scheduling mechanism and a UORA-based random competition mechanism. This does not mean that other scheduling methods or random-access methods are not applicable. TLP-MAC is suitable for all networks with the same characteristics.

3   Traffic Load Perception Based OFDMA MAC Protocol Design

3.1   Motivation

The scheduling-based access method or the UORA-based access method does not well meet the needs of the network at different times. We assume that only one user is allowed to transmit data in each RU. As shown in the Fig. 3, the AP divides the entire channel into 6 STAs for uplink scheduling access. At time i, only Two STAs have data to send to the AP, AID1 and AID2 are scheduled by the AP and the data transmission is successful. The remaining 4 UEs will have no data to be transmitted at this moment, which will result in the remaining 4 RU being vacant and the frequency resources being wasted. In this transmission, the utilization of the entire channel is only 1/3, so the overall performance of the network will decrease.

UORA-based access mode can effectively change the waste of frequency resources. However, if there are too many STAs to be sent at the same time, the RUs used for contention will frequently collide, and even all uplink transmissions will fail. As shown in the Fig. 4: When 5 users need to perform uplink transmission at the same time, only the first RU currently has only one user to select. Therefore, in this transmission, only one user can successfully transmit, and the channel utilization rate is only 1/3, and the service is also provided. QoS cannot be guaranteed.

In reality, the uplink traffic of wireless networks is constantly changing with location and time. For example, in some densely populated areas such as school dormitory buildings, the uplink traffic will be larger than the average area. Similarly, the nighttime business is better than the daytime. The amount is much larger. At this time, the uplink access mode selected by the AP is particularly important. Therefore, the network needs a service load evaluation mechanism to adaptively switch between different access modes.

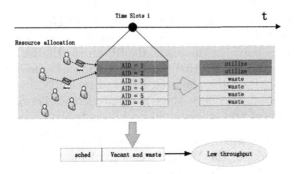

Fig. 3. Data transmission when scheduled access.

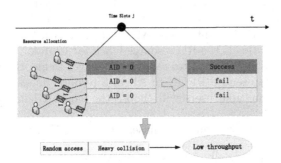

Fig. 4. Data transmission when random access.

3.2   Protocol Description

We propose a MAC layer protocol with a network traffic load perception mechanism. As shown in Fig. 5:

When the traffic is large, each STA has a high probability of performing uplink transmission. The AP adopts a scheduling-based access mechanism to arrange for each user to transmit data on the allocated RU:

(1) Buffer Status Report phase: The AP sends a BSRP. After receiving the trigger frame, the STA sends a BSR with the interval SIFS, including the current state information of the STA.
(2) Channel access phase: The AP monitors the channel state according to the carrier sense program of the IEEE 802.11 standard. When the channel is detected as an idle state, the AP performs a binary backoff procedure.
(3) Scheduling phase: After the AP backoff successfully, the AP performs scheduling according to the node information acquired in the BSR process, and then sends the result of the scheduling to the primary channel in the trigger frame, and the trigger frame contains several 5 bytes. The user information (User Info) mainly includes the AID of the scheduling user and the assigned RU location. At this stage, the RU for the UORA are not reserved.
(4) Data transmission phase: After receiving a trigger frame, the STA sends a PPDU to the AP on the allocated RU, and each RU is used for only one user transmission. Therefore, there is no interference between them.
(5) Acknowledgement transmission phase: AP sends MBA to each UL STAs.

When the traffic is small, each STA has a lower probability of uplink transmission. The AP adopts the UORA access mechanism, and each user freely competes with the RU for data transmission:

(1) Channel access phase: The AP monitors the channel state according to the carrier sense program of the IEEE 802.11 standard. When the channel is detected as an idle state, the AP performs a binary backoff.
(2) Scheduling phase: After completing the backoff procedure, the AP sends a trigger frame on the primary channel. The trigger frame contains 5 bytes of user information (User Info). The AID12 field in each User Info is set to 0, indicating that this is the RU resource block for UORA.
(3) Data transmission phase: After receiving a trigger frame, the STA randomly selects an RU to send a PPDU to AP in a resource block for UORA. It is possible that multiple users will choose the same RU and a conflict will occur.
(4) Acknowledgement transmission phase: AP sends MBA to each UL STAs.

The network dynamically selects the access type according to the amount of uplink traffic at different times. This is the working principle of the network service load evaluation mechanism. As shown in the Fig. 6, At time i, there are 6 STAs that need to perform uplink transmission. The AP adopts the method of scheduling access, and allocates RU resources to each STA. Each STA does not interfere with each other and successfully completes this. The secondary transmission fully utilizes the channel resources, avoids the unreliable transmission brought by the UORA access when the traffic is large, and ensures the service quality. At time j, only 3 STAs need to perform uplink transmission, and the AP adopts UORA access mode.

Allowing each STA to freely contend for the RU, saves the signaling overhead of the BSR compared to the scheduled access, and divides the entire channel into a smaller number of RUs. Therefore, each RU will have more subcarriers, which

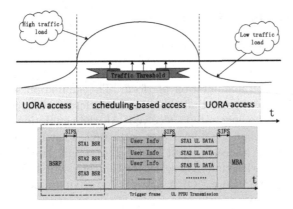

Fig. 5. The procedure of traffic load perception.

greatly increases the efficiency of a single transmission. Due to the small amount of traffic at this time, the probability of STA collisions is greatly reduced, and the quality of service is also guaranteed to a certain extent.

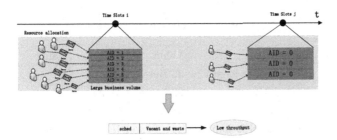

Fig. 6. Combination of scheduled access and random access.

3.3   Traffic Threshold

Obviously, the traffic threshold is a critical part of our protocol, and a suitable threshold can greatly improve throughput and MAC efficiency. If we set the threshold too low, the network is more inclined to schedule access. The threshold setting is too high and the network is more prone to UORA. Therefore, choosing a suitable threshold is critical. The choice of threshold is related to several factors, such as the number of STAs associated with the AP and the quality of the current network environment. In the next section, we try to find the optimal threshold through simulation.

4   Simulation and Results

4.1   The Simulation Configuration

In order to evaluate the performance of network service load evaluation mechanism, we constructed a simulation platform. The simulation scenario is 1 AP and several STAs. We assume that there is no interference between the RUs and the data frame can be successfully received. All the simulations are performed under the condition that the STA is not saturated. That is, the STA does not need to send data to the AP at all times. The uplink traffic of the network changes periodically with time. We select the network with TLP-MAC, the pure scheduling network and Pure UORA networks to compare network throughput and transmission delay.

The parameters in the simulation are shown in Table 1. The maximum number of aggregations is 64, and the maximum transmission time of TB-PPDUs is 4 ms. The two scenarios simulated are as follows:

1. The number of STAs has increased from 3 to 12, and UORA uses 20M-106TONE.
2. The number of STAs is 12, and the traffic threshold is gradually increased.

Table 1. Simulation parameters

Parameter	Value	Parameter	Value
MAC header length	30 Bytes	CWmin	15
Trigger length	22 Bytes	CWmax	63
Frequency	5 GHz	Slot time	9 μs
Max AMPDU number	64	DIFS	43 μs
Power per 20 MHz	15 dBm	TB-PPDU	4 ms

4.2   The Simulation Results in Scene I

Figure 7 shows the results of throughput change with the increase of STAs. Obviously, the network performance with TLP-MAC is significantly better than pure scheduling network and pure UORA network. As the number of STAs increases, the probability of collision of nodes through UORA access increases. When the number of cell nodes is small, the performance of TLP-MAC is 43% and 14% higher than that of scheduling network and UORA network respectively. When the number of STAs increases, the performance of TLP-MAC is 8% higher than that of scheduling network and UORA network respectively. 124%; When the traffic is at a low level, that is, when there are fewer STAs, it can be seen that the performance of UORA is better than that of UORA when the traffic is at a high level, that is, when there are many cell nodes due to scheduling performance.

Figure 8 shows the results of transmission delay with the increase of STAs. The transmission delay with the TLP network is clearly at a lower level. The transmission delay is reduced by an average of 6 ms compared to the scheduling network. Compared to UORA networks, the transmission delay is reduced by an average of 20 ms.

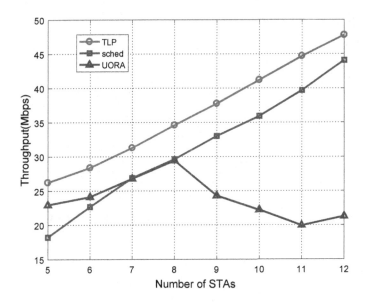

Fig. 7. Throughput varies with the number of STAs.

4.3   The Simulation Results in Scene II

Figure 9 shows the results of throughput change with the increase of traffic threshold. The performance of the network is best when the traffic threshold is around 1600 Kbytes. If the threshold is set too low, network performance will approach the scheduling network. If the threshold is set too high, the probability of collision will increase and the performance of the network will be greatly affected. Choosing a suitable threshold is important for TLP-MAC.

Figure 10 shows the results of transmission delay with the increase of traffic threshold. When the threshold is near 1600 Kbytes, the transmission delay of the network is the smallest. A threshold that is too high or too low will increase the transmission delay.

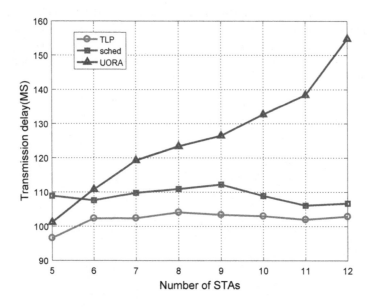

Fig. 8. Transmission delay varies with the number of STAs.

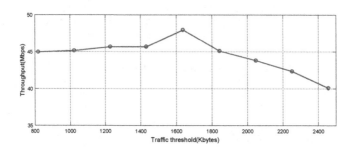

Fig. 9. Traffic threshold vs. transmission delay.

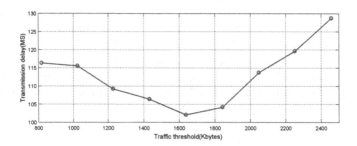

Fig. 10. Traffic threshold vs. transmission delay.

5   Conclusion

In this paper, the MAC protocol based on the evaluation mechanism of network traffic load is proposed, and the details of MAC protocol design are introduced. This kind of protocol makes good use of the advantages of two access methods and reduces the disadvantages brought by them to a certain extent. As far as we know, this is the first network service based on IEEE802.11ax. Load evaluation mechanism protocol design. In addition, this protocol is also very suitable for other systems, TLP-MAC has good compatibility. The simulation results show that TLP-MAC has better network performance than pure scheduling and pure free competition network. In the future research, the author will focus on the optimal traffic thresholds in different network environments and the relationship between them to further improve the versatility of TLP networks.

Acknowledgement. This work was supported in part by the National Natural Science Foundations of CHINA (Grant No. 61771390, No. 61871322, No. 61771392, No. 61271279, and No. 61501373), the National Science and Technology Major Project (Grant No. 2016ZX03001018-004), and Science and Technology on Avionics Integration Laboratory (20185553035).

References

1. Laya, A., Alonso, L., Alonso-Zarate, J.: Efficient contention resolution in highly dense LTE networks for machine type communications. In: IEEE Global Communications Conference (2016)
2. Bellalta, B.: IEEE 802.11ax: high-efficiency WLANs. IEEE Wirel. Commun. **23**(1), 38–46 (2016)
3. Deng, D.J., Chen, K.C., Cheng, R.S.: IEEE 802.11ax: next generation wireless local area networks. In: International Conference on Heterogeneous Networking for Quality (2014)
4. Bellalta, B., Kosek-Szott, K.: AP-initiated multi-user transmissions in IEEE 802.11ax WLANs (2017)
5. Yong, N., Yong, L., Jin, D., Li, S., Vasilakos, A.V.: A survey of millimeter wave communications (mmWave) for 5G: opportunities and challenges. Wirel. Netw. **21**(8), 2657–2676 (2015)
6. Studer, C., Durisi, G.: Quantized massive MU-MIMO-OFDM uplink. IEEE Trans. Commun. **64**(6), 2387–2399 (2016)
7. Dai, L., Wang, B., Yuan, Y., Han, S., Chih-Lin, I., Wang, Z.: Non-orthogonal multiple access for 5G: solutions, challenges, opportunities, and future research trends. IEEE Commun. Mag. **53**(9), 74–81 (2015)
8. Bjornson, E., Larsson, E.G., Marzetta, T.L.: Massive MIMO: ten myths and one critical question. IEEE Commun. Mag. **54**(2), 114–123 (2016)
9. Duarte, M., Sabharwal, A., Aggarwal, V., Jana, R., Shankaranarayanan, N.K.: Design and characterization of a full-duplex multiantenna system for WiFi networks. IEEE Trans. Veh. Technol. **63**(3), 1160–1177 (2014)
10. Bo, L., Qiao, Q., Yan, Z., Mao, Y.: Survey on OFDMA based MAC protocols for the next generation WLAN. In: Wireless Communications & Networking Conference Workshops (2015)

11. Lou, H., Wang, X., Fang, J., Ghosh, M., Zhang, G., Olesen, R.: Multi-user parallel channel access for high efficiency carrier grade wireless LANs. In: IEEE International Conference on Communications (2014)
12. Mishima, T., Miyamoto, S., Sampei, S., Jiang, W.: Novel DCF-based multi-user MAC protocol and dynamic resource allocation for OFDMA WLAN systems. In: International Conference on Computing (2013)
13. Lanante, L., Uwai, H.O.T., Nagao, Y., Kurosaki, M., Ghosh, C.: Performance analysis of the 802.11ax UL OFDMA random access protocol in dense networks. In: IEEE International Conference on Communications (2017)
14. Qiao, Q., Bo, L., Mao, Y., Yan, Z.: An OFDMA based concurrent multiuser MAC for upcoming IEEE 802.11ax. In: Wireless Communications & Networking Conference Workshops (2015)
15. Fernando, X.N., Srikanth, S., Pandian, P.A.M.: Orthogonal frequency division multiple access in WiMax and LTE a comparison. IEEE Commun. Mag. **50**(9), 153–161 (2010)
16. Shen, Z., Papasakellariou, A., Montojo, J., Gerstenberger, D., Xu, F.: Overview of 3G PP LTE-advanced carrier aggregation for 4G wireless communications. IEEE Commun. Mag. **50**(2), 122–130 (2012)

Environment Sensing Based Adaptive Acknowledgement and Backoff for the Next Generation WLAN

Yuan Yan, Bo Li, Mao Yang[✉], and Zhongjiang Yan

School of Electronics and Information, Northwestern Polytechnical University,
Xi'an, China
yanyuan2035@mail.nwpu.edu.cn, {libo.npu,yangmao,zhjyan}@nwpu.edu.cn

Abstract. Wireless LAN (WLAN) developed quite fast over the last two decades, and the next generation WLAN standard: IEEE 802.11ax will be released in 2020. IEEE 802.11ax needs to improve the performance and user experience under the ultra-high-dense deployment of cells. Thus, the concept of spatial reuse (SR) is introduced in IEEE 802.11ax by enabling more communication links to simultaneously transmit. This paper proposes an environment sensing based link adaptation algorithm (ESBLA). ESBLA introduces intelligent environment sensing and identifies the environment into several types: nice environment, serious collision, and severe channel fading. After that, ESBLA adjust the media access control (MAC) layer transmission strategy according to the sensed environment type. The simulation results show that ESBLA can reduce the impact of intensive deployment interference as much as possible while guaranteeing high throughput.

Keywords: WLAN · IEEE 802.11ax · ARF · MAC

1 Introduction

With the popularization of WLAN protocol IEEE 802.11ac, most of the devices have supported the protocol, which also represents the great improvement of people's daily network resource demand. At the same time, the next generation WLAN protocol IEEE 802.11ax [1], will be officially released. The technology of spatial reuse has greatly improved the throughput of cell [2].

In order to meet the requirements of ultra-high speed, high throughput, ultra-high reliability and ultra-low latency in future networks [3], emerging communication networks will be more and more heterogeneous, ultra-intensive and diversified, and the interference within the network system will become multi-level and complex [4,5]. This will lead to strong internal interference and resource collision, which will greatly limit the capacity and quality of service of the system. Because of the distributed characteristics, WLAN has to consider some wireless environment problems, such as channel fading is

D.-J. Deng et al. (Eds.): WiCON 2019, LNICST 317, pp. 249–259, 2020.
https://doi.org/10.1007/978-3-030-52988-8_22

serious, collision is serious, channel fading is serious and collision is serious. If the real-time environment around WLAN can not be accurately grasped, the MAC can not give the optimal configuration. Conversely, if we can accurately grasp the surrounding environment, we can let MAC and PHY support services with the optimal configuration, thereby improving the quality of network services.

This paper proposes a new link adaptation algorithm ESBLA based on wireless environment intelligent sensing. The MAC layer adjusts the MAC transmission configuration according to the environment state given by the wireless environment sensing module, so as to ensure the link quality. When the channel environment is good, the physical layer transmission rate can be increased rapidly; when the collision is serious, the minimum backoff competition window can be increased appropriately; when the channel fading is serious, the physical layer transmission rate can be limited. The simulation results show that compared with EDCA without environmental awareness mechanism, the throughput of the proposed algorithm can be increased by up to 30% and the packet loss rate can be reduced by up to 15%.

In this paper, for the first time, a novel pain point scenario optimization algorithm is proposed, which combines the intelligent recognition function of the environment with the transmission parameters of the wireless network. On the one hand, it guarantees the reliability of wireless network under ultra-intensive deployment, on the other hand, it reflects the trend of future wireless LAN towards intelligent development.

This paper is mainly divided into six parts: Sect. 2 protocol description. Section 3 protocol design. Section 4 simulation design and implementation. Section 5 performance analysis. Section 6 conclusion and future work.

2   Protocol Description

2.1   Related Work

In order to solve the degradation of QOS (quality of service) caused by the increasing complexity of wireless environment, most of the solutions proposed in the literature [6,7] are to feedback the channel environment according to the actual data packet reception and to ensure the stability of transmission by controlling the transmission rate of the physical layer of the sender. For example, AARF algorithm counts the number of successful or unsuccessful frames; MiRA algorithm [8] counts subframe error probability based on block confirmation; HA-RRAA algorithm [9] counts frame error rate in a short time. This method, which uses the statistical information value in a short time as the basis to measure the channel, has a lag and can not track the channel condition in real time.

ARF Algorithm. Among these algorithms, ARF algorithm is the most widely used. It counts ACK frame information to make decision on rate adjustment. If the sender does not receive Ndown ACK frames in succession, it immediately reduces the rate and starts a timer. If the node receives Nup [10] (default value is 10) ACK frames continuously or the timer timeouts, the rate will be increased by one level and the timer will be closed. If the first transmission (probe frame) fails after the rate increases, the rate is immediately lowered and the timer is started (Fig. 1).

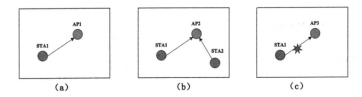

Fig. 1. SRP scene diagram.

BEB Algorithm. In MAC protocol, the random backoff mechanism decides who will get the channel occupancy, and the binary exponential backoff algorithm is the most widely used backoff algorithm. As shown in Fig. 2, the backoff management module randomly selects the backoff value from [0, CWmin]. If this transmission fails, the next transmission will double the competition window, and the probability of two nodes competing to the channel will be reduced at the same time, thus successfully avoiding the collision of adjacent nodes.

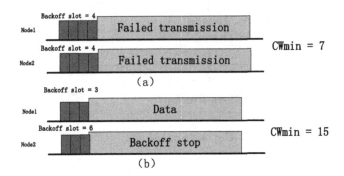

Fig. 2. Backoff mechanism.

2.2 Motivation

However, neither ARF nor BEB can effectively guarantee the quality of service in today's diverse channel environment. If the current channel environment is good, because ARF algorithm is more conservative for the promotion speed of MCS, nodes can not effectively utilize channel resources; if the cell deployment is highly centralized, the competition conflict between the nodes within the cell and adjacent cells will greatly reduce the link quality; if the current channel fading is seriously attenuated, ARF algorithm can not rapidly reduce the MCS, resulting in a higher packet loss rate. Therefore, this paper will propose the concept of channel intelligent sensing, and adjust the MAC transmission strategy in time on the premise of knowing the current channel state, so as to ensure the stability and effectiveness of data packet transmission in the diverse channel state.

3   Protocol Design

3.1   Protocol Flow

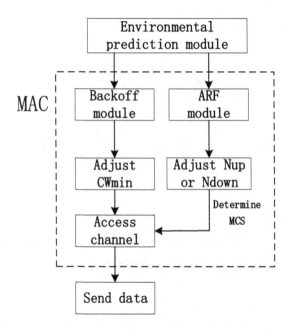

Fig. 3. Protocol flow.

Figure 3 describes the main flow of the MAC layer protocol. The environment-aware module relies on machine learning to determine the current channel state. The backoff module and ARF management module of MAC layer adjust CWmin, Nup and Ndown according to the channel state. When the node backoff ends and accesses the channel, the optimal MCS given by ARF management module is obtained and the data packet is sent.

3.2   Link Adaptive Design

This algorithm will design three different MAC layer transmission parameter adjustment schemes according to the three environment states given by the environment module: good channel state, serious conflict and serious channel attenuation. Plan A: Reduce Nup; Plan B: Increase Cwmin; Plan C: Reduce Ndown;

1. If the current channel state is determined to be good, then P (Environmental Perception Accuracy) probability executes Plan A, $(1 - P)/2$ probability executes Plan B, $(1 - P)/2$ probability executes Plan C.
2. If the current channel state conflict is serious, then P probability executes Plan B, $(1 - P)/2$ probability executes Plan A, $(1 - P)/2$ probability executes Plan C.
3. If the current channel state is determined to be seriously fading, then P probability executes Plan C, $(1 - P)/2$ probability executes Plan A, $(1 - P)/2$ probability executes Plan B.

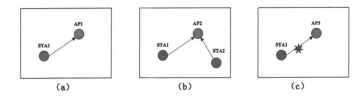

Fig. 4. Three possible scenarios.

As shown in Fig. 4(a), when the channel condition is good, reducing Nup will get higher transmission rate faster; as shown in Fig. 4(b), increasing CWmin will reduce the probability of each node getting the same back-off value to alleviate the conflict when the conflict is serious; as shown in Fig. 4(c), when the channel attenuation is serious, reducing Ndown will quickly reduce MCS when the link transmission fails to ensure link stability. The mode of adjusting transmission parameters according to channel perception will greatly reduce the impact of the lag of many link adaptation algorithms.

3.3   Pseudo Code

The core idea of this algorithm will be given in the form of pseudo-code. The first *Switch* represents the environment simulation algorithm, which changes the corresponding simulation parameters according to the random environment coefficients. The second *Switch* represents the adaptive algorithm, which adjusts the appropriate simulation parameters according to the perception results given by the environment simulation algorithm.

Algorithm 1. ESBLA Algorithm

Initialization: Parameter introduction: Environment is a stochastic simulation environment; Exponent is the channel attenuation coefficient; CWmin is the initial backoff window with an initial value of 7; Nup is the success threshold of ARF module speed-up with an initial value of 10; Ndown is the ARF module rate reduction failure threshold with an initial value of 2.

1: **switch** *Environment* **do**
2:      **case** 1
3:          $Exponent = 2.5$;
4:          $break$;

5:      **case** 2
6:          $CWmin = (Cwmin + 1)/2 - 1$;
7:          $break$;

8:      **case** 3
9:          $Exponent = 4.5$;
10:          $break$;

11: **switch** *Environment* **do**
12:      **case** 1
13:          $Nup = 5$;
14:          $break$;

15:      **case** 2
16:          $CWmin = Cwmin * 2 + 1$;
17:          $break$;

18:      **case** 3
19:          $Ndown = 1$;
20:          $break$;

---

4   Design and Implementation of Simulation

4.1   Related Work

In order to evaluate the performance of the above design and verify the expected effect, the simulation based on NS-3 platform[11] is carried out in this paper. NS-3 is a discrete event simulator, in which ARF algorithm has been implemented. According to the configuration requirements given by simulation platform, this paper only runs ARF management module under IEEE 802.11a protocol. In order to achieve performance comparison, the traditional DCF scenario configuration is also implemented on the platform as a comparison scheme.

4.2   Simulation Configuration

Make the configuration shown in Table 1 below on NS-3 platform[12].

Table 1. Simulation scenario configuration table

Parameter	Value
Parameter	SRP_CCA_DISALLOW
Cell topology	$4 * 8$
Distance between cells	$15\,\mathrm{m}$
Cell STA number	10
Traffic type	Uplink
Packet size	1500 byte
Protocol selection	IEEE 802.11a
Simulation time	$10\,\mathrm{s}$
Environmental change cycle	$0.5\,\mathrm{s}$
Exponent	$2.5/4.5$
Nup	$5/10$
Ndown	$1/2$

As shown in the above table, the environment simulation module is added to the simulation. Three channel states are simulated by periodically changing the channel attenuation parameters and the initial competition window:

1. Reduce the channel layer attenuation parameter Exponent to 2.5 in NS3 platform, and simulate the current wireless environment better;
2. Reduce the initial competition window of each node to simulate the serious competition conflict;
3. Increase the channel layer attenuation parameter Exponent to 4.5 to simulate the serious attenuation of the current wireless environment.

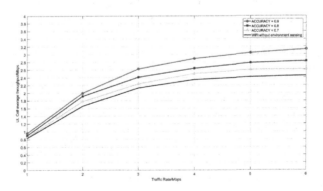

Fig. 5. Average throughput of the ESBLA algorithm.

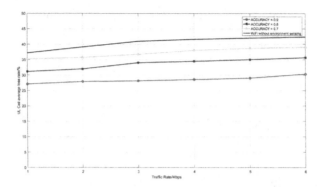

Fig. 6. Average packet loss rate of the ESBLA algorithm.

5   Performance Analysis

5.1   Trends in Performance Versus Service Rate

Figure 5 and Fig. 6 show the trend of performance versus traffic rate. Among them, the curve labeled "WiFi without environmental sensing" is the traditional DCF simulation curve, and the curve labeled "ACCURACY" is the simulation curve with the perception accuracy of 0.9/0.8/0.7 given by the environmental perception module. In order to use the traditional DCF mode as the contrast mode, this paper also adds the environment simulation module to it. Figure 5 shows the change of throughput; and Fig. 6 shows the change of packet loss rate.

In Fig. 5, throughput comparisons under four modes are presented. Overall, with the increase of traffic rate, the average cell throughput is increasing, in which the first half of the curve rises faster, the second half of the traffic rate tends to be saturated and the throughput tends to be stable. From the point of view of each mode, it is obvious that adding environmental awareness module will significantly improve the throughput. The higher the sensing accuracy, the greater the throughput gain. According to my laboratory research, the maximum accuracy of the environmental awareness module is 87%, and the maximum throughput gain can reach 30% with the optimal accuracy of 90%.

In Fig. 6, the comparison of packet loss rates under four modes is presented. Generally speaking, with the increase of service rate, the average packet loss rate of cell increases slightly, because the service rate from unsaturated to saturated state will bring more intense competition. However, the packet loss rate of the three precision modes of ESBLA algorithm shown in the figure is lower than that of the traditional DCF mode. The higher the accuracy, the lower the packet loss rate. As can be seen from the figure, ESBLA algorithm can reduce the packet loss rate by up to 15% under the 90% precision mode.

5.2   Trends in Performance Versus Number of Users

Figure 7 and Fig. 8 show the trend of performance changing with the number of cell users. Saturated traffic rate is used to simulate the curves. Figure 7 shows the change of throughput and Fig. 8 shows the change of packet loss rate.

In Fig. 7, as a whole, with the increase of the number of cell users, the throughput of the four modes is decreasing. This is because the simulation service is an upstream service, and the increase of the number of users will multiply the degree of fierce competition. It is not only the intra-cell link conflict, but also the natural concurrent links between the cell and the small cell will be more likely to produce high-power interference. Compared with the traditional DCF mode, the throughput of ESBLA decreases slowly. Similar to Fig. 5, the higher the perception accuracy of the algorithm, the higher the throughput. Under the 90% perception accuracy mode, the maximum throughput gain of the algorithm can reach 230%. It can be seen that when the number of cell users is large, ESBLA algorithm can better guarantee the successful transmission of adjacent links.

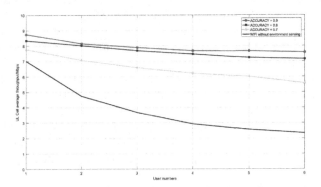

Fig. 7. Average throughput of the ESBLA algorithm.

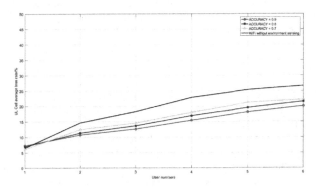

Fig. 8. Average packet loss rate of the ESBLA algorithm.

In Fig. 8, the loss rate of each mode is similar to that of Fig. 6. As the number of users increases, the packet loss rate increases, while ESBLA algorithm slightly alleviates the increase of packet loss rate.

Combining the above two simulation results, ESBLA algorithm can bring larger gains for cell regardless of the change of traffic rate or the number of cell users. In densely deployed cell environment, ESBLA algorithm can also bring 30% throughput gain and 15% packet loss reduction, which makes complex wireless environment more orderly and reliable.

6   Conclusion

Combined with the simulation results and analysis of the previous section, it can be concluded that the link adaptation algorithm based on environment awareness can greatly optimize the transmission parameters configuration of WLAN, and bring about 30% throughput gain while reducing the packet loss rate in the traditional DCF mode [13]. The gain can reach 230% in the moderate number of users, and the reliability of the link can be effectively guaranteed. In the future, with the gradual promotion of the IEEE 802.11ax protocol, more and more densely deployed cells will be deployed, which requires more real-time link adaptation algorithm. The idea based on environmental intelligent perception proposed in this paper will be widely used.

Although from the gain point of view, this algorithm has achieved remarkable results in improving the transmission quality, but in the future, the three channel states and solutions proposed in this paper are relatively preliminary in the high-or even ultra-high-density deployment environment of cell. Therefore, in the future research, the author will focus on the diversity of perception accuracy and environmental state, so as to propose more and more effective solutions.

Acknowledgement. This work was supported in part by the National Natural Science Foundations of CHINA (Grant No. 61771390, No. 61871322, No. 61771392, No. 61271279, and No. 61501373), the National Science and Technology Major Project (Grant No. 2016ZX03001018-004), and Science and Technology on Avionics Integration Laboratory (20185553035).

References

1. Wireless LAN medium access control (MAC) and physical layer (PHY) specifications amendment 6: enhancements for high efficiency WLAN, IEEE Draft 802.11ax/D2.0, October 2017
2. Qu, Q., Li, B., Yang, M., et al.: Survey and Performance evaluation of the upcoming next generation WLAN Standard - IEEE 802.11ax (2018)
3. Drieberg, M., Zheng, F.C., Ahmad, R., et al.: An improved distributed dynamic channel assignment scheme for dense WLANs. In: International Conference on Information, Communications & Signal Processing, pp. 1–5. IEEE (2008)
4. Zhang, D., Mohanty, B., Sambhwani, S.D.: Scheduling based on effective target load with interference cancellation in a wireless communication system (2014). US, US8676124

5. Bellalta, B.: IEEE 802.11ax: high-efficiency WLANs. IEEE Wirel. Commun. **23**(1), 38–46 (2016)
6. Deng, X., Li, X., Liu, Q., et al.: RAS: rate adaptation in IEEE 802.11 with receiver's SNR. Comput. Eng. Sci. **35**(12), 45–51 (2013)
7. Pang, Z., Wu, B., Ye, T.: Highly efficient rate adaptation algorithm for IEEE 802.11ac. J. Xian Univ. **43**(01), 120–126 (2016)
8. Pefkianakis, I., Lee, S.B., Lu, S.: Towards MIMO-Aware 802.11n Rate Adaptation. IEEE Press, Piscataway (2013)
9. Pefkianakis, I., Wong, S.H.Y., Yang, H., et al.: Toward history-aware robust 802.11 rate adaptation. IEEE Trans. Mob. Comput. **12**(3), 502–515 (2013)
10. Kamerman, A., Monteban, L.: WaveLAN-II: a high-performance wireless LAN for the unlicensed band. Bell Labs Tech. J. **2**(3), 118–133 (1997)
11. Simulation and analysis of an integrated GPRS and WLAN network
12. Ha, D.V.: Network simulation with NS3 (2010)
13. Ong, E.H., Kneckt, J., Alanen, O., et al.: IEEE 802.11ac: enhancements for very high throughput WLANs. In: IEEE 22nd International Symposium on Personal, Indoor and Mobile Radio Communications, PIMRC 2011, Toronto, ON, Canada, 11–14 September 2011. IEEE (2011)

Multi-BSS Association and Cooperation Based Handoff Scheme for the Next Generation mmWave WiFi: IEEE 802.11ay

Yue Li, Ping Zhao, Bo Li, Mao Yang$^{(\boxtimes)}$, and Zhongjiang Yan

School of Electronics and Information,
Northwestern Polytechnical University, Xian, China
lyjkf16@mail.nwpu.edu.cn, yangmao@nwpu.edu.cn

Abstract. Wireless LAN (WLAN) based on IEEE 802.11 protocol standard is widely used due to its advantages of low cost, fast speed, flexibility and convenience. Among them, the coverage distance of the millimeter wave (mmWave) WiFi such as IEEE 802.11ay is relatively short. In order to meet the needs of Virtual Reality (VR), high definition (HD) video and other emerging services, mmWave WiFi often adopts high-dense deployment. The mobility of nodes often causes multi-BSS handoff. MmWave WiFi handoff process is complex and consumes a lot of network signaling and time. Based on the advantages of multi-BSS association and cooperation, this paper designs a handoff protocol for mmWave WiFi to complete multi-BSS handoff without interruption of business continuity. Through simulation verification and comparison with other multi-BSS handoff technologies, proposed protocol improves the throughput and reduces the time delay.

Keywords: mmWave WiFi · AP clustering · Handoff · IEEE 802.11ay

1 Introduction

With the rapid growth of user business, WLAN has become one of the most important ways to carry data services. In order to satisfy the increasing needs of user business, academia and industry are focusing on the research and standardization of key technologies in the next generation WLAN standard.

High-frequency WiFi is suitable for ultra-high-capacity short-distance scenes, such as VR, HD video, etc. However, due to the short coverage distance of high-frequency, multi-BSS handoff is bound to occur as people move. The Handoff of traditional 802.11ad and 11ay requires that under certain conditions (such as poor signal quality), the connected AP should be broken first, and then the service will be interrupted if the new AP is added and scanned again. This problem becomes more and more serious in the case of high frequency and short

D.-J. Deng et al. (Eds.): WiCON 2019, LNICST 317, pp. 260–268, 2020.
https://doi.org/10.1007/978-3-030-52988-8_23

range [2]. How to improve handoff efficiency and ensure business continuity has become the focus of high frequency and high density deployment research.

In high-density deployment scenarios, there are often multiple AP resources around the STA that can be accessed, thus enabling a quick handoff to a BSS with better communication quality when the STA is moving. There are many research schemes for secure and fast handoff in WLAN, but there are few related researches in high frequency WLAN. Therefore, to overcome the challenge that the Next Generation mmWave WiFi: IEEE 802.11ay needs to realize fast handoff between multi-BSS, this paper proposes a MAC protocol based on multi-BSS association and cooperation based handoff. Specifically, this paper designs this MAC protocol flow, and plans simulation to verify its feasibility. From the simulation, it can be seen that the designed protocol can improve throughput and reduce delay.

This paper is structured as follows: Sect. 2 introduces medium access control (MAC) of IEEE 802.11ad protocol and AP Clustering, and draws out the core idea of the paper. Section 3 details the high frequency WiFi handoff protocol based on multi-BSS association and cooperation. Section 4 shows the simulation results and analysis. In Sect. 5, give conclusion for the paper.

2   Motivation

2.1   Introduction to High-Frequency BI Frames

IEEE 802.11ay protocol is suitable for high speed wireless communication in 60 GHz frequency band. Based on the 802.11 standard, the 802.11ay protocol redefines the physical layer(PHY)and the MAC. The paper designs the MAC layer for AP cooperation based on IEEE 802.11ay protocol. BI (Beacon Interval) frame is the basis of channel access in the 802.11ay protocol. BI frame is divided into four periods, and the access time and rules for every period are different. AP or STA schedules each period according to the planned schedule. As shown in Fig. 1, the four periods are: Beacon transmission interval (BTI), Association beamforming training (A-BFT), Announcement transmission interval (ATI), and Data transfer interval (DTI). Among them, BTI, A-BFT and ATI periods are all for beam training, which can be collectively called BHI period [3].

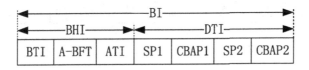

Fig. 1. Beacon interval frame.

In the BTI period, AP sends Beacon frames to STA. When STA receives the frame, it compares the different Beacon frames received, and finds out the best transmitting beam ID of AP. In the A-BFT period, STA takes up the channel according to the scheduling information in the received Beacon frame and sends the feedback frame to AP. AP receives the feedback frame to know its best transmitting beam ID, and compares different feedback frames to get the best transmitting beam ID of STA, and informs STA. In ATI period, AP and STA interact several times to confirm their best receiving beam ID [4]. And DTI consists of two periods: competition based access period (CBAP) and Service period (SP). Each sub-period communicates with the best beam ID trained in BHI period. CBAP is similar to EDCA competition mechanism; SP does not require competition, and nodes communicate according to time slot allocated [5].

2.2   Introduction of AP Clustering

1. The Principle of AP Clustering. AP Clustering is a new Clustering algorithm proposed by Science journal in 2007. The core idea of the algorithm is to automatically discover the clustering center by passing messages between data points and realize the automatic clustering of data points [6]. Compared with traditional clustering, it does not specify the number of classes and the initial clustering center in the initialization stage. On the contrary, it regards each data point as a potential clustering center equally, which can greatly reduce the impact of assuming the initial center on the clustering results [7].

2. AP Clustering Design in IEEE 802.11 ad/ay Protocol. In IEEE 802.11 ad/ay protocol, AP Clustering function is added and corresponding frame structure is designed. Its main purpose is to improve the spatial sharing ability of nodes and reduce the conflict with BSSs with the same channel.

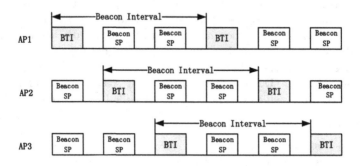

Fig. 2. Example of distributed AP clustering.

Figure 2 shows three PCP/AP distributed clustering flowchart, where PCP/AP1 is S-AP, the other two PCP/AP are slave AP. In the first BI, AP1 starts BTI at the beginning of BI, while others start BTI at the time of BI/n*(No. ID -1), where n means the number of AP. For example, when AP1 is in the BTI period, AP2 and AP3 are in the idle Beacon SP. During this SP period, AP2 and AP3 cannot communicate with their respective STA, in order not to interfere the sending process of AP1's Beacon frame. At the same time, AP1 needs to reserve two special SP periods in the its BTI period: Beacon SP2 and Beacon SP3, which are used to indicate that the STAs of AP1 are not allowed to send data to AP1 during the two SP periods, so AP1 doesn't affect the BTI transmission of AP2 and AP3.

2.3 Motivation

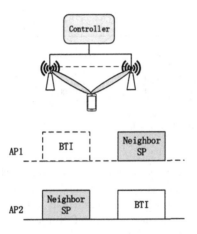

Fig. 3. Introduction of idea.

The coverage range of high-frequency WiFi is small. In order to meet the business requirements of VR and HD video, the AP in the coverage area of mmWave wireless LAN presents a very high density distribution. When the user position moves, the following two problems will occur: A. The communication quality between the user and the current BSS AP will become worse; B. The user has entered the coverage of another BSS and needs to switch the BSS [8].

Regardless of question a or b, the user needs to disconnect from the currently connected AP and then rescan and add a new AP. [9] Rescanning can cause disruptions, a problem that gets worse at high frequencies and short distances. The handoff process of WLAN is complex, which needs to consume a lot of signaling and process load [10]. If the handoff cannot be completed smoothly or the handoff delay is too long, the user's communication, especially for the service with strong real-time performance, will have interruption that the user can obviously perceive or even seriously affect the user experience [11].

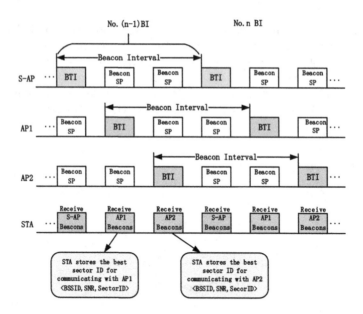

Fig. 4. STA looks for the new best AP

2. In the high-density deployment area, the coverage of the area is small, so the number of disconnection and reconnection must be more than the low frequency. The delay time in [12] is about 1.5 s, which will affect the business continuity and network throughput for the high-speed communication required by high-frequency WIFI [13]. How to improve handoff efficiency and ensure business continuity has become the focus of high frequency and high density deployment research [14].

To solve this problem, this paper proposes the idea of high frequency WiFi handoff based on multi-BSS association and cooperation, which is called HAC (Handoff based on AP Clustering) for short, to complete the BSS handoff without interrupting the connected AP.

3   MAC Protocol

3.1   Idea

In IEEE 802.11 ad/ay protocol standard, Beacon frame and SSW frame in the beam training stage are omnidirectional transmission, that is, through Beacon frame and SSW frame, all AP and STA can conduct brief interaction from Fig. 3. Nevertheless, only the BTI interaction information with the current communication AP is used in the DTI period, and the BTI interaction information between STA and other AP is useless.

1. Considering this point, can this paper use the BTI interaction information between STA and other AP to make handoff?

Using BTI interactive information in question 1, information between STA and new AP can be obtained before handoff, but there is no communication between AP. How to complete BSS handoff without cutting off the current service? [15].

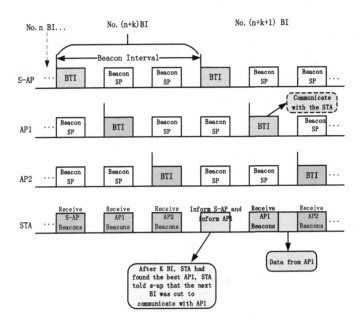

Fig. 5. STA confirms and switches the best AP

2. For the above two problems, this paper involves the high frequency WiFi handoff based on multi-association cooperative BSS. As shown in the Fig. 4, multiple aps under the control of the same controller, STA can communicate with the controller and STA can be associated with all the APs of the controller. After STA has moved, extract useful information to switch to the new BSS from the BTI period interaction information with all AP, tell the controller this information, the controller tells the corresponding BSS, STA switches to the new BSS at the start of the new BI.

In AP Clustering, STA can communicate with other aps within the Beacon SP stage. When STA sends movement, the BSS handoff process is as follows:

1) In Fig. 4, when STA moves, SNR is bound to change. In the next BI BTI stage, beam training is conducted again to update the best sending and receiving sectors.

If the signal quality of all beam in this BTI is less than a threshold, this BI shall listen to every neighbor SP, namely BTI stage of other AP, listen to the signal strength of beam in STA and other communities, and record the strongest signal between STA and other AP, that is, the best beam ID.

2) In Fig. 5, after the above process lasts for K BI, it will feed back to the current BSS in its SP, and the current BSS will inform the target BSS through the controller decision. The target BSS will officially work in the next BI of the target BSS without business interruption.

3) The buffer of the current BSS is migrated to the destination BSS to continue business transmission. In order to ensure the correctness of BSS handoff, the duration of 2 BI was interception, but the time from the original BSS to the current BSS was one BHI length (Fig. 6).

4   Simulation

4.1   Design of Simulation Scenario

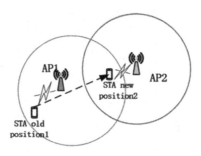

Fig. 6. Simulation scenario

The IEEE 802.11 ad protocol is suitable for multiple dense scenarios. All nodes can get the best beam ID through beam training. AP Clustering scenario includes two PCP/AP, and the interval SIFS time between DATA and ACK within SP. When STA starts to communicate with AP1, it moves to position 2 and enters the new BSS2.

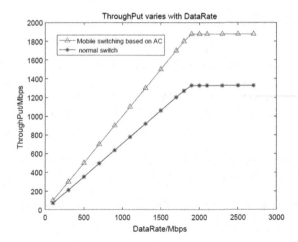

Fig. 7. ThroughPut with DataRate

4.2   Simulation Results

PCP/AP1 and PCP/AP2 start the BI frame at the time of 0/2*BI and 1/2* BI. Simulation time is 4S, packet size is 30000 Bytes, BI frame is 0.5 s, and BHI duration is 1 ms. When STA enters the BSS2, under the HAC protocol, the communication with the current BSS1 will not be disconnected after STA moves. In the two BI, the BHI period of AP2 is used to interact with AP2, and the optimal sector for communication with AP2 is obtained, and then the next BI switches to the BSS2. However, ordinary handoff will directly break the connection with the current BSS, and reconnect with AP after two BI (Table 1).

Table 1. Switch time comparison.

Switch methods	Switch time
Handoff based on AC	5 ms
Normal switch	1.24 s
Method of reference [9]	1.5 s

Analysis: From results in the Fig. 7, it can be seen that with the increase of the Data rate from 0, the network throughput also increases with the increase of the two simulation conditions. When the service rate reaches about 2000 Mbps, the throughput increases gradually and reaches saturation. The saturated throughput of HAC protocol is about 1.4 times of that of ordinary handoff, and its performance is better than that of ordinary handoff.

5 Conclusions and Future Work

Multi-BSS Association and Cooperation based Handoff Scheme for IEEE 802.11ay has been introduced in this paper. By controlling multi-AP with controller, STA is connected to multi-AP, and the new BSS can be switched to without disconnecting the current STA connection, which ensures the continuity of service and reduces the handoff delay. The simulation results turn out the designed protocol reduces the time delay and improves the throughput by 40%.

Acknowledgement. This work was supported in part by the National Natural Science Foundations of CHINA (Grant No. 61871322, No. 61771390, No. 61771392, No. 61501373, and No. 61271279), the National Science and Technology Major Project (Grant No. 2016ZX03001018-004), and Science and Technology on Avionics Integration Laboratory (20185553035).

References

1. Yan, H., He, C.: A fast security switching scheme for wireless LAN. J. Shanghai Jiaotong Univ. **38**(11) (2004)
2. Ni, W., Dong, Y., Xia, Q.: Station based IEEE 802. J. Southeast Univ. (English Edn.) **24**(2), 149–154 (2008)
3. Shi, L., Fapojuwo, A., Viberg, N., Hoople, W., Chan, N.: Methods for calculating bandwidth, delay, and packet loss metrics in multi-hop IEEE802.11 Ad Hoc Networks. In: VTC Spring 2008 - IEEE Vehicular Technology Conference (2008)
4. Wang T.: Beamforming based on IEEE 802.11n [D]. Xidian university
5. ISO/IEC/IEEE ISO/IEC/IEEE International Standard for Information technology-Telecommunications and information exchange between systems-Local and metropolitan area networks-Specific requirements-Part 11: Wireless LAN Medium Access Control (MAC) and Physical Layer (PHY) Specifications Amendment 3: Enhancements for Very High Throughput in the 60 GHz Band (adoption of IEEE Std 802.11ad-2012). ISO/IEC/IEEE 8802–11:2012/Amd. 3:2014(E) (2014)
6. Cold, Y.: Distributed AP clustering algorithm based on MapReduce. Comput. Modern. **2014**(10), 104–107 (2014)
7. Xu, X., Wang, W.: Research on WiFi based seamless access technology for roaming switching. Ind. Mining Automat. **37**(2), 6–8 (2011)
8. Research on switching technology of wireless LAN based on IEEE 802.11
9. Cao, Q., Wu, Q.: Comparison of wireless LAN active switching technology and pre-switching technology. J. Chifeng univ. (Nat. Sci. Edn.), 2017(13) (2017)
10. Liu J.: IEEE 802.11 wireless LAN media access control technology research
11. Liu, J.: Multi-rate control of heterogeneous wireless network cooperative access. South China university of technology
12. Zhao, Z., Feng, J.: Research on wireless LAN switching technology based on IEEE 802.11. Comput. Technol. Devel. **28**(10), 8–14 (2018)
13. Yuan, M., Huang, S.: Security and fast switching scheme based on 802.11 wireless LAN. Sci. Technol. Eng. **8**(14), 4000–4003 (2008)
14. Wu, F., Chu, E., Li, J.: Based on IEEE 802. Research on fast switch of 11r wireless LAN. Electron. Sci. Technol. **27**(4), 54 (2014)
15. Zeng Z.: Research on wi-fi access control technology based on physical layer information (2016)

Services and Applications

A Plug-in Framework for Efficient Multicast Using SDN

Yu Zhang[(⊠)], Tim Humernbrum, and Sergei Gorlatch

University of Münster, Münster, Germany
{yu.zhang,humernbrum,gorlatch}@uni-muenster.de

Abstract. The great variety of modern networked applications, e.g., online computer games, cloud host backups, video conferencing, etc. bring significant differences in their usage scenarios. Therefore, they impose very different QoS (Quality of Service) requirements on network communication. In particular, traditional multicast implementations cannot react adequately to the potentially very dynamic application requirements at run time. In this paper, we suggest a novel Plug-in Multicast Framework (PiMF) placed on top of an existing multicast framework. PiMF can modify the topology of the multicast tree during the application's run time, thus providing QoS guarantees for multicast communication. We design our plug-in framework using the emerging SDN (Software-Defined Networking) technology, and we especially address the challenge of non-interfering behavior of PiMF with respect to the underlying multicast implementation. We evaluate the correctness and performance of our plug-in framework in detailed simulation experiments.

Keywords: Plug-in muliticast framework · Software-defined networks · Multicast group management

1 Introduction

The rapid development of the Internet has spawned many applications which make heavy use of multicast communication, i.e., when a single host sends the same packet to multiple hosts in the network at once. Traditionally, multicast mechanisms do not consider the specific needs of a particular application. However, applications of multicast, such as cloud host backups, video conferencing, and online games, may have very different scenarios. These scenarios, together with different needs of particular groups of users, impose very different QoS requirements on multicast communication. For example, in video conferencing and online games, the topology of the multicast members is dynamic during the lifetime of the multicast group; the multicast packets do not need to arrive at the receiver in strict accordance with the order of their transmission, they are allowed to be dropped during the transmission process; and it is generally a multi-source multicast. In contrast, in cloud host backups, multicast packets need to arrive at the receiver in strict accordance with the sending order, and the multicast data packets are not allowed to be dropped during the transmission process.

D.-J. Deng et al. (Eds.): WiCON 2019, LNICST 317, pp. 271–284, 2020.
https://doi.org/10.1007/978-3-030-52988-8_24

Due to the diversity of applications and the complexity of their QoS requirements, Multicast Routing Algorithms (MRA) are traditionally used to design multicast trees with different criteria of optimality. MRA and multicast trees are the main characteristics of a particular multicast framework, while Multicast-IP address allocation, MAC address mapping and Internet Group Management Protocol (IGMP) are other aspects of multicast framework, all of which interact with each other. For an efficient multicast framework, these aspects should be considered together as much as possible. Our focus in a multicast framework is on three modules: Multicast Group Management (MGM), IGMP and MRA, while MGM consists of multicast-IP address allocation and MAC address mapping.

The traditional multicast frameworks have the drawback that the existing multicast routing algorithms, for example Reverse Path Forwarding Multicast Routing Algorithms (RPF-MRA), do not take into account the specific QoS requirements of particular applications. Moreover, corresponding multicast frameworks, for example RPF-MF, are designed to be closed, without considering scalability and flexibility. Therefore, Customized Multicast Routing Algorithms (CMRA) cannot be deployed in RPF-MF to satisfy the specific QoS requirements of a particular application.

In order to overcome the above drawback and not to interfere with the operation of RPF-MRA, we suggest to deploy an additional multicast framework (Plug-in Multicast Framework, PiMF) at the network layer in the network, such that a CMRA can be deployed in PiMF.

This paper is organized as follows. Section 2 discusses related work. We describe the idea and the main challenges of our plug-in framework in Sect. 3, and then we address the major challenge - designing the MGM for PiMF - in Sect. 4. Next, we describe the experiments to evaluate the performance of our PiMF and report our results in Sect. 5. Finally, Sect. 6 concludes the paper and discusses future work.

2   Related Work

Multicast communication is implemented under the support of a multicast framework in the network, and the multicast framework provides MGM services and MRA for multicast application. Many researchers have studied MGM services and MRAs at network layer in classic networks [1–7]. These existing multicast frameworks are designed to be exclusive and closed for particular application scenarios at the network layer, and only the corresponding MRAs can be deployed on them. However, multicast member usually needs to trigger different MRAs for different application scenarios. Therefore, a CMRA, which is suitable for dynamic application scenarios, cannot be deployed on these existing multicast frameworks to satisfy the specific QoS requirements of particular applications.

Traditional approaches deploy a particular multicast framework and manage the multicast group at the application layer, and then deploy the CMRA on the application-layer multicast framework. Lee et al. [8] deploy an MRA for highly dynamic application scenarios on the application-layer multicast framework. The auxiliary protocol and MRA assist the newly joined multicast member to form a new multicast tree. Each node can only obtain information from other nodes connected to it, but cannot obtain information from all nodes in the entire network. Although this algorithm can be used to improve the performance of multicast communication in dynamic application scenarios, it cannot modify a multicast tree according to the real-time changes of the network state.

Based on an application-layer multicast framework, Alkubeily et al. [9] propose a reconfigurable multicast framework. The framework deploys dedicated application-layer protocol for the rendezvous point [10]. When a new member requests to join existed overlay, it should report the rendezvous point for its expected membership duration within the multicast group through a dedicated protocol. The rendezvous point precomputes how to modify the multicast tree structure according to the duration of stay of each member in the multicast group, in order to minimize the multicast packet drop during the multicast tree update. However, according to Zhang et al. [11], although the application-layer multicast frameworks can deploy appropriate MRAs to improve the performance of multicast communication in different application scenarios, the host as a multicast member cannot obtain the topology of the entire network. What is worse, the application-layer multicast framework cannot locate the newly joined multicast members in the network quickly and accurately.

Wang et al. [12] propose an application-layer multicast framework for data centers in a cloud network. Compared with the previous application-layer multicast frameworks, their framework has the following two advantages: 1) it exploits SDN architecture to implement and control the overlay which caters to the features of future data center networks; 2) there is no special protocol that needs to be established, and it reduces the consumption of bandwidth and computing resources. It adopts the topology of fat tree [13], and all nodes are assigned the regular IP addresses. Then the distances are calculated between the network devices depending on the IP address information of each node. Finally, a degree-constrained multicast tree is established based on the distance information.

In order to adapt the multicast communication to the requirements of different application scenarios, the existing mainstream approach [8–11] is to deploy an application-layer multicast framework in the network and appropriate MRA on top of it [14, 15]. Since the previous approaches avoid conflicts with RPF-MF by migrating the MGM to the application layer, the developers of multicast applications have to develop dedicated application-layer protocols for MGM, which increases the cost of using multicast communication.

3 Plug-in Multicast Framework: The Idea

Inspired by [12], we use the advantage of SDN (Software-Defined Networking [16]) centralized control, to deploy our PiMF (Plug-in Multicast Framework) as an SDN-programmable application at the network layer. Consequently, it can modify the topology of the multicast tree during the run time of the multicast communication, thus providing QoS guarantees for the transmission of multicast packets.

As with RPF-MF, we suppose that PiMF implements all the functions of the IGMPv2 protocol at the network layer, so we do not discuss the technical details of implementing the IGMPv2 protocol.

However, there is a conflict between the PiMF and RPF-MF in the MGM process. The MGM process is organized as follows: 1) each multicast querier in PiMF and RPF-MF (which is a switch and is selected to periodically query the number of multicast members in the multicast group) sends a General-Query IGMP message to multicast members within the network, and its starts the Timer-General-Query at the same time; 2) the multicast member sends Membership-report IGMP messages to multicast group after receiving the General-Query message; 3) the multicast querier stops sending the General-Query message after receiving the Membership-report message; 4) after that, MGM module calls the MRA module to update a multicast tree after receiving the Membership-report IGMP message. If there are two multicast frameworks in the network, these two frameworks may conflict in two ways. On the one hand, if there is a multicast member in the multicast group, then: 1) the multicast member will receive the General-Query IGMP message from two multicast frameworks; 2) the Timer-General-Query would start after receiving the first General-Query IGMP, and the multicast member would send Membership-report IGMP messages to multicast group; 3) after receiving the second General-Query IGMP message, the Timer-General-Query of the multicast member would be reinitialized, which suppresses other members to send Membership-report IGMP messages. As a result, it causes that the querier cannot obtain the real information about the existence of the multicast members in each multicast group. Eventually, the multicast datagram would be lost or even the multicast group would be deleted by mistake. On the other hand, each multicast framework will call its own MRA to update the multicast tree for each multicast group after receiving the Membership-report IGMP message from multicast members. Thus, the same multicast member within a multicast group would be connected by two completely different multicast trees, and the same multicast datagram would be sent repeatedly.

The traditional method to avoid such conflicts between two multicast frameworks is to deploy a multicast framework and manage the multicast group at the application layer, and then to deploy a CMRA on the application-layer multicast framework. While the RPF-MF (which is based on the IGMP protocol) works at the network layer, the application-layer multicast framework works at the application layer. As a result, RPF-MF and application-layer multicast frameworks can be isolated at different layers of the network, thus avoiding the transmission conflicts. Since the application-layer multicast framework does not use the standard IGMP protocol to manage multicast groups, this results in the incompatibility between the application-layer multicast frameworks and the majority of classic multicast applications developed in the past. Developers of multicast applications have to develop dedicated application-layer protocols and corresponding application-layer program for each MRA, which violates the reusability principle of the software industry. Therefore, the deployment of a CMRA (which is suitable for dynamic application scenarios and maintains compatibility with classic multicast applications) is a challenge in the field of multicast research.

To address this challenge, we take advantage of the SDN centralized control, and propose a PiMF for efficient multicast based on SDN at network layer.

Specifically, we design and implement the PiMF as an SDN-programmable application at the network layer, with the following advantages:

1) The SDN controller obtains the access information of a multicast member and the information about the bandwidth. Thus, the MGM process can be designed according to the real-time changes of network state.

2) The topology of the multicast tree can be adjusted according to the programmable characteristic of the SDN application. And the CMRA can be more easily deployed on the network layer using the northbound interface of SDN.

Additionally, PiMF takes over specific multicast groups from RPF-MF and allows a CMRA to be deployed for these specific multicast groups. PiMF can be embedded into the underlying network without modifications of the architecture and hardware.

4 Multicast Group Management Module Based on SDN

Figure 1 shows that our PiMF consists of three modules - MGM, CMRA and IGMP. As an example, let us analyze the multicast data transmission in one multicast group. In order for a multicast member to be able to send or receive multicast packets within a multicast group, there are two conditions to be satisfied. First, the newly joined multicast member must apply to join a specific multicast group. Second, PiMF explicitly obtains the existence of multicast members in this multicast group, and then PiMF mobilizes CMRA to establish a multicast tree which is based on the topology of the multicast members. The above two points are usually summarized as MGM. The IGMP is a signaling mechanism which is specially developed for MGM. We describe in the following three aspects of MGM in our PiMF: the joining process of multicast member, the departure of multicast member, and the maintenance of multicast membership, with the aim that PiMF can deploy a CMRA to meet the specific QoS requirements of particular applications.

Different from the previous work, we embed the process of the multicast address mapping in the MGM mechanism of PiMF. In particular, we take over the specified multicast group from RPF-MF and manage this multicast group in the new address space. Although PiMF still manages multicast groups using the IGMP protocol at the network layer, PiMF and RPF-MF do not interfere with each other because of the different address spaces. Moreover, PiMF is seamlessly compatible with the existing classic web applications, and it does not require additional application-layer protocols and dedicated application-layer software to support. As a result, network administrators can deploy a CMRA on PiMF, adapting to the specific needs of different application scenarios, without modifying and interfering with RPF-MF at the network layer.

Figure 1 shows how PiMF runs as an SDN application in parallel with RPF-MF on the SDN controller. PiMF and RPF-MF share the northbound interface of the SDN controller. They can obtain the status of the SDN switch (A, B, D, E) and then install flow entries at the SDN switch via the northbound interface in the network. The user configures the multiple bigram for PiMF of the form <Multicast Address, Delay Bound>: it explicitly indicates that the specific multicast group needs to be taken over from the RPF-MF by PiMF. Since every host should be able to send or receive multicast data through a multicast group as soon as possible, the delay of takeover process must not exceed a certain threshold.

The SDN controller uses the Link Layer Discovery Protocol (LLDP) [17] to periodically discover the link and the location of the switch. The SDN controller firstly commands one of the SDN switches connected to it, for example SDN switch B, to broadcast the LLDP packet to all of the switches. If there is a link between two switch,

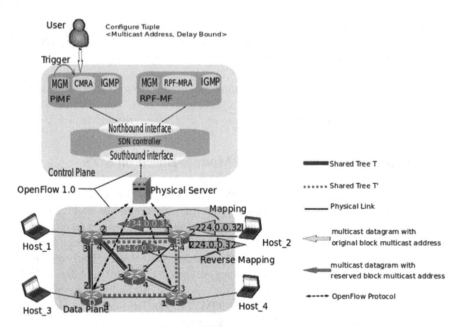

Fig. 1. PiMF based on SDN.

the SDN switch reports this LLDP packets to SDN controller. Then all the rest SDN switches (A, D, E) perform this operation. After the SDN controller receives the LLDP packet from the last SDN switch, it completes a cycle. In the meanwhile, the MGM module of PiMF periodically checks the topology of the underlying network and the change of bandwidth via the OpenFlow 1.0 protocol, and it passively monitors whether there are some multicast members that want to join/leave the multicast group or not. If there is one or more multicast members that want to join/leave a multicast group, the MGM module triggers the CMRA module. The CMRA module then updates the multicast tree of the multicast group according to the current topology of the underlying network and its bandwidth.

4.1   The Joining Process of Multicast Members

Classic multicast applications generally work in the LAN multicast address space (224.0.0.0–224.0.0.255) and the Internet multicast address space (224.0.1.0–224.0.1.255), while the multicast addresses in the space 234.0.0.0–238.255.255.255 are reserved but not used [18], network administrators can use these multicast address spaces to multicast communicate flexibly. The multicast packets, which are taken over in the specific mutilcast group, have their own addresses.

Our PiMF maps these multicast addresses from the LAN multicast address space or the Internet multicast address space to the reserved multicast address space. Then PiMF transmits these multicast packets to specific multicast groups through SDN. Since this reserved multicast address space is not managed by the RPF-MF, RPF-MF does not manage these multicast packets. Consequently, the specific multicast group is taken over and managed by PiMF successfully.

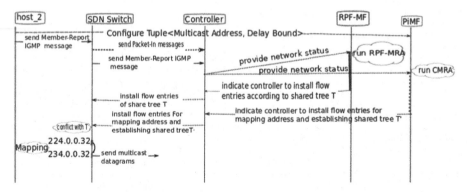

Fig. 2. The timing diagram of the joining process.

Figure 1 illustrates the joining process of multicast members in PiMF. Figure 2 shows the timing diagram of the joining process. We suppose that the LAN multicast address 224.0.0.32 has been configured into PiMF through bigram, and host_1, host_2, host_3 and host_4 attempt to join the multicast group. Taken host_2 as an example, it firstly sends a Member-Report IGMP message to switch B through port 2, and then it informs PiMF that it is trying to join the multicast group with the multicast address 224.0.0.32. At the beginning there is no flow entry which matches the Member-Report IGMP message at switch B. Switch B does not know how to handle this Member-Report IGMP message, thus it firstly sends a Packet-in message to the SDN controller, according to the OpenFlow protocol. Packet-in message indicates that Switch B receives an abnormal message, and then Swith B secondly sends this Member-Report IGMP message to SDN controller. As a result, SDN controller is responsible for handling this Member-Report IGMP message. Since PiMF is installed as an SDN application on the SDN controller, it can obtain information from the SDN northbound interface that host_2 is trying to join a multicast group with the address 224.0.0.32. In the meanwhile, the RPF-MF also obtains the information that host_2 is trying to join a multicast group with the address 224.0.0.32 from the SDN northbound interface. Next, RPF-MF triggers its RPF-MRA module to modify the multicast tree T. Host_2 will be added to the multicast tree T = <{A, B, C, D, E}, {(A, B), (A, C), (C, E), (A, D)}>, which is not required by PiMF. However, since the address 224.0.0.32 has been explicitly configured into PiMF, PiMF will perform a "mapping" operation at the access switch B. More precisely, PiMF prompts switch B to change the multicast address of the joining multicast packets from 224.0.0.32 to 234.0.0.32, and to send these multicast packets from port 1 and port 4 to the multicast tree T' = <{A, B, D, E}, { (A, B), (B, E), (D, E)}> which is established by CMRA of PiMF.

Flow entry (a) reflects the operation of mapping in Fig. 3. A "reverse mapping" operation will also be performed at switch B: PiMF prompts switch B to change the address of the packets, which are sent to host_2, from 234.0.0.32 to 224.0.0.32 correspondingly. Consequently, host_2 can receive multicast packets from the multicast address 224.0.0.32 in this way. Flow entries (b) and (c) reflect the operation of reverse mapping in Fig. 3.

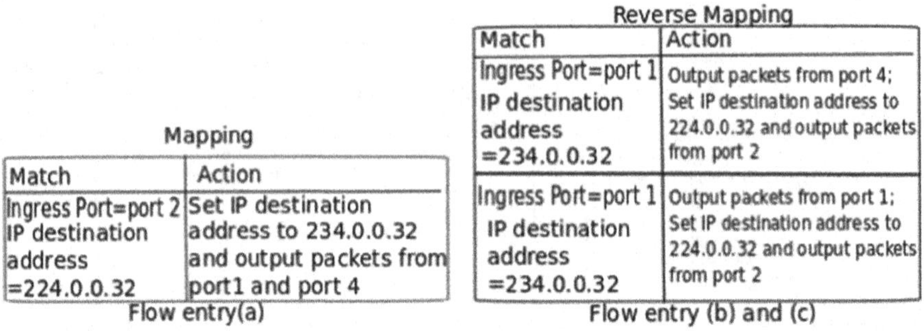

		Reverse Mapping	
		Match	Action
		Ingress Port=port 1 IP destination address =234.0.0.32	Output packets from port 4; Set IP destination address to 224.0.0.32 and output packets from port 2

Mapping	
Match	Action
Ingress Port=port 2 IP destination address =224.0.0.32	Set IP destination address to 234.0.0.32 and output packets from port1 and port 4

Match	Action
Ingress Port=port 1 IP destination address =234.0.0.32	Output packets from port 1; Set IP destination address to 224.0.0.32 and output packets from port 2

Flow entry(a)   Flow entry (b) and (c)

Fig. 3. Flow entry.

As a result of the "mapping - reverse mapping" operation, the multicast querier of the RPF-MF will not receive the Member-Report IGMP message issued by host_2. Furthermore, a Timer-General-Query is set for the multicast group with the multicast address 234.0.0.32 at the beginning according to the IGMP protocol, and RPF-MF will automatically delete the host_2 branch from T after the Timer-General-Query expires. Similarly, the same "mapping - reverse mapping" operation will be performed by PiMF at SDN switches A, D and E in the network. As a result, the multicast tree T' is set up, and multicast tree T which is not needed is completely removed from the network. Finally, the RPF-MF abandons the management of the multicast group with the multicast address 234.0.0.32, in accordance with the IGMP protocol, while PiMF completely takes over the multicast group from RPF-MF.

Note that the multicast addresses 224.0.0.1 and 224.0.0.2 are two exceptions in the operations of mapping - reverse mapping. They will not be mapped to the reserved space by PiMF, because both of them are reserved for supporting the IGMP protocol. For example, General Query type of IGMP messages are broadcast to the network. If they are mapped, the entire multicast management mechanism would be paralyzed.

Figure 4 shows the timing diagram of how PiMF takes over the multicast group from RPF-MF without conflict. When PiMF installs flow entries at the SDN switches A, B, D and E, which reflects the operation of "mapping - reverse mapping", there might be conflicts between the flow entries at switches for multicast tree T' and the flow entries installed for T. To solve this problem, each of the access switches sends an ofg_error_msg message to the SDN controller according to the OpenFlow protocol, to notify the occurrence of an abnormal situation. Then, PiMF raises the priority of the flow entries installed at switches, to be higher than the priority of the flow entries installed by RPF-MF for the multicast tree T. Next, RPF-MF deletes the flow entries which are installed for multicast tree T. Finally, the flow entries are installed at switch successfully.

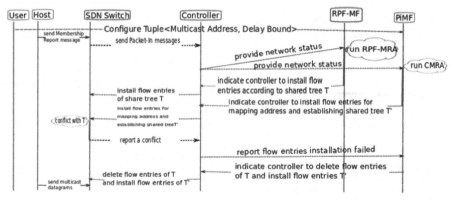

Fig. 4. The timing diagram of how PiMF takes over the multicast group from RPF-MF without conflict.

4.2 Departure of Multicast Members

When a multicast member leaves its multicast group which is taken over by the PiMF, it sends a Leave-Report type of IGMP message to the multicast address 224.0.0.2 according to the IGMP protocol. Thus, the MGM module is notified. Since the multicast address of the multicast group is encapsulated in the IGMP message, the SDN switch cannot match the sender of the IGMP message through the flow entry. As a result, it is impossible to know which member of the multicast group is going to leave. In order to manage such type of messages and parse out the multicast group whose member is about to leave, we pay attention to the SDN controller and the SDN application itself.

Figure 5 shows the delivery of multicast members' leaving messages. PiMF pre-installs a special flow entry at the access switch for a multicast member after it joins the multicast group. The special flow entry prompts the access switch to send the packets to the SDN controller, only when the multicast packets satisfy the following requirements: 1) the packet is sent from the multicast member; 2) the IP header of the packet's destination address is 224.0.0.2. When the packet arrives at the access switch, it is encapsulated into a Packet-in message and sent to the SDN controller. Next, PiMF obtains this packet through the northbound interface of the SDN controller, and then it parses out the address of the multicast group in the IGMP message. Additionally, if PiMF does not take over this multicast group, it instructs the access switch to flood the IGMP message to port 2 through the SDN controller. Consequently, it ensures that RPF-MF receives this message successfully.

If PiMF takes over the multicast group, it prompts all access switches, which are directly connected with the multicast group members, to send the Group-Specific-Query IGMP message. Therefore, PiMF can query whether there are any other multicast members in this multicast group or not. If so, then the multicast members in this group respond to the access switch with the Member-Report IGMP message. The multicast querier of PiMF knows that there are still multicast members in the multicast group after receiving the first message of such type. Next, PiMF prompts the access switch to stop sending Group-Specific-Query IGMP messages. As a result, the process of query is finished. Finally, the CMRA module is triggered, and the multicast tree is updated according to

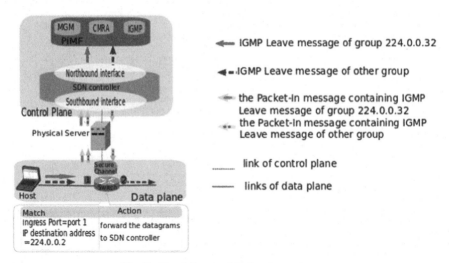

Fig. 5. The delivery of the leaving message

the current membership of the multicast group. If there is no other multicast member in the multicast group, PiMF does not get any feedback from the access switch. Then, the MGM module of PiMF knows that the multicast group is already empty. Next, PiMF immediately deletes the multicast tree for the multicast group and the corresponding flow entry at the SDN switch. Finally, the multicast group is returned to RPF-MF.

4.3 Maintenance of the Multicast Membership

The maintenance of the multicast membership is implemented by a multicast querier. The multicast querier periodically broadcasts a General-Query IGMP message to query the current situation of multicast members in the network. Since the control plane of SDN is separated from the data plane, the SDN switch that acts as the multicast querier can only forward data. The SDN switch neither creates General-Query IGMP messages nor it sets a timer for multicast groups. Therefore, there are two differences of the MGM module between PiMF and RPF-MF: 1) the SDN switch, which is selected as a multicast querier, does not set a timer for the multicast group, instead the timer is set in the MGM module of PiMF; in contrast, each of the access switches, which can be selected as a multicast querier in RPF-MF, set a timer for the multicast group after broadcasting the General-Query IGMP message; 2) although the Membership-Report IGMP message of the multicast member is sent to the multicast querier, the multicast querier of PiMF directly transfers this message to the SDN controller after receiving, and the SDN controller parses and further processes the information of the multicast member; in contrast, the multicast querier of RPF-MF directly triggers its RPF-MRA module to modify the multicast tree after receiving the Membership-Report IGMP.

The maintenance of the multicast membership in PiMF is organized as follows: 1) in order to know whether there are any members in every multicast group, the SDN controller periodically sends the Packet-out message of OpenFlow to SDN switch, thus it prompts the SDN switch, which serves as multicast querier, to send the General-Query message. Furthermore, the timer Timer-General-Query of MGM is started; 2) in any of the multicast groups, the multicast member sends Membership-report IGMP messages to multicast group after receiving the General-Query message; 3) then the multicast querier stops sending the General-Query message and it reports the Membership-report message to the SDN controller after receiving the Membership-report message from the specific multicast group; 4) next, the MGM module of PiMF knows that there are some members in this specific multicast group after parsing this message; 5) afterwards, the CMRA module is triggered, and a multicast tree is updated for this specific multicast group; 6) finally, the relevant flow entry at the SDN switch is installed. Besides, if there is no member in this multicast group, the multicast querier cannot receive the Membership-report message. After the timer expires, the router deletes the multicast link automatically.

5   Experimental Evaluation

In order to evaluate the performance of PiMF, two experiments are conducted to compare the performance of the multicast communication regarding packet loss ratio and throughput. First, we run RPF-MF and PiMF separately, and then we run them together; we call the latter scenario the Combined-MF. We verify that PiMF can act on the underlying network in parallel with RPF-MF, and that it does not interfere with each other.

We evaluate PiMF, RPF-MF, and their implementation in the Floodlight SDN controller [19], on the platform of Mininet [20]. Moreover, we use Wireshark [21] to test the network performance, and we use the network performance test tool iperf [22] to record the experimental results.

In order to verify whether PiMF generates additional packet loss when it works together with RPF-MF, we set the bandwidth of physical link to 10 Mbps in the experimental environment. Then we test the packet loss ratio of multicast communication, when a multicast member sends multicast packets to the multicast group at rate from 20 MBit/s to 60 MBit/s, respectively.

Figure 6 shows the average packet loss ratio of the switch in three experimental scenarios, which run RPF-MF, PiMF, and combined-MF separately. In the figure, P1 is the average packet loss ratio of the switches when we run RPF-MF. P2 is the average packet loss ratio of the switches when we run PiMF. P3 is the average packet loss ratio of the switches, which are in RPF-MF, when we run combined-MF. P4 is the average packet loss ratio of the switches, which are in PiMF, when we run combined-MF. We observe that when multicast member sends multicast packets to the multicast group at the same rate, the packet loss rate P3 or P4 is almost twice as high as P1 or P2. Specifically, compared to the data traffic of the multicast in the network when we run RPF-MF and PiMF separately, there will be doubled data traffic in the network when we run combined-MF. However, the data-forwarding capability of the switches does not change. Consequently, the packet loss ratio will be double, which is consistent with the experimental results.

Our second experiment is to verify whether RPF-MF and PiMF interfere with each other if they are deployed together on the same physical network. We set the link bandwidth of the network to 10M bps. The multicast packet is transmitted at 10 Mb/s continuously through iperf tool.

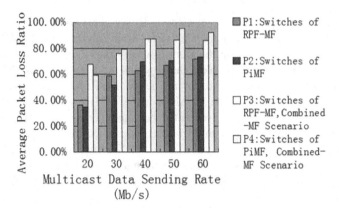

Fig. 6. The average packet loss ratio of the switches

Figure 7 shows the average throughput of the switches in three experimental scenarios, which run RPF-MF, PiMF, and combined-MF separately. We observe that when we run RPF-MF or PiMF separately, the average throughput of the switches reaches a peak around 1.7 Mb/s at about 0.5 s, and then it floats around 1.2 Mb/s. When we run combined-MF, the average throughput of the switches reaches a peak around 1.7 Mb/s at about 0.2 s, and then it floats around 1 Mb/s. The average throughput of switches gradually increases to peak before the switch buffer memory is exhausted. Specifically, compared to the data traffic of the multicast in the network when we run RPF-MF and PiMF, correspondingly, there is a doubled data traffic in the network when we run combined-MF. As a result, it takes about half the time to reach the peak for the average throughput of the switches, which is consistent with our experimental results. We can conclude that when PiMF is deployed with RPF-MF in the same physical network, there is no negative effect on the throughput of the RPF-MF.

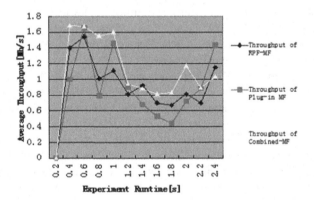

Fig. 7. The average throughput of the switches

6 Conclusion and Future Work

Our main contribution in this paper is the design and implementation of a novel Plug-in Multicast Framework (PiMF) that allows to dynamically deploy a customized multicast routing algorithm (CMRA) depending on a particular application scenario. We also show how to solve the potential conflicts between the existing multicast framework and our plug-in framework. Our experiments show that PiMF can deploy CMRA without interfering with the existing multicast framework and at the same time, it maintains compatibility with classic multicast applications.

While we prove that PiMF does not cause additional packet loss in the existing framework, we have not yet designed the packet loss avoidance mechanism in the module of CMRA. This could result in high packet loss ratio. For further work, we plan to consider: 1) the packet loss avoidance mechanism in CMRA, and 2) combining the social relationship information in the network with the packet loss avoidance mechanism.

Acknowledgments. This work is supported by a scholarship from CSC (China) and by the BHBF project HPC^{2}SE at the University of Muenster.

References

1. Bueno, M., Oliverira, G.: A dynamic multiobjective evolutionary algorithm for multicast routing problem. In: 2013 IEEE International Conference on Systems, Man, and Cybernetics on Proceedings, Manchester, UK, pp. 841–846. IEEE (2013)
2. Ghaaboosi, N., Haghighat, A.: A path relinking approach for delay-constrained least-cost multicast routing problem. In: 19th International Conference on Tools with Artificial Intelligence on Proceedings, Patras, Greece, pp. 383–390. IEEE (2007)
3. Xu Z., Chen L.: An effective heuristic algorithm for dynamic multicast routing with delay-constrained. In: 9th International Symposium on Computers and Communications on Proceedings, Alexandria, Egypt, pp. 1024–1031. IEEE (2004)
4. Bauer, F., Varma, A.: ARIES: a rearrangeable inexpensive edge-based on-line steiner algorithm. IEEE J. Sel. Areas Commun. **15**(3), 382–397 (1996)
5. Zhang, B., Mouftah, H.: Forwarding state reduction for delay-constrained multicasting in IP networks. In: 2003 IEEE Global Telecommunications Conference on Proceedings, San Francisco, USA, pp. 4191–4195. IEEE (2003)
6. Rammohan, N., Murthy, C.: On-line multicast routing with QoS constraints in WDM networks with no wavelength converters. Comput. Netw. **50**(18), 3666–3685 (2006)
7. Lee, D., Youn, C., Jeong, S.: RP reselection scheme for real-time applications in delay-constrained multicast networks. In: 2002 IEEE International Conference on Communications on Proceedings, New York, USA, pp. 1290–1294. IEEE (2002)
8. Lee, J., Ahn, C., Lee, Y.: Instant distributed minimun diameter tree construction for scalable application layer multicast. In: 12th International Conference on Computer and Information Science on Proceedings, Niigata, Japan, pp. 23–28. IEEE (2013)
9. Alkubeily, M., Bettahar, H., Bouabdallah, A.: A new Application-Level Multicast technique for stable, robust and efficient overlay tree construction. Comput. Netw. **55**(15), 3332–3350 (2011)
10. Rendezvous Point Engineering, Cisco White Paper. http://www.cisco.com/c/en/us/products/collateral/ios-nx-os-software/ip-multicast/whitepaper_c11-508498.html

11. Zhang, X., Gu, W., Yang, M., Geng, G., Luo, W.: A distance-heuristic tree building approach in application layer multicast. Comput. Inform. **31**(6), 1481–1510 (2013)
12. Wang, H., Caic, J., Luc, J., et al.: Solving multicast problem in cloud networks using overlay routing. Comput. Commun. **70**, 1–14 (2015)
13. Lee, G.: Understanding Cloud-based Data Center Networks. Morgan Kaufmann, Burlington (2014)
14. Liao, S., Hong, X., Wu, C., Wang, B., Jiang, M.: Prototype for customized multicast services in software defined networks. In: 22th International Conference on Software, Telecommunications and Computer Networks on Proceedings, Split, Croatia, pp. 315–320. IEEE (2014)
15. Lin, H., Lin, M., Wu, C.: Constructing application-layer multicast trees for minimum-delay message distribution. Inf. Sci. **279**(279), 433–445 (2014)
16. Haque, I., Abu-Ghazaleh, N.: Wireless software defined networking: a survey and taxonmy. IEEE Commun. Surv. Tutor. **18**(4), 2713–2737 (2016)
17. Liao, L., Leung, V.: LLDP based link latency monitoring in software defined networks. In: 2016 12th International Conference on Network and Service Management on Proceedings, Montreal, Canada, pp. 330–335. IEEE (2016)
18. Cotton, M., Vegoda, L.: IANA Guidelines for IPv4 Multicast Address Assignments, RFC5771 (2010)
19. Project Floodlight. http://floodlight.openflowhub.org/
20. Mininet. http://mininet.org/
21. Goyal, P., Goyal, A.: Comparative study of two most popular packet sniffing tools-Tcpdump and Wireshark. In: 2017 9th International Conference on Computational Intelligence and Communication Networks on Proceedings, Girne, Cyprus, pp. 77–81. IEEE (2017)
22. Iperf - The TCP/UDP Bandwidth Measurement Tool. http://sourceforge.net/projects/iperf2/

Cross-Border E-Commerce Intellectual Property Protection in China-U.S. Trade Friction

Zhou Ping Ying[1] and Ye Xiuwen[2(✉)]

[1] School of Business Administration, Baise University, Guangxi 533000, Baise, China
[2] Yulin Normal University, Yulin, China
18677588510@qq.com

Abstract. Along with the fast development of Internet technology, cross-border E-commerce is also exhibiting an extremely strong growth trend. Among the many problems derived from this new type of cross-border trade, the intellectual property issue is even more complex, and there are many difficulties emerging in governance and rights protection. These difficulties lie in the fact that the conflict between E-commerce and regional intellectual property protection also comes from the lag of technological innovation and legal regulation, with conflicts arising from inadequate international coordination and other realistic causes. The snags in intellectual property protection are also due to the conceptual factor of the conflict between efficiency and fairness. Thus, in order to effectively solve these difficulties, this paper holds that the government, cross-border E-commerce enterprises, intellectual property holders, civil collective forces, and governance bodies at home and abroad should conduct diversified collaboration with one another. In addition, relevant data and an expert talent database should be established, a framework for cross-border E-commerce intellectual property governance and protection must be jointly built, and greater efforts can be made for the sound development of cross-border E-commerce.

Keywords: Cross-border E-commerce · Intellectual property · China-U.S. trade friction

1 Introduction

Global economic development has gradually weakened via the economic value-adding ability of industrial innovation technology. Moreover, the institutional dividends and technological dividends in globalization are in a clear decline, and economic development in the developed countries of Europe and North America is weakening, while Chinas foreign trade surplus keeps growing. After coming into power, the U.S. government under President Donald Trump is eager to solve such an economic dilemma, hence generating China-U.S. trade friction.

Under the election slogan of "America First", the U.S. government has implemented unilateralism and a trade protectionist policy for the sake of its own priority interests, but this policy has put the whole world at high risk. Such adventurous decision-making

© ICST Institute for Computer Sciences, Social Informatics and Telecommunications Engineering 2020
Published by Springer Nature Switzerland AG 2020. All Rights Reserved
D.-J. Deng et al. (Eds.): WiCON 2019, LNICST 317, pp. 285–293, 2020.
https://doi.org/10.1007/978-3-030-52988-8_25

adds to the uncertainty in the development of global economies. In the game and negotiation process between China and the United States concerning trade, China's insufficient efforts over the regulation and protection of intellectual property are often attacked by the United States. In recent years, cross-border E-commerce transactions have been booming, but the intellectual property issue involved is more complex and problematic. Therefore, China needs to pay more attention to the governance and protection of intellectual property, especially in cross-border E-commerce transactions.

1.1 Causes of the China-U.S. Trade Friction

The rapid development of China's economy has expanded its trade surplus with the United States. From 1979 to 2017, the China-U.S. trade volume increased from US$2.5 billion to US$583.7 billion, or an increase of 233 times, and the China's trade surplus with the U.S. hit US$275.8 billion in 2017 [1]. Moreover, as the U.S. economy is not performing well, its government is eager to solve this problem and hence the friction. The causes and the most profound background of the China-U.S. trade war are rooted in the threat posed by the rapid rise of China's economic strength.

1.2 China-U.S. Intellectual Property Disputes

As the China-U.S. trade surplus increases, the trade competition friction between the two countries keeps rising. Starting from 2000, the United States began to put continuous pressure on China. For example, the United States has been requiring and forcing China to substantially appreciate its RMB since 2003 and has repeatedly launched "Section 301" (Section 301 of the Trade Act of 1974) trade investigations against China (see Table 1).

Table 1. History of U.S. Section 301 investigations against China (Source: Compiled by this study)

Starting and ending time	Events
April 1991–January 1992	The United States initiated a special 301 investigation against China, and an agreement on intellectual property protection was signed in January 1992
October 1991–October 1992	The United States initiated a special 301 investigation against China, and the Memorandum of Understanding on Market Access between China and the United States was signed in October 1992
June 1994–February 1995	China and the United States reached the second agreement on intellectual property
April 1996–June 1996	The United States re-initiated the special 301 investigation, and China and the United States reached the third agreement on intellectual property in June 1996
October 2010–December 2010	The United States launched a special 301 investigation against China once again, and in 2010 the two countries settled disputes through the WTO dispute settlement mechanism
March 23, 2018	The U.S. government announced a 301 investigation against China

With the dramatic increase of China's foreign trade volume, Chinese enterprises are also being confronted with investigations by the United States International Trade Commission (USITC) under Section 337 of the "Tariff Act of 1930" of the United States ("Section 337"). These investigations are aimed at whether the imported products involve infringement of the U.S. intellectual property, and whether there are acts of unfair competition like antitrust acts involved in import trade.

According to statistics for 16 consecutive years from 2001 to 2017, the annual average proportion of Chinese enterprises investigated by the United States among all foreign enterprises hit 33.25% (see Table 2). As previously mentioned, investigations on intellectual property disputes can be launched under both "Section 337" and "Special 301". In the "2017 Special 301 Report" [2], the United States placed China at the top of the "Priority Watch List". As a result, the United States has repeatedly used intellectual property disputes to launch trade attacks against China, and the latter has been at a disadvantage over the issue.

Table 2. Number and proportion of "337 Investigation" cases of the United States

Year	Total number globally	Number of Chinese enterprises involved	Proportion of Chinese enterprises
2001	24	1	4.2%
2002	17	5	29.4%
2003	18	8	44.4%
2004	26	10	38.5%
2005	29	10	34.5%
2006	33	8	24.2%
2007	35	10	28.6%
2008	41	11	26.8%
2009	31	8	25.8%
2010	56	19	33.9%
2011	69	16	23.2%
2012	40	13	32.5%
2013	42	14	33.3%
2014	39	13	33.3%
2015	36	8	22.2%
2016	54	18	33.3%
2017	59	22	37.3%

Source: http://news.zhichanli.cn/article/5774.html

In other countries (regions) than the United States, Chinese enterprises often face legal proceedings into foreign intellectual property due to a lack of intellectual property consciousness, or inappropriate reference, or having the mentality of a free rider. Legal disputes over intellectual property have become one of the important competitive means for foreign enterprises to restrict Chinese enterprises. The most essential reason why Chinese enterprises are in such a weak position is the lack of intellectual property protection consciousness and incompleteness of a standard legal system.

2   Cross-Border E-Commerce Intellectual Property

With the rapid growth of China's trade, Chinese enterprises have accelerated their pace towards taking a great piece of the global market, and the intellectual property issue has been elevated to a strategic height of national policies. Network virtualization and trade remoteness of cross-border E-commerce transactions enable intellectual property to play a positive role in this transaction process.

First, intellectual property can demonstrate the quality of the commodities and services provided by E-commerce, reduce the cost of searching for high-quality commodities with E-commerce traders, and improve the quality of transactions. If the element of intellectual property is added to a commodity or service, then the value of the commodity or service may be increased. The brand logo on a commodity, together with its patented technology, is also a production cost. In addition to raw materials and all the expenses from production and processing to output, the production cost of commodities includes the value cost of intellectual property such as trademarks and patents. When the intellectual property value of a commodity is higher, the selling price will be higher and the commodity will be favored more. Even E-commerce commodities sold through the Internet exhibit this nature.

Second, in all E-commerce activities the trademark in intellectual property can be used as a reliable stamp of a commodity. Buyers use patents, trademarks, and copyrights to judge the information of the commodities to be purchased. Even if they cannot check the commodities in person, most buyers will identify the reputation and quality of a seller thousands of miles away through the brand name. Therefore, intellectual property (especially a trademark) is of particular importance in cross-border E-commerce marketing activities. The value of intellectual property is more prominent in a cross-border E-commerce platform. The sales of commodities with intellectual property are booming, while commodities without intellectual property might be unpopular. This is exactly what gives rise to the fluke mentality of "free rider" in the intellectual property issue (especially trademark rights) by dishonest merchants. As a result, the issue of intellectual property infringement appears.

2.1   Types of Intellectual Property Infringement in Cross-Border E-Commerce

In the process of cross-border E-commerce transactions, the intellectual property risks faced by market participants are mainly trademark infringement risks, patent infringement risks, and copyright infringement risks.

(1)   Trademark infringement. It refers to the fraudulent use of well-known brands, or the use of words and graphics similar to famous trademarks as the trademark of their own commodities, or the adding of words like exclusive store, franchise store,

agent, direct selling, and authorized store without the authorization of the famous trademarks, which is enough to confuse consumers; or legal disputes over intellectual property caused by arbitrary use, dissemination, and plagiarism of famous commodity web pages, or the setting of deep links and other infringements.

(2) Improper plagiarism of commodity patent. It refers to the plagiarism of a patentee's invention, appearance, structure, smell, and/or other patented items without the legitimate permission of the patentee for the purpose of producing and selling commodities to seek illegal profits.

(3) Copyright infringement. It refers to the exploitation, modification, reproduction, and/or dissemination of a copyright owner's work without the legitimate authorization of the copyright owner for the purpose of seeking illegal profits with such illegal means.

2.2 Current Situation of Intellectual Property Protection in Cross-Border E-Commerce

With the increase of cross-border E-commerce transaction volume, the number of infringement cases is also gradually rising due to the lack of complete laws and regulations on intellectual property and protection awareness. Such acts not only impair the image of Chinese enterprises in foreign merchants, but also hinder the healthy development of China's cross-border E-commerce industry in addition to damaging their goodwill. At present, the intellectual property governance and protection of China's cross-border E-commerce are not adequately implemented.

2.2.1 Dilemma in Intellectual Property Governance

The dilemma in cross-border E-commerce intellectual property governance is caused by multiple factors, including root cause, realistic cause, and conceptual cause [12].

(1) Root cause: The most typical feature of intellectual property is regionalism, and its rights can only be guaranteed and developed by law after being confirmed by law. Rights are the principle of territorialism. When it comes to cross-jurisdictions, intellectual property in a jurisdiction cannot be protected outside the borders unless there is regional collaboration between different regions or stipulated by international convention. For example, a Chinese E-commerce enterprise has legally registered a same or similar trademark in China, but the trademark products might cause infringement if they are sold across borders.

(2) Realistic cause: The contradiction between risks arises due to the following factors: the innovation of science and technology, the rapid development of a sales model, a serious lag in the redesign of a legal norm system, and the lack of coordination among countries or regions across the globe.

The rapid development of science and technology has promoted vigorous development of cross-border E-commerce and demonstrated a variety of innovative business modes. Innovations related to information services and payment patterns are also derived in the process of cross-border E-commerce transactions. Without due intellectual property protection, these innovative methods might cause risks and practical difficulties. For example, Alibaba Group once pointed out that in dealing with counterfeit commodities, it encountered such difficulties as abuse of the safe harbor rules by enterprises, poor operability of commodity information ex-ante review, and an incapacity to determine whether a commodity is a counterfeit by price alone.

2.2.2 Dilemma in Intellectual Property Protection

The cost of intellectual property protection is surging, but the economic benefit generated is decreasing gradually. This is also the reason why cross-border E-commerce intellectual property protection cannot be fully implemented. The main causes are free use and income protection, object protection, gratuitous law, and other factors.

(1) Dilemma of free use and income protection

In the Internet context, many people want to obtain the intellectual achievements of others free of charge via easy access to the Internet. In the development of the Internet, the public has been accustomed to obtaining intellectual property for free, which has prevented the intellectual property holders from obtaining creative benefits, severely discouraged the enthusiasm toward creation, and further affected the reproduction of intellectual property commodities. The conflict between free use and income protection is getting increasingly tense.

(2) Dilemma of object protection and gratuitous law

In cross-border E-commerce under the Internet context, intellectual property commodities are easy to be copied, and the objects of intellectual property protection are facing multiple crises. The economic cost paid by infringers to obtain the information of the intellectual property-related objects is very low. Infringers do not have to pay the innovation cost or the operating cost, and so it is easy to obtain the market competition advantage and seek illegal huge profits. If the intellectual property objects cannot be effectively protected, then the due interests of intellectual property holders cannot be effectively guaranteed, and the illegal acquisition of intellectual property cannot be effectively contained; thus, the principle of interest equity will be out of the question.

3 The Path to Break Through the Dilemma of Cross-Border E-Commerce Intellectual Property Governance and Protection

3.1 Establishment of a Reasonable Governance Relationship in Domestic and Overseas Fields

In terms of the establishment direction of intellectual property governance, the China government should pay equal attention to encouragement and supervision. In terms of overseas intellectual property governance, the China government and the governments of other countries (regions) should promote cross-border governance by joining international agreements on intellectual property through negotiation and cooperation. Specifically, the improvement of the legal system on cross-border E-commerce intellectual property mainly includes the following four aspects.

(1) Fill the legal vacancy, establish the concept that efficiency takes precedence and fairness is taken into account, and improve the relevant legal system. The provisions of the "Trans-Pacific Partnership" can be invoked in the legal protection of cross-border E-commerce. The intellectual property clauses in this agreement reflect some consensuses on intellectual property protection reached among these member states (regions). The intellectual property issues involved in cross-border E-commerce are greater in quantity and more complex, such as database sharing, protection of private intellectual property rights, and business secrets. If China wants to become an intellectual property powerhouse, then more attention should be paid to the protection and development of intellectual property of various countries for the construction of a legal system, so as to fill the gaps in its own legislation.

(2) Improve efficiency and lay emphasis on fair competition. The efficiency of cross-border E-commerce customs clearance can be improved by clarifying and simplifying the procedure of intellectual property protection system, and by means of a positive list or ex-post review. When intellectual property disputes occur between E-commerce enterprises and consumers, it is also very important to establish a mechanism that can quickly resolve disputes and effectively protect legitimate rights and interests. In terms of fair competition, attention must be paid to the anti-monopoly supervision of intellectual property to avoid the abuse of a dominant position by cross-border E-commerce platforms or the abuse of power by intellectual property holders to practice a monopoly.

(3) Establish a diversified cooperation mechanism. The intellectual property issues involved in cross-border E-commerce are extremely complex, and the identity of each transaction subject is also multiple. Therefore, in combination with the multi-cooperation and joint governance mechanism of all parties, the government, intellectual property holders, licensees, commercial users, cross-border E-commerce platforms, and civil forces should cooperate with one another, which would be more important not only at home, but also abroad. Only in this way can sharing, win-win results, mutual supervision, and proper checks and balances be achieved.

3.2 Idea of Constructing the Path to Break Through the Dilemma of Cross-Border E-Commerce Intellectual Property Governance and Protection

By establishing an ex-ante early risk warning mechanism and an ex-post protection mechanism, the dilemma of protecting the intellectual property objects can be effectively broken through. The content of this mechanism includes such resources as a big data database, professional consultation, regulators and dispute settlement authorities, and scientific and legal professionals to build the early risk warning and protection mechanism.

This mechanism must be open to administrative organs, intellectual property holders, consumers, and other subjects. It is also necessary to meet the needs of the administrative subjects in order to exercise their regulatory authority, of the copyright holders to protect their rights, and of consumers to perform supervision. Professional functions such as an early warning of intellectual property copying, discovery of intellectual property infringement, and settlement of intellectual property disputes should be integrated into one-stop services.

The establishment of the early warning and protection platform for cross-border E-commerce intellectual property can integrate such functions as "risk warning, complaint and report, dispute resolution, information release, consultation and guidance" into one place and open the platform to various social parties. This platform can provide an effective channel for information communication and transmission by relevant parties and combat intellectual property infringements on the Internet in a timely and effective manner.

In order to support the long-term and effective operation of the platform, it is necessary to establish an early warning center and a dispute settlement center, which will be responsible for conducting comparative retrieval analysis of patents and trademarks from the perspective of prevention and dispute resolution, respectively. A long-term intellectual property protection mechanism for Internet E-commerce should be established. This platform can effectively integrate basic resources such as relevant laws and regulations, standards, subject information, product information, intellectual property information, cases and experts on intellectual property infringements, and the production and selling of counterfeit and shoddy commodities in the network environment and can provide open and professional public services to society. The crackdown on and governance of cross-border E-commerce intellectual property infringements can be achieved by relying on such function modules to be early risk warnings, reports and complaints, supervision and investigation, rights protection, consultation, and guidance and through the integrated and overall supervision via online and offline linkages.

4   Conclusions

Only by effectively protecting the legitimate rights and interests of intellectual property holders in accordance with the law can more creative workers be encouraged to input, share, and disseminate the achievements of innovation, return such achievements to all members of society for reasonable sharing, and thus maximize the public interests of intellectual property. This concept is the most important consideration in the design of an intellectual property protection system in cross-border E-commerce activities.

One of the significant ideas in the formulation of national intellectual property protection policy is how to reconcile the conflicts of various ideas in the intellectual property system, give equal consideration to private rights protection and public interests, and make the most appropriate institutional adjustment in long-term development relationships. Ever since China's accession to the WTO, intellectual property protection has always been the focus of worldwide attention. As China deepens its reform and opening-up efforts, all topics surrounding intellectual property protection are an indispensable part of its participation in international trade competition.

It is therefore imperative to formulate a set of appropriate intellectual property protection strategies, promote the culture and concept of intellectual property protection, balance the interests and values of all parties, and develop the idea of multi-dimensional, inclusive, active, and open intellectual property, so that Chinese enterprises can be in a dominant position under fierce international trade competition.

Acknowledgments. This work was supported by Foundation for Advanced Talents of Yulin Normal University (G2019SK02).

References

1. China.org.cn. http://guoqing.china.com.cn/zhuanti/2018-11/13/content_72164727.htm
2. Office of the United States Trade Representative. https://ustr.gov/sites/default/files/301/2017%20Special%20301%20Report%20FINAL.PDF
3. http://news.zhichanli.cn/article/5774.html
4. Shiral, A., Schemlzer, R.: Bricks and clicks-kicking the tires of an e-commerce company: issues to consider when setting up, or investing in an E-business. J. Internet Law **4**, 1–16 (2000)
5. Peter, K.Y.: Intellectual property geographies. WIPO J. **6**, 1–15 (2014)
6. Hammond, H.J., Cohen, J.S.: Intellectual property issues in E-commerce. Texas Wesleyan L. Rev. **18**, 752 (2012)
7. Haines, A.D.: Why is it so difficult to construct an international legal framework for e-commerce? The draft hague convention on jurisdiction and the recognition and enforcement of foreign judgments in civil and commercial matters: a case study. Eur. Bus. Organ. Law Rev. **3**(1), 157–194 (2002)
8. Yang, G., Maskus, K.E.: Intellectual property rights, licensing, and innovation in an endogenous product-cycle model. J. Int. Econ. **53**, 169–187 (2001)
9. Robert, M.: Sherwood: Intellectual Property and Economic Development. Westview Press, Boulder (1990)
10. Maskus, K.E.: Regulatory standards in the WTO: comparing intellectual property rights with competition policy, environmental protection, and core labor standards. World Trade Rev. **02**, 135–152 (2002)
11. Li, Z.: Protection of intellectual property in e-commerce. J. Polit. Sci. Law **19**, 5–9 (2002)
12. Zheng, L.-Y.: Intellectual property governance in cross border e-commerce: dilemma, causes and solutions. China Bus. Market **31**, 110–118 (2017)

A Framework for Big Data Analytics on Service Quality Evaluation of Online Bookstore

Tsai Jich-Yan[1], Ye Xiu Wen[2(✉)], and Wang Chien-Hua[3]

[1] School of Computer Science and Engineering, Yulin Normal University, Yulin, China
jytsai@ylu.edu.cn
[2] Yulin Normal University, Yulin, China
2315405512@qq.com
[3] Department of Information Management, Yuan Ze University, Taoyuan City, Taiwan
thuck@saturn.yzu.edu.tw

Abstract. With the advancement of Internet technology and the rise of e-commerce, Big Data Analytics can be applied to assess service quality for e-commerce industry achieving customer relationship improvement and reflecting the service quality of transaction. Online bookstore is a form of electronic commerce which allows consumers to directly buy books or services from a seller over the Internet using a web browser or a app program. Most researches are focus on expert opinion or few sample to measure the critical criteria. The goal of this study is to explore and demonstrate the utility of big data analytics by using it to study core online bookstore service quality variables that have been extensively studied in past decades. Text analysis method to extract a large number of consumer reviews from Amazon to deconstruct the bookstore customer experience and examine its relationship with satisfaction. This paper proposed a framework that integration of big data analytic and SERVQUAL model to measure the importance and relationship of service quality criteria. How to provide a level of service quality that satisfies consumers is an important issue for operators of online bookstores. Further research will apply Amazon data set to evaluate the criteria.

Keywords: Big data analytics · E-commerce · SQUEQUAL

1 Introduction

With the widespread use of the Internet and the rapid growth of smart device applications, the rapid growth of e-commerce has been promoted. The growing popularity of the mobile devices, the increasing number of internet user that facilitate the e-commerce development. Electronic commerce is supporting of customers, supplying of services and commodities, portion of business information, manages business transactions and maintaining of bond between suppliers, customers and vendors by devices of telecommunication networks [13]. Online bookstore is a form of electronic commerce which allows consumers to directly buy books or services from a seller over the Internet using a

D.-J. Deng et al. (Eds.): WiCON 2019, LNICST 317, pp. 294–301, 2020.
https://doi.org/10.1007/978-3-030-52988-8_26

web browser or a app program. At first, organization focus on buying and selling product or service on the Internet. Laterly, business realized that digital information gathering, processing and distribution is influence to management, finance, negotiation, purching. However, consumers' requirements for the service quality of online bookstores have been increasing. How to provide a level of service quality that satisfies consumers is an important issue for operators of online bookstores.

As the growing the e-commerce, there are many online retailers was forced to shut down business. In a competitive business environment, it is important to understand customer need. Customer need is directly influenced by customer satisfaction. Therefore, how to improve customer satisfaction has become a very important concern for business organizations. Spreng and Mackoy [15] mention about customer satisfaction and service quality are two core concepts at marketing theory and practice. Service quality is about whether a service meets customer needs or not by comparison of a customer expectations with their perception of actual service. It is believed that provided high quality service lead to satisfied customers. Service quality is an important indicator to measure competitive advantage and can determine a business success or failure [12]. Therefore, how to measure service quality in e-commerce has become a very important task.

Big data can be defined based on large volumes of extensively varied data that are generated, captured, and processed at high velocity [1]. To efficient processing these digital information would yield high returns for the organization [14]. The use and analysis of big data can increase its competitive advantage for each industry, government units, business organizations, medical institutions and e-commerce. Adopting big data technologies, business like e-commerce can gain benefits from big data analytic. Big data analytics is a technology to process the data and realize the value drived from big data. Especially for e-commerce, a large amount of data is generated every day. Collecting and analyzing these data can not only enhance the competitive advantage, but also improve the consumers' satisfaction.

Usually user satisfaction can be achieved by measuring the quality of service. This is a multi-layered problem. Coupled with the intangible nature of the service itself, there are more personal subjective factors and vague concepts in assessing consumers' perception of the experience, and the use of accurate values may not be able to express the evaluation of consumer services in online stores. Because services have intangible characteristics that are difficult to measure, consumers' subjective cognitive judgments are often ambiguous when evaluating service quality. Therefore, this study applied Wang's research method [16] to the online bookstore service quality evaluation model, and then integrated various evaluation aspects and standards.

This research is organized as follows: Sect. 2 reviews some of the theories and previews studies related to Big data analytics, e-commerce, and service quality. Section 3 describes the research methodology that shows the exact road map of the study. This research mainly proposes a preliminary framework that integrates big data analytics and SERVQUAL service quality models. The online bookstore customers'review data that will be further used in the future and improve this structure. Section 4 concludes the paper and draws direction to future work.

2 Research Method

2.1 Big Data Analytic

Data is everywhere. Big Data refers to humongous volumes of data that cannot be processed effectively with the traditional applications that exist. The initial definition given by Gartner [1] is,

> *"Big data is high-volume, and high-velocity and/or high-variety information assets that demand cost-effective, innovative forms of information processing that enable enhanced insight, decision making, and process automation."*

Laterly, Veracity has been reiterated by Gartner [2] and NIST [3] expanded upon by IBM [4]. Veracity includes questions of trust and uncertainty with regards to data and the outcome of analysis of that data. Big data can be defined based on large volumes of extensively varied data that are generated, captured, and processed at high velocity.

Big Data refers to our newfound ability to crunch a vast quantity of information, analyze it instantly, and draw sometimes astonishing conclusions from it and Big data analytics focuses on the collection of data with an unprecedented breadth, scale, and depth to solve actual problems [5]. Big data analysis is often a complex process that examines large and various data sets (big data) to discover hidden information patterns, unknown correlations, market trends, and customer preferences to help organizations make informed business decisions. Big data analytics can provide many other information and data correlations that can be used to detect business trends, understand customer satisfaction, avoid the spread of disease, fight crime, and measure current traffic conditions. This is why big data analytics are prevalent. There are many big data surveys in the literature, but most surveys tend to Algorithms and methods for processing big data rather than technology [22].

2.2 E-Commerce

Since the 1990s, the Internet has been born and has begun to develop rapidly. In the past, the physical business model of the Internet, due to the booming development of the Internet, has led to the emergence of Internet-based e-commerce. With the widespread use of Internet and rapid growth of intelligent device application, the methods of consumer shopping also undergone tremendous changes. E-commerce is a commercial activity dealing directly with the trading of goods and services and with other related business activities, in which the electronic communication medium plays a central role [23]. Typical e-commerce transactions include the purchase of online books (such as Amazon) and music purchases (music download in the form of digital distribution such as iTunes Store), and to a less extent, customized/personalized online liquor store inventory services [6]. E-Commerce can be defined as a modern business methodology that addresses the needs of organizations, merchants, and consumers to cut costs while improving the quality of goods and services and increasing the speed of service delivery [7].

2.3 Service Quality

Grönroos [8] defined service quality as "the outcome of an evaluation process, where the consumer compares his expectations with the service he perceives he has received." Technical quality, functional quality and corporate image are further suggested by Grönroos. In recent researches [9, 10], reveal that service quality is close related to customer satisfaction and good service quality lead to high service quality. Since service quality is highly related to customer satisfaction, it is essential for service providers to measure and assess customer satisfaction.

So far, many techniques and methods have been developed to measure service quality. Parasuraman et al. [11] considered that for consumers, service quality is not easy to evaluate compared to product quality, and service quality perception is compared between consumer expectations and actual service performance. They proposed the SERVQUAL model measured service quality in terms of ten dimensions including access, communication, competence, courtesy, credibility, reliability, responsiveness, security, tangibility, and understanding/knowing the customer. Parasuraman et al. [12] purified and distilled these ten dimensions of service quality into five dimensions: tangibility, reliability, responsiveness, assurance, and empathy, SERVQUAL, that included 22 evaluation items to assess service quality. SERVQUAL has been widely used and verified in traditional business services. There are many researches directly use SERVQUAL to assess the service quality in online stores. Traditional measurement models like SERVQUAL often require the design of questionnaire-based research models for analysis. In this study, we propose a preliminary framework that integration big data analysis technology and SERVQUAL model to study the relationship between dimension and criteria for online shopping service quality, and to measure its weight to understand its importance. Make relevant recommendations for e-commerce companies.

3 Research Method

3.1 Research Design

Because the online store is a virtual transaction environment built on the Internet, the way products and services are presented, online transaction payment processes, and product distribution channels are all different from traditional physical stores. These activities include the communication of information, the management of payment, the negotiating and trading of financial instruments, and the management of transport [23]. A framework that integration of big data analytic and SERVQUAL model to measure the importance and relationship of service quality criteria. The SERVQUAL model is based on Wang [16] and Lin [17] to assess online bookstore service quality. It uses factor analysis to build a hierarchical structure of online bookstore service quality, so each level structure is complete, and it has certain validity. Five dimensions were identified in Online bookstore service quality hierarchy structure as follows:

1. Website design: The overall design features provided by the online store and how easy it is to operate. WebPage Design, Operational usability, Rich in information content, Linking ability, Layout, Variety of choices, Search ability, seven criteria were included.

2. Reliability: Whether the information content provided by the online store and its product distribution process have fulfilled the commitment to customer service. Clear transaction process, Transaction correctness, Commitment to customers, Information correctness, Data protection capability, Transaction Security, six criteria were included.
3. Responsiveness: The ability of online stores to respond to customers' questions or complaints in a timely manner. Reply Timeliness, Tracking consumption records, Information immediacy, three criteria were included.
4. Trust: Whether the transaction mechanism provided by the online store can make customers feel the ability of confidence and trust. Website trustworthy, The internet is honest, Sincerely care for customers, three criteria were included.
5. Personalization: The ability of online stores to flexibly respond to individual customer needs. Personalized service, Understanding Customer Preferences, Post-purchase information notice, three criteria were included.

Instead of questionnaire-based or survey-based research to measure the relationship and weight between these five dimensions and 22 criteria. Big data analytics based on customer review framework is introduced. A framework structure of integration of big data analytics and SERVQUAL model is proposed (see Fig. 1). Our framework is mainly to extract linguistic attributes from the big data set of customer, and through the keyword analysis, find the corresponding dimension and criteria to calculate the weights.

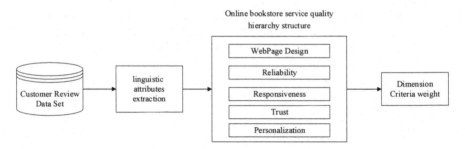

Fig. 1. Online bookstore evaluation framework

Online customers' review usually with an open-structure from that need to extract the linguistic attributes. Zhao et al. [18] mentioned that customer satisfaction is predicted by the linguistic characteristics of reviews. Almost 85% customers read online reviews before making a purchase [19], sentiment analysis to convert textual reviews into the visual representation, to improve efficiency and to determine the attitude of mass towards the subject of interest. Sentiment analysis [21] usually determines whether the content of a document is positive or negative or neutral to the content of a paragraph or sentence. How to find the corresponding keyword in the customer's review, as the input of each criterion of our service quality model is a big challenge.

3.2 Data Analysis

Real e-commerce product data that were available on-sale at Amazon on-line market place on November 17–19, 2014 [20]. The dataset covers products from 6 main categories, Automotive, Books, Electronics, Movies, Phones and Home including 1529 sub-categories. All products are listed over 334 independent attributes & the size 2000K of value space. This dataset includes reviews (ratings, text, helpfulness votes), product metadata (descriptions, category information, price, brand, and image features), and links (also viewed/also bought graphs). Pre-category Books product reviews json file is apply to assess our framework. The json file format is shown as below (see Fig. 2). Four attributes (helpful, reviewText, overall, summary) are selected to measure the weight of criteria in our framework.

```
{
    "reviewerID": "AH2L9G3DQHHAJ",
    "asin": "0000000116",
    "reviewerName": "chris",
    "helpful": [
        5,
        5
    ],
    "reviewText": "Interesting Grisham tale of a lawyer that takes
    millions of dollars from his firm after faking his own death. Grisham
    usually is able to hook his readers early and ,in this case, doesn't
    play his hand to soon. The usually reliable Frank Mueller makes this
    story even an even better bet on Audiobook.",
    "overall": 4.0,
    "summary": "Show me the money!",
    "unixReviewTime": 1019865600,
    "reviewTime": "04 27, 2002"
}
```

Fig. 2. Book review json format

4 Conclusion

This is a preliminary framework for our combination of big data analytics and online bookstore service quality measurement models. We hope that through the input of massive data, combined with natural language processing, instead of questionnaires or expert interviews, we will calculate the weights of the dimensions and guidelines for the service quality of the bookstore. Further work will be to apply big data for analysis, and to purchase machine learning algorithms, to adjust our customer satisfaction model, according to the analysis results to provide e-commerce vendors to propose to improve their competitive advantage.

However, the following are the remaining works and challenges, to take into consideration, and improve the efficiency of the proposed system during the evolution of this research:

1. This research represented the Big Data Analytics techniques. However, further studies of the linguistic attributes extraction are needed to improve the support of data preprocessing for the text analysis.

2. Amazon generates huge amount of feedback data. Reviews need to be analyzed for building machine learning algorithms to calculate the weight of dimensions and criteria. In our work, we present the analyses of customer book reviews from amazon.com to evaluation our combined SERVQUAL model. Different machine learning algorithm should be developed to evaluate their performance.

References

1. Laney, D.: 3D Data Management: Controlling Data Volume, Velocity and Variety. META Group Research Note, 6(70) (2001)
2. Beyer, M.A. Laney, D.: The Importance of "Big Data": A Definition. Gartner (2012)
3. NIST Big Data Working Group (NBD-WG). http://bigdatawg.nist.gov/home.php
4. IBM, What is big data? - Bringing big data to the enterprise July 2013. http://www-01.ibm.com/software/data/bigdata/
5. Mayer-Schönberger, V., Cukier, K.: Big Data: A Revolution That Will Transform How We Live, Work, and Think. Houghton Mifflin Harcourt, Boston (2013)
6. Statista: Retail e-commerce sales CAGR forecast in selected countries from 2016 to 2021, October 2016. Accessed 1 Jan 2018
7. Kalakota, R., Whinston, A.B.: Electronic Commerce: A Manager Guide. Addison-Wesley, New York (1997)
8. Grönroos, C.: A service quality model and its marketing implications. Eur. J. Mark. 18(4), 36–44 (1984)
9. Mukherjee, A., Nath, P., Pal, M.: Resource, service quality and performance triad: a framework for measuring efficiency of banking services. J. Oper. Res. Soc. 54(7), 723–735 (2003)
10. Ramanathan, R., Karpuzcu, H.: Comparing perceived and expected service using an AHP model: an application to measure service quality of a company engaged in pharmaceutical distribution. Opsearch Indian J. Oper. Res. 48(2), 136–152 (2011)
11. Parasuraman, A., Zeithaml, V.A., Berry, L.L.: A conceptual model of service quality and its implications for future research. J. Mark. 49(4), 41–50 (1985)
12. Parasuraman, A., Zeithaml, V.A., Berry, L.L.: Servqual: a multiple-item scale for measuring consumer perceptions of service quality. J. Retail. 64(1), 12–40 (1988)
13. Nanehkaran, Y.A.: An introduction to electronic commerce. Int. J. Sci. Technol. Res. 2(4), 190–193 (2013)
14. Viehland, D.: Principles for e-business success. In: PACIS 2000 Proceedings, vol. 7, pp. 78–87 (2000)
15. Spreng, A.R., Mackoy, D.R.: An empirical examination of a model of perceived service quality and satisfaction. J. Retail. 72, 201–214 (1996)
16. Wang, C.H.: A study of fuzzy multiple criteria evaluation on service quality of online bookstor. Web J. Chin. Manage. Rev. 20(1), 1–18 (2017)
17. Lin, H.F.: The application of fuzzy analytic hierarchy process on service quality evaluation of online retailers. J. e-Bus. 8(3), 347–372 (2006)
18. Zhao, Y., Xu, X., Wang, M.: Predicting overall customer satisfaction: big data evidence from hotel online textual reviews. Int. J. Hosp. Manag 76, 111–121 (2019)
19. Jinturkar, M., Gotmare, P.,: Sentiment analysis of customer review data using big data: a survey. In: IJCA Proceedings on Emerging Trends in Computing, pp. 3–8 (2016)
20. Amazon product data. http://snap.stanford.edu/data/amazon/productGraph/
21. Aljoharah, A., Sahar, B., Alshehri, D., Alzahrani, S., Munirah, A.: Sentiment analysis and visualization of Amazon books' reviews. In: Conference: 2019 2nd International Conference on Computer Applications & Information Security (ICCAIS), pp. 1–6 (2019)

22. Ali, A., et al.: Big data for development: applications and techniques. Big Data Anal. **1**, 2 (2016)
23. Heng, M.S.H.: Understanding e-commerce from a historical perspective. Commun. AIS **12**, 104–118 (2003)

Author Index

Printed in the United States
By Bookmasters